The Complete
English Springer Spaniel

Colin Muirhead

RINGPRESS

Published by Ringpress Books Ltd,
POBox 8, Lydney, Gloucestershire GL15 6YD

Discounts available for bulk orders
Contact the Special Sales Manager at
the above address. Telephone 01594 563800

First Published 1996
© 1996 RINGPRESS BOOKS
AND COLIN MUIRHEAD

ISBN 1 86054 095 3

Printed and bound in Singapore
by Kyodo Printing Co

CONTENTS

4

bitch; Preparations for whelping; The birth; Essential whelping equipment; Problem whelpings; Examining the litter; The early days; Weaning; Worming; Abnormalities; Pick of the litter; Selling puppies.

***This book is dedicated to the English Springer
– past, present and future.***

Acknowledgements

I would like to express my gratitude to everybody who, over the years, has contributed to my "magpie's hoard" of breed records, photographs, etc., some well-known, some unknown, some professional, some amateur – the latter category including many of my friends overseas. I am especially grateful to Viv Rainsbury for translating my "doodles" into the line drawings used to illustrate the Breed Standard.

Colin Muirhead

Title page photograph: Strathnaver Barley Wine (Bowswood Barleycorn – Dallowgill Wood Wych).

Photo: Diane Pearce.

Introduction

THE ENGLISH SPRINGER CHARACTER

THE PERFECT COMPANION

The English Springer is a Breed that can be all things to all people, and perhaps the best way I can describe its character is to dip into my own experiences. Probably the most important use of the Breed is as companions, and my first introduction to the English Springer was, like most other owners, as a pet. Dinah was acquired as a two-year-old in 1937. Her curriculum vitae included the qualification Gundog (failed) – and a showdog she certainly wasn't! However, to a five-year-old boy these things were incomprehensible, and over the next decade she taught me that the breed was the ideal family dog. The gentle nature of her immediate successor enhanced my love of the breed, whose laid-back, even temperament is, without much doubt, the main reason for the breed's continuing popularity. This benevolent disposition was why Springers became popular as gundogs. For many country families, in the years between the two World wars, rabbits were the main source of meat, and the Springer doubled up as a pot-filler and a family pet. Over the past four decades my own Springers have associated with various, widely-differing breeds including Whippets, Beagles, Bassets, Pyrenean, Bouviers, Scotties, Smooth Fox Terriers and Border Terriers, as well as gundogs such as Labradors and most of the Spaniel sub-group. They have got on well with all of them, proving the equable nature of the Breed.

THE WILL TO WORK

This temperament has always been a feature of the Spaniel family as a whole, the innate desire to please making them ideal candidates for training in work on flushing game, or in the case of the smaller types, development into Toy Spaniels, or "comforters". Over the centuries, selective breeding for sagacity and fidelity produced the archetype of the faithful Spaniel. However, breeding for these points alone could have produced dogs of all shapes and sizes – but somewhere, sometime, somehow these desirable traits were found to exist very strongly in dogs equating to the Spaniel type, which were also physically suited to the work they were required to perform. With the passing of time, the general Spaniel type has been refined into the handsome breed we know today. This gradual evolution is in contrast to some of the manufactured gundog and guarding breeds. For some reason or other, back in the dim past, Spaniels had developed a penchant for fetching and carrying things – a useful attribute when shooting superseded working with hawks, greyhounds or the net. During this long period of development, permission to keep dogs, especially sporting dogs, was only granted to a minority of privileged individuals. This led to localised strains and types, which were known by various names, such as English Water Spaniel, Norfolk Spaniel etc. In some cases other breeds were assimilated into a strain to give certain points, these included Pointers and a French Poodle. One aspect of the Springer temperament that

Int. and Nordic Ch. Mustela P. Auktoritet (Int. and Nordic Ch. Ambridge Bystander of Stubham – Sh. Ch. Mustela M. Petronella): The English Springer's desire to please is a great asset when training a gundog for the field.

endears the dogs to so many fans is the breed's innate cheerfulness. This optimistic outlook on life manifests itself in many ways, from the bustling worker zipping backwards and forwards, convinced there is game behind every blade of grass, even though the dog's eyes, nose and the guv'nor's whistle try to persuade otherwise, to the proud arrogance and showmanship setting off the glamour of the top show dogs. Most owners of companion Springers out for exercise will know that self-satisfied glance back up to their owner's face.

In recent years the working ability of the breed has been sharpened to a great extent by the keen competition in Field Trials, although this has turned out to be something of a two-edged sword. While the performances at Trials have improved in style and speed, this has meant that the average owner finds that stock from the more high-powered lines is too much to cope with. It is a matter of some debate as to whether this hyperactivity is of benefit to the breed as a whole, or just to the competition dogs. Many general shooting men have, in fact, taken to using Labradors, as they have found them more sedate. Having said this, a good Springer from sensible, trainable lines is still the best all-round gundog for most people.

THE SHOW DOG
Prior to World War Two, Cockers were probably the glamour dogs of the show scene with regard to General Championship Show Best in Show wins, holding their own at a time when terriers were fairly dominant. Springers, I think, only mustered two such awards during this period. Post-war, the picture changed somewhat, and, starting with the late Joe Braddon's Ch. Invader of Ide, followed by several of the Boxer progeny, the breed began to assert itself in the challenge for the

The English Springer has an excellent sense of smell coupled with good concentration which makes it ideal for detecting drugs and explosives.

SNIFFER DOGS AT WORK
Photos courtesy of the Metropolitan Police.

top spot, although exhibits from the top Cocker kennels, such as Ware, Colinwood and Lochranza, continued to provide competition. In the sixties and seventies, the breed hit a purple patch with BIS wins by the Moorcliff pair, Dougal and Gamecock, and also the brothers Majeba Mac and Lochardils Ghillie of Bramhope. These all shared the same sire, Douglas of Freetwood. The two Dougal sons, Hawkhill Royal Palace and his younger brother Connaught (more than once), were also BIS winners. More recently, the supreme award has eluded the breed, although the Springer still holds its own in the group. In the USA under, admittedly, somewhat different rules, Springers are no strangers to the top place, the great Salilyns Aristocrat notching up, I believe, 45 BIS in one year. Of course the most spectacular BIS win of recent years has to be that of Salilyns Condor topping Westminster. In Australia, the breed often figures prominently in the top placings. Among the various Springers with top awards at the numerous "Royal" shows, the black and white Azucroft Jumping Jack took top spot at the prestigious Sydney Royal.

SNIFFER DOGS

The breed has now added another raison d'être to its score, as more and more Springers are being used as "sniffer" dogs on drugs and explosives. In the early part of 1992 there were upwards of 200 Springers trained for this purpose. Currently the Bedford police force has four Springer bitches working as "sniffers", two on drugs and two on explosives. The two disciplines require slightly different techniques. The dog seeking drugs works like a normal Spaniel up to the "freeze and point" stage when the quarry is discovered, stopping short of the actual "flush". With explosives, for obvious safety reasons, a much more sedate approach is required, with just a general indication given of the area where the explosives are hidden – ready for the Bomb Disposal squad to take over. Training is on the basic lines of the preliminary gundog exercises, except the dummy contains a quantity of the target substance. Springers are superseding many of the Retriever breeds in this department because, generally, they have better scenting powers and, also, they are capable of sustaining their concentration for much longer periods. Many of the Springers used by the various Police Forces are obtained via the Breed Rescue and Welfare schemes.

TRACKING

In Norway, for many years there have been tracking trials, in which dogs are tested on their ability to trail and find wounded deer or elk. A trail is laid using blood. It is about 600yds long with right-angle turns and breaks in the track and is laid 12 to 24 hours before the tests. The dogs are tested individually. The trail must be followed at a reasonably sensible pace, not too fast, and silence is essential. Awards are given for First, Second and Third. Three Firsts are required for the Tracking Champion title. The more common breeds participating are Dachshunds and Elkhound but, since the early 1980s, Springers have taken part and in 1987 were permitted to compete for the title of Tracking Trial Champion. Prior to this it had been restricted to Dachshunds. The first English Springer to gain the title was Norwegian Trial Ch. Revirets Silver Shadow, a daughter of the imported Cliffhill Gossips Fieldday. As upwards of 50,000 deer and elk are shot each season in Norway, there will be a fair proportion of these which are only wounded, and will need to be found.

In these situations a reliable dog is needed with the same attributes required as for the sniffer dogs – a good nose and dedication to the job in hand. This use of trackers for wounded game has now in fact become a legal requirement from the 1994 season, and the Norwegian Department of Agriculture together with the Hunting and Fishing Association have instituted an Official Register of qualified dogs, and all persons going out to hunt elk or deer must have access to a Licensed dog.

*Nu Ch. Lajbans Firecracker: Tracking wounded
game in Norway.*

For inclusion on the register a dog must have been awarded at least a second prize at an official Trial and also have been tested on live game.

The first Spaniel to be entered on the register was the English Springer Spaniel Norwegian Sh. Ch. Stormbirds Final Whistle (N. Ch. Shipden Fiorello – N. Sh. Ch Shipden Oonagh). Three others have at present been licensed: Final Whistle's brother, S. Treble Chance, N. Sh. & Tr. Ch. Brigadoon St Toreador (Cliffhill Huggy Bear – Cleavehill Scotch Isla) and Salix Black Mist (sired by Calvdale Beau Geste). These English bench lines have proved successful at this type of work because not only do they have good noses, but they have an equable temperament and good powers of concentration – the attributes all good English Springer Spaniels possess.

Chapter One

ORIGINS OF THE BREED

Spaniel types were thought to have been brought from Spain by the Romans – hence the name, which derives from Hispania, the Latin for Spain. But it is a moot point as to which breed is the oldest, with most specialist writers claiming that honour for their particular group. As all Spaniels would appear to derive from the same source, I suppose they are all correct! The claim of "ancient and pure origins" in the Breed Standards certainly applies to the Spaniel family as a whole. The names Field Spaniel and Springer were originally generic terms denoting purpose, rather than a separate breed. Field dogs were working Spaniels, as opposed to the Toy Spaniels (or "comforters" as they were known), although at least one source says that the original Blenheim Spaniels of the Duke of Marlborough were "liver and white" and larger than the normal Toy Spaniels. Having watched some of my Cavalier King Charles Spaniel puppies carrying their playthings in a style very much like the Field Trial Spaniels, and showing great drive and willingness to address cover on the odd occasion that I have taken them "beating", I am more than willing to acknowledge their place as a link in the evolutionary chain. The term Springer is derived from the action of springing the game for the net or falcon. They were also used to start ground game for the Greyhounds and were sometimes known as starters, although this term was latterly used to refer to their Welsh cousins.

FIRST LITERARY ALLUSIONS

Spaniels made an appearance in literature early on, with mentions in Chaucer's *Wife of Bath's Tale* and Shakespeare's *King Lear* as well as references in sporting books. As far back as the 1570s, Caius classified the various groups of dogs, splitting his 'fowling' group into 'Index' (the Setters) and 'Aquaticus' (the Spaniels). Those two well-known diarists John Evelyn (his Spaniel was lost or stolen) and Samuel Pepys (he was somewhat less than complimentary about King Charles's dogs) both mention Spaniels, although the latter would have been the Toy variety. The Toys were most likely to have been produced by selective inbreeding from the larger Spaniels. There is a reference in an American book of the early 1600s, *Journal of the English Plantation at Plymouth* by G. Mourt, in which he reports that there were two dogs on the *Mayflower*, a Mastiff and a Spaniel. Surprisingly, in view of the fact that it is an American publication, there is no mention of this in Maxwell Riddle's book *The Springer Spaniel*. What he does mention, however, is the Irish laws of 17 AD where Water Spaniels were given as tribute to the king. But my friend Nick Waters does not give too much credence to this connection in his book *A Bundle of Rags in a Cyclone* (The Irish Water Spaniel) as he discovered that the term Spaniel had been used rather loosely to cover various breeds of dog. Mr Riddle also quotes the Welsh laws of 300 AD as mentioning Spaniels. Since he wrote his book, another of my friends, John Phillips, in the course of his research for *The Essential Welsh Springer*, discovered that this story was based on a 19th century mis-translation of an unauthenticated fourteenth draft or copy of these laws of Hywel Dda. Ted Orton, in one of his Monographs on the Sussex Spaniel, also mentions these laws, but, like Maxwell Riddle, his booklet pre-dates the Welsh book.

Both John and Ted mention the French claim that the word Spaniel is derived from the French word "S'espagner", to crouch. On reflection, I am inclined to agree. Bearing in mind the Moorish influence in Spain and the Mediterranean, I think any Spanish dogs of the times would be of the hound types still found in that area. Perhaps both derivations are feasible and the gifts in the Irish reference were indeed "Dogs of Spain" – but of a hound type, foundation of the great Irish tradition in running dogs.

In the absence of any official records for the various breeds, a great deal of trust must be placed on the contemporary literature of the times. One southern French nobleman, Gaston de Foix, who lived in the late 1300s, wrote *Le Livre de Chasse* which gives a description of Spaniel work that equates well with modern Spaniel tasks – quartering the ground, flushing game (albeit for hound or falcon and not the gun) and retrieving waterfowl. Obviously hounds and hawks are not water-minded (times haven't changed much – even on modern shoots Springers get called on to sort out the muddles). The reference by Mourt in the 1620s to the Spaniel on the *Mayflower* quotes the fact that it chased a deer! I have no doubt that John Goodman, the Spaniel's owner, had thoughts similar to those voiced by the Norfolk "beater" whose dog was coursing a hare on a pheasant drive – "d'yu catch ut you can damwell carry ut"! Another early reference to Spaniels in America is in a 1780 publication called the *Sportsman's Companion* which describes different varieties. Here again, as with all the early references, the accent is on the working abilities. Although there is no reference anywhere to Spaniels on the American continent prior to Mourt's account, I have often thought it highly likely that sometime between Columbus landing and the arrival of the Pilgrim Fathers, some of the Spanish grandees would have taken their sporting dogs with them to the new colonies and, with the Spaniel group's presumed Spanish derivation, surely Spaniels would have been included?

Of a similar period to Mourt's *American Journal*, an English book on fowling, *Hungers Prevention*, divides the Spaniel into land and water dogs. The author, the English writer Markham, goes on to subdivide the land Spaniels into crouching and springing, and splits the latter into two sizes, calling the smaller of the two Cocking Spaniels. A few phrases quoted verbatim from Markham's description of the land Spaniel's nature show that the dog's character has not changed much in three and a half centuries and that the breed remains "evermore loving and desiring toyle". Anybody who has known a Springer on a shooting morning will agree that "he is a strong, lusty, and nimble raundger, both of active foote, wanton tayle, and busie nostrill, that his toyle is without wearinesse". In 1638 Aldrovanus gives us a physical description that also sounds familiar: "Spaniel dog with floppy ears, the chest, belly and feet white, picked out with black, the rest of the body black" – which is a good description of a blue roan. In the 1700s there was a small black Spaniel in existence in England known as a Gredin. These were black, or black and tan, and they are of passing interest as a possible source of the tan in the other varieties of Spaniel.

PORTRAITS OF SPRINGER SPANIELS

Art is also a fruitful source of material of canine history. Those who have painted Spaniels in their works include Titian and Sir Anthony Van Dyck. One of the dogs in a Van Dyck portrait of the Royal children, Charles II, James II and Mary, looks to be quite tall. Of the sporting prints, one of the earliest, reproduced in my copy of Maxwell Riddle, is by Francis Barlow and shows a very definite Springer type which would not have looked out of place at shows a few years ago. The late Dorothy Hooper, in her book on the breed, mentions a portrait painted in 1712 of a little American girl named Darnall, of Baltimore, Maryland, with a Springer. As this was over half a century before the Declaration of Independence there had obviously been other Spaniels taken to the colonies by the settlers. What a pity no records appear to exist of those early days! Information is even scarcer concerning the rest of the world. Europe generally had its Spaniel types but these, through close breeding, had settled into their own localised breeds and varieties such as the Wachtelhund and the Brittany, although a lot of them bear more than a passing resemblance to the Springer. The different types of sport in those districts also had some bearing on the development of certain characteristics.

Towards the end of the 18th Century the Spaniel family was beginning to split into three groups. First the Toys, then came the two sporting branches, the Cockers for woodcock and smaller game – this section was up to 25lbs weight (about 13kgs) – and above them the Field Spaniels (at this time the term was a blanket description covering all the Spaniels that worked). As this was done purely on size, a "runty" Cocker could be a Toy, and some of our present-day Cavalier King Charles would definitely be Cockers. The same applied between the other two grades. With maturity a dog could progress from one grade to another.

SEPARATING THE VARIETIES OF SPANIELS

The early 1800s saw the gradual evolution of the idea of classifying and separating the different varieties of Spaniel by bloodlines rather than by size. The owners of the large estates were creating their own strains of sporting dogs with regard to their own special local conditions. Two examples of how these local strains became specific breeds in their own right are Sussex Spaniels and Gordon Setters. Some landowners, like the Boughey family of Aqualate, in Shropshire, started keeping their own stud records. In about 1800 the Aqualate strain of English Springers was founded and in 1813 a stud book was commenced, thus pre-dating the Kennel Club by some sixty years! Of course, the records were only for their own Spaniels and, when they had to have recourse to other people's stud dogs, all that appears on the records is an indication of the dog's name and the owner.

Over a century later, in 1903, Sir Thomas Boughey bred FT Ch. Velox Powder (owned by C. Eversfield of the Denne affix), who was fourteen generations descent from the original Mop I, of 1812, the first to appear in the Aqualate register. His breeding is shown as Sire: Lord Talbot's breed. Dam: Follett's Busy. With keeping their own breed records, I would have expected the Boughey family to have used Aqualate as an affix in much the same way as hound kennels did, but, although there are many references in pedigrees to the Aqualate strain, I cannot trace many dogs actually carrying the prefix, even after the formation of The Kennel Club. I also feel sure that, if the Boughey family were keeping their own private records, other breeders would have done the same, although none of them seem to have survived.

SHOWS AND THE KENNEL CLUB

This early period was still something of a melting pot as regards Spaniels generally, and it was not until the advent of dog shows in 1859 that the various breeds really began to separate. Admittedly, the divisions were still by size and colour rather than anything else, but the formation of the Kennel Club in 1873 would eventually help to change this with their official registrations and the creation of the Stud Book. During the transitional period the accent was still mainly on the sporting side. The breeds were still being intermingled and, even in the KC Registrations, puppies from the same litter would appear in more than one breed. However, separate breed clubs were gradually appearing and breed standards being formulated.

One of the early clubs was the Sporting Spaniel Club, which later changed its title to the Sporting Spaniel Society. It was founded in the late 1880s at a meeting at the Bull Hotel, Woodbridge, Suffolk, specifically to arrange competitive matches in the field, for hunting Spaniels. I believe that Ernest Wells, who later emigrated to the United States and had the Mahwire kennels there, was one of the persons present. They held the first Field Trial on Mr W. Arkwright's Derbyshire estate on January 3rd, 1899. Unfortunately there was no Springer, as such, among the awards, but this was hardly surprising as the breed would not officially exist for another two years. The Setters and Pointers had already been holding trials for over thirty years, their first being at Southill, Bedfordshire, in 1865 – a certain W. Arkwright being one of the instigators! Arkwright did have an assortment of other breeds in his kennel as well as his gundogs, including Dachshunds and Collies.

A lot of the breeders at this time were involved with more than one variety of Spaniel, mainly due to the idea of segregation by size and looks and not by breeding, and most of the Spaniel breeds of the period carry the blood of a dog called Bebb, bred by Phineas Bullock. Bebb was owned by T. Bowers and was registered as a liver-coloured Sussex. His sire was Old Bebb, described as "Lord Derby's breed", which were said to be Water Spaniels, probably liver or liver and white. Bebb's dam, Flirt, was the product of two black Cockers who were descended from the pairing of Burdett's Frank (black/tan) with Mousley's Venus (liver/white), a mating which appears quite a lot in Spaniel pedigrees. Bebb changed owners late in life and appears to have changed breed as well. He was exhibited as a Norfolk Spaniel, as were some of his progeny.

NORFOLK SPANIEL

The origin of the name Norfolk Spaniel is somewhat obscure. James Farrow, the Cocker breeder, went out of his way to disprove the connection with the Duke of Norfolk (for the benefit of overseas readers the ducal seat of the Norfolk family is in the county of Sussex, and very probably the gundogs used on the estate in the early 1800s would have been forebears of the present Sussex breed – the family were also involved with black and tan Toy Spaniels). Farrow dismisses the Norfolk Spaniel as a "myth and a delusion". He does not mention the more likely theory, which I prefer, that the term was used loosely to cover the many parti-coloured Spaniels used as gundogs in what is my home county, Norfolk. The name was still being used in the early days of shows and one of the first Tissingtons to be shown, Tissington Flush, was exhibited as a Norfolk Spaniel. There is a painting of her by Maud Earl. A Norfolk Spaniel, Dash II, was shown at the New York Fanciers Show at Madison Square Garden in 1886.

One of the many estates in Norfolk to use Springers during this time was the Royal Estate at Sandringham, which, undoubtedly, was one reason why they were called Norfolk Spaniels. In the early part of the 1860s the then Prince of Wales, later Edward VII, had purchased Sandringham and developed driven game shooting there. The grandsire of Ranger of Ranscombe, Ben, owned by Earl Fortescue, was a present to the Earl from the Prince of Wales. Other large estates in or on the fringes of Norfolk such as Holkham, Euston, Merton and Elveden, all used Spaniels in the same way as the Sandringham Estate. The famous Caistor strain was owned by Mr H. Green of Caistor St Edmond on the outskirts of Norwich. The Horsford strain derived from Caistor stock. I believe Mr Green originated from Sussex and owned a Sussex bitch called Chloe in the mid-1870s. She, in due time, was mated to one of the popular stud dogs of the time and produced a dog, Chance II, who did quite a lot for the Sussex. His brother started life as Guess but was renamed Caistor and as such appears in many of the old Sussex pedigrees. Presumably the change of name came about when Mr Green moved to Norfolk, and it makes one wonder whether it was intended as an affix, and also whether, during the next twenty or so years, he was assimilated into the Norfolk/Field Spaniels in the kennels. Norfolk Spaniels were classified as a separate breed by the Spaniel Club at one time, although, thanks to Farrow's intervention, they were eventually deleted and came under the heading of Springers. I understand one reason why Farrow was against the Duke of Norfolk's connection was the fact that the Duke would not part with, nor let anybody else breed from, his line.

ENGLISH WATER SPANIEL

The old English Water Spaniel is another component breed of the modern English Springer that has become extinct as a separate entity. As has been mentioned, the sire of the ubiquitous Bebb was believed to have been an English Water Spaniel. Sir Hugo FitzHerbert of the Tissingtons also bred them, as he did Norfolks, so very probably these were incorporated in his strain. These English Water Spaniels were slightly larger than the Springers then in vogue. One of his later Champions was alleged to be a straight cross between a Cocker and an English Setter. Winton Smith was another who kept English Water Spaniels, in his Beechgrove kennels. The Ware kennels came into being during this time, founded by H. S. Lloyd's father, Richard. It was basically a Cocker kennel, with some Field Spaniels. In view of the kennel's subsequent involvement with Springers, I surmise that these Fields were most likely of the type that evolved into the Springer.

THE START OF FIELD TRIALS

The Spaniel Club, which published breed standards, had been formed in 1885 and was registered with the Kennel Club on June 2nd 1891. The Sporting Spaniel Society had also been formed and was the first of the two clubs to run a Field Trial – as I have said, this was in January 1899. The winner is recorded as Isaac Sharpe's liver/white Cocker, Stylish Pride, although she is probably behind some of the Stylish Springers.

The Sporting Spaniel Club's second Trial was held in the December of 1899 and, officially, no Springer was amongst the awards. However, the winner, Burton Duchess, was a liver and white Spaniel bitch, so perhaps we can chalk it up on our side of the fence! The Spaniel Club decided to run Field Trials to help counteract the breeding of exaggerated show points. Basset hound blood had been introduced into some Field Spaniel lines to produce longer and lower dogs, and, of course, the Spaniel varieties were still all being interbred. The Spaniel Club's first Trial, held in

F. Winton Smith with Harrington, head keeper at Clumber Park and trainer J. Alexander, with Clumber Spaniels Beechgrove Annette and Beechgrove Bee.

January, 1900, was won by Mr F. Winton Smith with a Clumber, Beechgrove Bee. Winton Smith later exported some of his famous Beechgrove Springers to Canada, one of which (Beechgrove Teal) carried some Clumber blood. The Spaniel Club's second Trial a year later saw the first official mention of a Springer winning the stake (not English Springer Spaniel, for this was still several months before official KC recognition) in the shape of Tring, owned by Mr J.P. Gardner. This is the same Mr Gardner of the Hagley kennels.

Winton Smith also dabbled in other breeds such as Pointers, Setters, Retrievers, Beagles and several varieties of Terrier. Apart from his Clumbers and his English Water Spaniels, his other Spaniel breeds, prior to 1902, were listed as Norfolk, Field, and Cockers. Obviously the Norfolks and, doubtless, some of the Field and Cockers, would be assimilated into the new breed. I believe he built up his Beechgrove strain on breeding type to type, rather than close inbreeding, to fix points. Winton Smith was lucky in having J. Alexander as his trainer, who had his own quite well-known strain, and used the affix of Suddern Warren – his S. W. Bob was from the same dam as Beechgrove Mark'em.

RECOGNITION FOR THE ENGLISH SPRINGER SPANIEL

The ingredients having been assembled now seemed a good time to stir the pudding. The resulting dish was the English Springer Spaniel, and in 1902 the English Kennel Club granted the breed full recognition in its own right in the official KC Stud Book. This was as a result of a meeting held on November 19th 1901, with Mr Harding Cox, Harry Jones and Dr J. Sidney Turner as Kennel Club appointees, and Mr W. Arkwright, Mr S. Smale and Mr B. J. Warwick representing the various interested clubs. This new breed would include dogs from various sources – some, such as the Aqualates, with reasonably authenticated documentation, others, no doubt, kept equally pure as a strain but without breeding records. The rest would consist of those that had been classified as other breeds for lack of a suitable slot, and those of indeterminate parentage but which looked like Springers.

At this time the Welsh Springer was acknowledged as a separate breed, although their purity of type had been fixed for quite a long time before. Up till then they had been known as Welsh Cockers. I mention this because one of the original entries in the KCSB as a WSS also appears in a previous volume as a Welsh Cocker. This is Corrin of Gerwn who is important by reason of the fact that some of his progeny are registered as ESS e.g. Guy of Gerwn and Rover of Gerwn. Rover sired the black and white Don Juan of Gerwn, who was exported to Canada.

AMERICA

Apart from the earlier Springers mentioned, more Springers seem to have been introduced to the US in the first decade of the 1800s, although the numbers appear to have declined later in the century. These early Spaniels were quite common and were to be found in most towns and villages, especially where there was close proximity to game areas. The Spaniels were usually worked in the swamplands and brambles on wildfowl and partridge, much as in England. The decline in numbers was caused by a drop in the numbers of game and the growing popularity of the Setters and Pointers, which increased with the spread westward into the plains area where quail were numerous. Later on, the development of the pheasant as a game bird increased the breed's popularity again.

After the breed had been separately classified in England, the first recorded imports to the US, under the new title, were to New Jersey for a Mr R. D. Foot. This was in 1907. Ernest Wells of the Mahwire Kennels, Mahwah, New Jersey, who imported the two dogs on behalf of Mr Foot, wrote in the *American Dog World* in March and April 1949 claiming that his family had Springers for over one hundred years and that he had been given his first puppy by his father, sixty-five years previously. I think this should be Springer with a small "s", as this pre-dates the official designation by several decades. The two imports were Trimbly Trick, a dog that was looked upon as a model for the breed, and reported to be of pure Springer blood for over fifty years, which puts him in line with the Aqualates etc., and the bitch Blythburgh Bess. I assume she came from the area of that name on the East coast of Suffolk and, quite possibly, carried Caistor and Horsford blood.

CANADA

The breed appears to have started in Canada at about the same time. The first recorded showing of a Springer was at the Victoria Show in 1913. This was M. Coleman's Jack, no breeding or age being given. In 1914 a dog called Longbranch Teal was registered in the Canadian Stud Book. He was bred in Canada from Beechgrove stock, being by Beechgrove Owen out of B. Teal, who carried Clumber blood. Some further Beechgroves appeared in Canada at about this period. Mr Wolfe of Toronto imported B. Bounce and B. Fly (both liver/white – but their son Niagara Prince was black/white/tan!). B. Nutty and B. Florette went to Hoyes Lloyd of Toronto (not to be confused with the Wizard of Ware). Also Toronto-bound was B. Roddy, to Mr E. J. Marsh. At about this time too, Mr W. Gardiner of Winnipeg imported the afore-mentioned Don Juan of Gerwn. Don Juan was instrumental in firing the enthusiasm for the breed of Eudore Chevrier. The appearance of a tri-colour from the Beechgrove pair, although it contradicts one of the widely-held genetic myths, should not be too much of a surprise, as this was quite a common colour in the early dogs. Many of the Caistor strain were of this colour, as were a lot of the Horsfords.

BENCH CHAMPIONS

Meanwhile, back in England, the first pair of Bench champions had been made up, in the shape of Beechgrove Will (Winton Smith) and Fansome, owned by Jones. The bitch Fansome was also of Beechgrove breeding, and her sister later became Ch. Beechgrove Alexandra. She was bred by Sir Hugo FitzHerbert. Another sister was Tissington Flush. The first Challenge Certificates for the breed were offered by the KC at their show at the Crystal Palace in October 1902. The classes were for ESS over 25lbs and under 50lbs. Judged by Mr Arkwright, the winners were the aforementioned pair, Will and Fansome. The next two shows with CCs were in 1903 at the Crystal Palace and in Birmingham. Will was victorious at both, getting made up at three straight shows. Fansome took longer to finish, winning the tickets at Birmingham in 1903 and 1904.

Pictured left to right: Beechgrove Will, Beechgrove Primrose and Beechgrove Alexandra.

FIELD TRIAL CHAMPIONS

The first FT Chs. were Velox Powder, bred by Sir Thomas Boughey of pure Aqualate strain, and Rivington Sam, bred by C. A. Phillips by Spot of Hagley ex one of his Cocker bitches, Rivington Riband. Riband was oversized for a Cocker. Velox was owned by Mr C. C. (Bethune) Eversfield and, for a while, he named his dogs after various makes of gunpowder; later he used the affix Denne. Apart from the Aqualate blood through Velox, many of his dogs were of Beechgrove breeding, FT Ch. Cannonite Powder being by Ch. Beechgrove Will. Mated to Denne Nitro, a son of Velox, Cannonite produced Denne Punch, whose most influential son was Ch. Little Brand.

Another sire of great importance owned by Eversfield was FT Ch. Denne Duke. Duke's sire, Bosh, was a son of Dash of Hagley. Beechgrove Nelly, when mated to Duke, produced Beechgrove Mark'em. This dog (apart from being father to several of the Horsfords) was mated to Beechgrove Vera and sired a dog who was to have a profound influence for many years on both sides of the Atlantic. I am, of course, referring to the great Ch. Springbok of Ware. Unfortunately, Eversfield died in 1915 and his kennel was disbanded. Probably his last triumph was the winning of the first Spaniel Championship Field Trial organised by the Spaniel Club on behalf of the KC at Wytham Abbey, Oxon, in January 1914, when Duke beat Rivington Sam. The judges were Lt Col. C. Heseltine and Mr Lewis Wigan. Eversfield also won the Brace stake with Duke and D Jester. This pair, together with V Powder and D Normal, took the Team stake to give the kennel a clean sweep of all three stakes.

For the first ten years the Spaniel Championship was truly that – an any-variety Spaniel stake, with entry by qualification. The first stake had nine English Springers, three Cockers and one Clumber competing. Following the death of Bethune Eversfield, his dogs were sold by auction and Velox Powder and Duke were withdrawn from stud. Denne Lucy, dam of Nitro, had already gone to the US in 1910.

INFLUENTIAL DOGS

Contemporaries of C. C. Eversfield whose dogs were to have an influence on later generations were, among others, Mr Gardner (Hagley), Sir Hugo FitzHerbert (Tissington), Isaac Sharpe (Stylish) and William Humphrey (Horsford). The latter was living in Norfolk at this time, at Black Park, in the village from whence he took his affix. Horsford lies about five miles north of Norwich, so it is not too surprising that he should use the Caistor dogs of H. P. Green, who lived a similar distance to the south of the city at Caistor St Edmond Hall. Mr Green owned the CC-winning Thorington Flush, by his Caistor Gunner out of Ch. Fansome.

Prior to using the Horsford affix, William Humphrey had registered one or two dogs with the prefix of Will's. There were also other members of the family involved, registering Springers under the Wilful or Bradshaw labels, although the breeding was all the same. Many of the well-known Springers seem to have changed hands several times. C. Mackay Sanderson is on record as stating that six main lines are responsible for today's Springer. In chronological order these are: FT Ch. Velox Powder, Dash of Hagley, Denne Duke, Caistor Rex, FT Ch. Rivington Sam and Cornwallis Cavalier. In practice, this is really only four lines, as Duke is a grandson of Dash of Hagley and Cavalier's grandmother was by Velox Powder ex Rivington Romp.

FT Ch. Denne Duke, through his son Beechgrove Mark'em, appears behind all the Bench winners of today, especially via the lines descended from Int. Ch. Springbok of Ware. Dash of Hagley also sired Foel Jock, whose progeny is spread through both Bench and Trial sides of the breed. From Jock's son, Foel Poncho, derive the Bryngarw, Tedwyns and O'Vara Field Trial lines. His other son, Chancefield Jock, was the sire of the first American Field Trial winner, Am. FT Ch. Aughrim Flashing. More importantly, however, he was the father of Chum of Chancefield who

Ch. Velox Powder.

FT Ch. Rivington Sam.

sired Rufton Flirt, dam of Rufton Recorder. FT Ch. Velox Powder also has more Bench descendants than on the Trial side. His son, Slinfold Mac, was the sire of Ch. Andon of Leam, who fathered Int. Ch. Nuthill Dignity. The dam of Dignity, Ch. Banchory Tranquil, was by Ch. Little Brand. Brand, who was a great-grandson of Velox Powder, also appears in many other lines. Velox's influence on the trial lines comes mainly through Cornwallis Cavalier via the Cairnies, Avendale and Fintry lines. Aughrim Flashing's dam, Rose of Avendale, was by Cavalier. She was also descended from Caistor Rex on her dam's side.

FT Ch. Rivington Sam is of far more importance to the Trial lines, especially through his sons Rivington Bobstay and Rivington Samson. Bobstay sired, among others, Dalshangan Dandy Boy, who left his mark on the Trial world on both sides of the Atlantic. Samson was the sire of FT Ch. Rex of Avendale, grandsire to Rufton Recorder. Sam is also behind most of the Avendales, Banchorys and the Cairnies. Caistor Rex owes his main lines to his grandson Gunner of Crombie (formerly Horsford Hunt), sire of Horsford Hetman (who had at least three lines to Rex) and great-grandsire to Flint of Avendale whose sire, Bob of Crombie, was by Hetman's brother and probably carried four lines to Rex.

By one of those strange quirks of fate, just after the breed lost Mr Eversfield, a young teacher, who was later to became one of the staunchest supporters of the dual-purpose Springer, purchased her first English Springer. Ranger of Ranscombe was born in 1915 and founded the Ranscombe dynasty that lasted well over half a century in an unbroken line which only ended with the death of Dorothy Morland Hooper in 1970. Miss Hooper purchased a bitch, Rival of Ranscombe, in 1917 and in her first litter, to Ranger, produced Ch. Reipple of Ranscombe. Amongst the Crufts CC winners of the period up to the start of the First World War we find Ch. Beechgrove Donaldson won four times, Ch. Tissington Frocks three, Tissington Bounce two and Ch. Tissington Fact and Ch. Bush (grandmother of Horsford Hetman) appear once each. This would be virtually the last of these two great strains that had given so much to the breed in the previous fifty years. Beechgrove Lalia was Best of Breed at Crufts 1917 with no "tickets", and a Tissington bitch, Fragrants, mated to Horsford Hetman in the 1920s, was the dam of Am. Ch. Horsford Historical.

A line that was influential at this time was the Leam kennels of J. Anderson. A combination of Tissington and Beechgrove blood, when later allied to the Rivington and Denne lines, would give us Chs. Little Brand and Nuthill Dignity. Anderson also owned and bred Ch. Andon of Leam. Cornwallis Cavalier, latterly owned by Mr L. D. Wigan (of the Cairnies), was found by Tom Gaunt (then trainer for the Duke of Hamilton) running behind a butcher's cart! Whether or not this tale is

Int. Ch. Springbok of Ware.

Avendales: FT Ch. Prince, Rag, Reva and Rex.

apocryphal, he acquired the dog, who sired many of the Avendale FT Chs. – his progeny proving far more important than his antecedents. He did much the same job of founding a line for the Of Cairnies.

During this period there were many less well-known kennels and strains that provided a link with the older bloodlines and a solid basis for some of the lines that would follow. Among these was J. Dalgleish of Galashiels, in the Scottish Borders, who exported several of his Ellwyns to Canada and the US, one of which was Ellwyn Lady who went, in whelp, to Robert Fox of Ottawa. There was also J. Wood, whose dogs all carried the word Fire as the first part of their name. His Fireworks was the first of many dual-purpose dogs owned by him. She was a daughter of Rex of Avendale. The litter resulting from her mating to Cornwallis Cavalier contained Firecrest, grandmother of the immortal Rufton Recorder. At this time, too, the Chancefield strain had come into being. This was based on C. Cleo (Rivington Sam ex Susan of the Cairnies) and a dog, C. Jock, by Foel Jock out of Foel Dacia. A son of this pair was Chum of C. who, when put to Firecrest, sired Rufton Flirt. The Foel line was owned by H. W. Carlton (who wrote one of the early books on Spaniel training) and was predominantly the old Hagley strain. Like most of these early bloodlines, it is behind both Bench and Trial lines of today. Carlton's 1914 book, *Spaniels: Their Breaking for Sport and Field Trials*, which had an introduction by W. Arkwright, was the first of its kind, and is generally recognised as the pattern for the various books that followed.

In these first two decades of the "new" breed, good foundations were being laid for future generations by some of the kennels that would become famous. Horsford Hyssop was bred by the Boughey family and was, presumably, pure Aqualate, and Horsford Heiress was out of Thorington Flush and thus was grand-daughter to Ch. Fansome. Reva of Avendale was a daughter of Hyssop and Denne Jester and was dam of many Field Trial winners. This was the period when the Ware kennels of Mr H. S. Lloyd became prominent in the breed. However, this was not, as in the case of the Ware Cockers, as a specific strain, but rather in Lloyd's other guise as a fancier. By a series of astute purchases of likely-looking Springers, either for show or trials, he brought to the fore several dogs that would prove to be extremely beneficial to the breed. Ch. Springbok of Ware belonged to this era. Bred by Major Paine, he was a son of Beechgrove Mark'em, his dam, Beechgrove Vera, being by Ch. B. Donaldson ex Ch. Tissington Frocks. Luckily he sired several litters in this country before he went to Canada.

Other "seedlings" that would mature into influential strains over the next few years were Lady Iris Portal's Laverstokes; the Little/L'ile kennel of David MacDonald; A. McNab Chassels' famous Inveresk dogs (these too had a definite transatlantic influence), the Banchorys, owned by Countess Howe (as Mrs Quintin Dick she showed and made up Ch. Hemlington Kalgar, a Springbok son), and the start of Florrie Turner's respected Renrut strain. The Banchorys of Countess Howe, apart from the Bench Ch. B. Tranquil (Little Brand ex a Springbok daughter) were best known as Trial dogs, although bred on dual-purpose lines. Her early dogs were B. Jock, a grandson of the trial-winning Tellax, and B. Mick by Rivington Sam. Banchory Gloss, who is behind many Field Trial winners, was bred by J. Hulme by Little Brand from his Withington Duster, a Rivington Bobstay daughter. Gloss, apart from breeding FT Ch. Banchory Bright from her mating to Tedwyns Trex, produced FT Ch. Bryngarw Jock and Noranby Rhys when put to J. Wood's Fireflash. The Countess later concentrated on her Labradors in which she made up several Dual Champions – a feat which eluded her in Springers. Her forthright and autocratic personality held the Bench and Trial factions of the Labradors together for a longer period than in Springers.

Lady Portal started her strain with a bitch, Laverstoke Sapphire, by Beechgrove Mark'em out of B. Gyp, and a dog L. Bustler, whose parents were also Beechgroves, Gamester and Vanda. Soon after came L. Nell, litter sister to Horsford Hella, dam of Hetman. The foundations of David MacDonald's kennels were based on L'ile Merle by Rivington Sam and Little Sunray from unregistered parents. However, the success of his line is undoubtedly due to his stud dog of that time, Ch. Little Brand, who was almost pure Beechgrove breeding. He also owned the famous Ch. Nuthill Dignity.

It is hard to pinpoint where Bailie McNab Chassels did in fact start. He had previously owned a well-known kennel of King Charles Spaniels and had also done well in Airedales and Alsatians (German Shepherds). The first Inveresk English Springer I can trace would seem to be Inveresk Countess, by Stylish Bounce out of Cherry. Bounce was a son of Ch. Roverson of Gerwn. Countess owned amongst her progeny many who were to be an influence overseas. The title Bailie is a purely Scottish one, meaning a Scottish municipal magistrate, which is loosely equivalent to the American town Judge. Besides breeding, McNab Chassels also made one or two astute purchases and changed their names. Major of Craigie, by Little Brand became I. Caruno, originally obtained to mate to Countess, but I cannot, in fact, find whether she had a litter to him. A son of Springbok of Ware, originally called Dilkusha Punch, was later acquired, renamed, and became a top sire on both sides of the Atlantic as I. Chancellor.

Chapter Two

DEVELOPMENT OF THE ENGLISH SPRINGER SPANIEL

The twenty-five year period from 1920 to 1945 was arguably the most important in the Breed's history, even more so than the first ten years to the outbreak of the First World War. The increase in the number of shows and Field Trials in the post-war years led to the consolidation of the breeding programmes of those pre-war breeders still extant. It also saw the foundation and growth of many of the well-known kennels which influenced the breed in future years. It was a period when the dual-purpose Springer was still a reality, before the quest for perfection in both Bench and Field and, therefore, specialisation in both spheres, led to the divergence of type seen today.

The first five years produced the three UK Dual Champions – Horsford Hetman (he was actually born in 1919, but for practical purposes can be counted in this section), his son, Thoughtful of Harting, and Flint of Avendale. There were several dogs too that gained both CCs and Field Trial awards but just fell short of the target on one side or the other. An Eng. FT Ch., Tedwyns Trex, exported to the Ferguson family of New York, became an Am. Dual Ch. at about this same time. There were also three recorded Dual Chs. in the US in the mid to late 1930s – Green Valley Punch, King Lion and Fast. Newcomers to the breed, seeking a bit of sport in the shooting field or relaxation at dog shows after the upsets of the 1914-1918 years, included F. Warner Hill (Beauchief), Maj. H. Doyne Ditmas (Boghurst), Col. F. Carrell (Harting), G. A. Taylor (Carnfield), W. D. Edwards (Pierpoint), H. Ogden (Merlin) and, on the purely Field Trial side, Messrs. Trotter and Byrne of the Dalshangan and Tedwyns kennels respectively. Some of these had perhaps bred prior to this, but were new to competition. George Taylor had been involved with Field Spaniels successfully. The English Springer Spaniel Club was formed at a meeting held at Crufts Show in 1921. This was an exciting day for William Humphrey – not only had he won BoB with Horsford Hetman but he was also elected Secretary of the new Breed Club. Other events of importance in the first full year of activity after the War were the foundation of the Beauchief kennel, the gaining of the title of FT Ch. by Horsford Hetman and, most

Walton Ferguson with Am. Dual Ch. Tedwyns Trex and Trex of Chancefield.

important as far as transatlantic breeding was concerned, the kindling of the interest of Eudore Chevrier in the working capabilities of the Springer. Apart from Hetman getting well on the way to his Dual Title, this was the year that Flint of Avendale first saw the light of day.

THE CANADIAN CONNECTION

Flint was one of several Avendales that went to Canada to found the North American kennels of a similar name, Avandale, owned by Eudore Chevrier. These imports, and others, augmented the previous bloodlines brought in earlier. Together with Flint went numerous other top Field Trial and Bench winners. Eudore Chevrier's ancestry is as interesting as that of the breed which he so successfully popularised in Canada and the American Midwest as he was a descendant of Breton stock on his father's side and had a Scottish mother. In 1914 he owned the imported Ch. Don Juan of Gerwn. This Spaniel was also in the ownership of Mr W. Gardiner of Winnipeg for a time. Don Juan fired the enthusiasm of Chevrier for the dual-purpose English Springer. At the end of the First World War, Chevrier, whose family owned one of the largest fur businesses in Canada at that time, decided that the Springer was the ideal dog for sportsmen in the area and set out to found a top dual-purpose kennel of the breed.

In three and a half years up to 1925 he imported no less than 250 dogs, including English Bench and Field Trial winners such as Dual Ch. Flint of Avendale, FT Ch. Flush of Avendale, FT Ch. Dan of Avendale, Ch. Springbok of Ware, Ch. Boghurst Rover, Ch. Laverstoke Powderhorn and many more of almost equal calibre. In 1925 there were around 600 Springers in his kennels, he had his own team of trainers and had puppies out being "walked" on about 100 prairie farms! At New York's Westminster Show in 1925 he showed 11 Springers (in 1993, when Ch. Salilyns Condor was Best in Show, the total breed entry was 18). His team at a Field Trial that year numbered 10. Chevrier bred and reared many puppies and most were sold either part or fully trained. Nowadays he would be termed a puppy farmer, or factory breeder, but his profound influence on the breed in the years between the Wars was undoubtedly of great benefit to breeders in Canada and the US. Many of the later top kennels were based on Avandale stock which provided a solid foundation for breeding to the later imports. It is a pity, from the aspect of canine genealogy, that he could not have found an affix (Avandale) a bit further removed from that of the Duke of Hamilton (Avendale), but he was an entrepreneur par excellence.

FORMATION OF THE CANADIAN BREED CLUB

In 1922 Chevrier, together with some of the other Canadian Springer breeders, founded the English Springer Spaniel Club of Canada and, in the fall of that year, they organised the first Field Trial held in North America, at Ste Agathe, thirty miles south of Winnipeg. The judges were W. Lee, W. McCall and Freeman Lloyd who was a canine journalist and writer on outdoor sports of long standing. His career had started nearly forty years previously in the kennel section of a London weekly, *The Stock-keeper*, reporting on shows and Field Trials and also contributing some items to the canine gossip column 'Whispers of Fancy'! The Trial was fixed for September 30th and was run on the same lines as English Trials with live game. Unfortunately, in their enthusiasm, the organisers overlooked the fact that the official season for prairie chicken (sharp-tailed grouse) did not open until October 15th. However, the Department of Agriculture gave special permission for the Trial to be held. The novice stake was won by Patty of Avendale, second came Miss Lucy of Avandale and Ch. Springbok of Ware took third place. In the Open stake the placings were: Winner Ch. Laverstoke Powderhorn, followed by Ch. Don Juan of Gerwn with Flight of Blockley third. The interesting thing about this is that Powderhorn was a fairly recent import, Don Juan was over ten years old, and Flight had only arrived from England five days before the Trials.

THE US BREED CLUB

The parent breed club in the US, the English Springer Spaniel Field Trial Association, was also formed in 1922. The founders were three brothers, Walton, Henry and Alfred Ferguson, together with Samuel Allen and William Hutchinson. Their consultant and general adviser was Wm. Humphrey who just happened to drop by. They held their first Field Trial in October 1924. First and second were both owned and handled by Mr Humphrey. The winner, Aughrim Flashing, was later sold to Mrs Walton Ferguson and, in 1927, had the honour to become the first American Field Trial Champion. Horsford Hale was second and, I believe, later became a Bench champion. Flashing was by Chancefield Jock, and Hale by Horsford Hetman.

The first Specialty Show was also held in 1922, in New Jersey, and, a year later, the first general championship Show to specially classify English Springers was held at Madison Square Gardens. The winner was Horsford Highness, another son of Hetman. In 1927 the American Kennel Club formally recognised the Association as the parent club and, therefore, responsible for such things as breed standards and the organisation of Trials and Shows. The original standard formulated by the Association stood until the mid-1950s with very little change. It was adopted on July 12th 1932. The committee of five enlisted to draw it up were determined that it would reflect the differences between the various Spaniel breeds. It was felt that the English KC had been rather lenient in permitting some of the inter-breeding with different varieties. It is quite possible that, by breeding from the basic general type of Springer available, the early American dogs were nearer the desired Standard than some of the UK dogs which had had the benefit of some well-meant outcrosses. I believe one of the Rufton imports was taken as the archetype, although back in the UK this strain was generally criticised as being too cockery. It is ironic that some of the points those who formulated the US Standard were trying to avoid, such as over-round heavy bone, deep stops and Clumbery forefaces, too low a set to the ears like Cockers and too short a back spoiling the movement, have crept into some of the Bench strains over the last fifteen or so years, leading to the UK parent Club thinking that perhaps the modern American Show-type of Springer should be classed as a different Breed. In view of the above it is interesting to note that the Breed Standard in the UK was not stabilised until May 16th 1934! Up until then there were four standards in existence – those of the ESSC of England, the Spaniel Club of England, and their Scottish counterparts. One significant difference between the two new Standards was in height, the US standard asking eighteen and a half inches (27cms), whereas the English standard stated up to twenty inches (31cms). This was one reason why the Rufton strain was so successful in the US.

UK REGISTRATIONS

Resumption of competitions in the UK after the War meant that the number of registrations with the Kennel Club increased dramatically from 29 in 1919 to over 150 in 1920 and just short of 400 the following year. By 1925 registrations had soared to around 1400, although by 1930 they had dropped back to 1100. There were, naturally, many more unregistered Springers, that did quite a bit for the breed, appearing in the stud books as parents or grandparents of some of the top Bench or Trial winners, a case in point being the foundation bitch of the Beauchief kennels. She was B. Lady Barbara, by Allestree Pride, who was quite a well-known sire by Ch. Little Brand. However, his dam, Ruby, was unregistered. Barbara's dam, Ashbourne Kit, is recorded as "pedigree unknown". As Barbara's litter sister, Ashbourne Splendour, produced Ch. Standard, the lack of paperwork did not seem to affect the genetic makeup of the line. Standard was bred in 1934 by A. V. Blake, of Derbyshire, who used the Ashbourne prefix on occasions, sometimes abbreviating it to Ashbon, but quite often using no affix at all. Standard was purchased and campaigned by George Taylor of Carnfields. He also did this with more stock from Blake, who was then using the prefix Albvic after the Second World War.

INDIAN INTEREST

Mention of Ch. Standard leads to thoughts of India, which was then still part of the British Empire. The British living there at the time had introduced Shows and Trials, with Springers being one of the more popular breeds for these events. Foremost among the Indian nobility to take an interest in the breed was H. H. the Maharajah Dhiraj of Patiala. His first acquisition from England was a bitch called Cidger, a grand-daughter of Ch. Rivington Bobstay, sent out by David Macdonald of the L'ile kennels. Other imports soon followed – Ch. Standard (CC winner at the 1926 Crufts), Ashbourne Stroller and Ch. L'ile Buccaneer. Buccaneer had, as parents, the two Champions Little Brand and Reipple of Ranscombe.

Int. Ch. Inveresk Coronation.

From him and Cidger the Maharajah bred Crusader of Malwa who, after gaining his Indian title, was sent to England and campaigned to his English Championship by the Ware kennels. Crusader also ran in Trials. Another purchase by the Rajah was Ch. Inveresk Coronation but, probably, his most famous dog was the Field Trial winner Wakes Wager. The dog stayed in England until he had won his English crown in 1937. He was next campaigned in 1939 to his Indian title and then, on the death of His Highness, finally joined the Greenfair kennels of Joseph Quirk in Connecticut, who, in 1941, collected the title of Am. FT Ch. with him. To be a FT Ch. in three continents must have made him a rather special dog and I have often wondered about the different types of game and cover he must have experienced in his career. During the twenties and thirties the Maharajah had many of his dogs kennelled in England and they figured prominently in the Bench and Trial awards. The litter brother to Wakes Wager, FT Ch. Busy Lad of Ware, stayed in England, under the ownership of the Maharajah. The Field Trial dogs, like all those connected with the Ware kennels, were trained and handled by Reg Hill.

Triple Int. FT Ch. Wakes Wager of Greenfair.

GEORGE TAYLOR OF CARNFIELDS

Soon after the resumption of Shows, George Taylor of the Carnfields made a re-appearance. As I have mentioned, prior to the First World War he had owned and shown Field Spaniels, among them Ch. Carnfield Queen. His foundation bitch in Springers, Carnfield Cassie, was by Horsford Hetman. By mating Cassie to Little King, Taylor bred the winners Nancy, Doll and King. The latter was quite a popular stud dog, as Little King was by Ch. Little Brand out of Ch. Little Sunray. At one time the kennel owned and made up Ch. Standard, and a daughter of C. King, put to Standard, whelped the two sisters Lily and Lucy. Ch. Boghurst Bristle spent some time in the kennel and left behind some winning stock. One, C. Gem (out of Lily) was covered by Ch. Marmion, and their daughter, C. Betty, was the dam of Sadie of Shotton. Lucy's daughter by Bristle, Dual Chance, when paired with Marmion, produced Ch. Fanshawe Fury, again owned by the Shotton kennel. A further connection with the Shottons was through the sister of Dual Chance, a bitch called Farm Blossom. She had a litter by Carnfield King Again, which contained the bitch Ridgeway Brenda, who won CCs for the Shotton kennel. C. King Again was by Carnfield Bristle out of Lily; Bristle was by Boghurst Bristle out of Judy of Marmion. There was some gossip that some of the original Carnfield Field Spaniel blood had been introduced into the later Springers by means of a re-registration of a bitch, although Warner Hill of Beauchief thought the cross was beneficial. George Taylor left the breed at the end of the thirties, but re-appeared in the mid-forties with some stock descended from his old lines.

THE TRANSATLANTIC TRADE

By 1925 a lot of the "pillars of the breed" had made their mark and some of them had left the UK shores for Canada, the US and elsewhere. Fortunately, most of them had left behind some good stock. When Mr H. Placey took Ch. Inveresk Chancellor to Quebec it meant that four generations in tail male descent had crossed the Atlantic – Chs. Springbok, Jambok and Jamson of Ware, plus Chancellor, who had started life as Dilkusha Punch. As well as Chancellor, Mr Placey also imported Inveresk Cocksure, and the bitches Fleur of Orford and Sequence, to both of which he added his prefix of Belmoss. Fleur of Orford was one of the ubiquitous Beechgrove Mark'em/Vandala litter which also contained Floss of O., grandmother of Ch. Timperley Gunmaster. But the most important of the crop was the bitch Vandoreen. Among her progeny were Am. Ch. Maid of Honour (dam of Fod Seeta – also a prominent matron) by Andon of Leam, Rufton Reece (by N. Dignity) and the litter by Rex of Avendale which was probably the most influential and contained Breckonhill Vanlotta, Rex of Glasnevrin and his brother Boss of G. She had also had a litter to Flint of A., a dog from which, Hatch Viceroy, was the sire of Dilkusha Velvet.

Ch. Inveresk Cocksure was a son of Dual Ch. Flint out of Ch. Inveresk Careful whose parents were Ch. Little Brand and Ch. Inveresk Countess. Cocksure does not seem to have sired anything of importance before he left, but, crossed with the Belvidere lines bred from the original Beechgrove pair imported by Hoyes Lloyd, he helped to found the Belmoss kennels which were fairly well-known in Canadian circles at the time. They produced many Canadian and American Champions including the prominent sire Belmoss Chessman, who was actually by Chancellor, owned by Fred Hadley of Ohio. Others to benefit from the Belmoss blood were A. M. Nichter's Avalon kennels in Ohio; the Tuscawilla kennels of Dana Knight at Charleston, W. Va; Freeman's Lammond Springers based in Ontario and also the Shagmoor kennels owned by Dr W. Rohrkaste of Pittsburgh. Dr Rohrkaste had also imported Ch. Advent of Solway from Tom Meageen of the Mockerkin kennels and piloted him to his American and Canadian titles. Inevitably, he was by Chancellor.

THE IRISH CONNECTION

Advent was BIS at Manchester Championship Show in 1930. He was bred by Bob Grierson, who handled him for Tom Meageen as he did most of the Meageen-owned gundogs, the Mockerkins being primarily a terrier kennel. At this time the Solway dogs were doing quite a lot of winning. Chs. and CC winners included Dairymaid, Winning Number, Third Degree, Advent, Admiration, Miss Amy, Lovebird and Sensation. Admiration and Winning Number were also owned by Tom Meageen. The Mockerkins were based in the north-west corner of England and the Solways situated just across the border into Scotland. This proximity to the Stranraer to Larne ferry meant that Ireland was as conveniently reached as a lot of the southern England Shows. This proved to be important in the period after World War Two when some of the bloodlines returned. Other dogs that Tom Meageen was campaigning at this time were Flashdale, one of the widespread Andon of Leam/Vandoreen litter, and Inveresk Comforter. This last pair were behind Pasture Juanita, one of the early dogs owned by Mrs Dixon-Johnson.

AMERICAN IMPORTS
Jamson of Ware had gone to the Avalon kennels of A. M. Nichter of Ohio, as had Belmoss Fleur of Orford. After getting her Can. Ch. with H. Placey, she had gone to the Shagmoor kennels of Dr Rohrkaste, where she finished her Am. title. Jamson had also added the American and Canadian crowns to his English one. Others of Miss Pike's Dilkushas went to the US. One of these, D. Velvet, was mated to Banchory Bosun before exportation and produced her litter in California. One of this litter, a bitch called Trixie Cox, was the foundation of Robert Elliott's Elysian strain. Trixie's daughter E. Elf, by N. Dignity, was the dam of five Champions in one litter, including Dual Ch. King Lion. This litter was sired by the imported Adcombe Yakoub (Eng. and Am. Ch.), a son of L'ile Buccaneer, who held his English and Indian titles. Digressing a little, I am intrigued by the naming of Trixie, bearing in mind that Bob Elliott himself was an English export, ending up in California after doing some breeding and training in Canada. The name is so obviously English, I wonder whether she was a real person he had known back home, whose name has now gone down in the archives of American Springer history?

The Breeze kennel of Mrs C.M. Buchanan, in Colorado, was also founded on a daughter of Velvet (D Darkie) mated to Dignity. Two of this litter, Woodelf of B and Miss Dignity of B, when later mated to Rufton Recorder, would have a deep and lasting effect on the breed. Apart from Darkie, Mrs Buchanan also owned Dilkusha Dazzler. E. Leffingwell imported Dilkusha Roy, by D Chum, litter brother to Chancellor's dam. A separate line descending from Jambok appeared in California. His son, Beauchief Major, was the grandsire of Am. Ch. Inveresk Clip, who was a fairly well-used stud on the West Coast, particularly in conjunction with the stock from Adcombe Yakoub and Nuthill Dignity, with successful results.

Another English kennel, Boghurst, which came into prominence between the wars and found a ready market in America was that of Major Doyne Ditmas. The Boghursts were founded on the 1922 Crufts CC winner Woolton Bramblebush, whose dam, Lindley Bess, had been BoB at Crufts in 1916 when no CCs were on offer. Bramblebush had two litters to Dual Ch. Horsford Hetman, and a son from each of them finished their English titles as well as running in Trials. Rover, winner of the dog CC at Crufts in 1924, was exported to Eudore Chevrier and made his Can. title and later his Am. Ch. He was sold to George Higgs of Los Angeles and became the foundation sire of the American Boghurst kennels. Other notable inmates of the English Boghurst kennel were Boghurst Signoretta, winner of the Bitch CC at Crufts in 1926, and her son Ch. Boghurst Bristle (by Jambok). Bristle at one time was owned by the Inveresk kennels and had also spent a short time with the Carnfields. A son of Bristle, Dalshangan Goldigger, was also exported to the US, to the dual-purpose Clarion kennels of Charles Toy, and gained his Am. FT Championship. Goldigger was out of Inveresk Chita. Bramblebush was also bred to the CC and Trial Winner Beeding Buckle, which produced Renrut Rosery Brambletyke, the foundation bitch for Florrie Turner's Renrut strain. She mated Brambletyke to Chancellor prior to his exportation, and the bitch she retained from this litter, Renrut Patsy, appears both in Bench and Field Trial lines through her various litters to such dogs as FT Chs. Banchory Boy and Busy Podge of Ware.

The bitch CC winner at the 1924 Crufts, Ch. Inveresk Careful, also found her way to the USA, being purchased by the well-known American breeder Dr A. C. Gifford of Oshkosh, Wisconsin. Her son Inveresk Cadet went to Canada at the same time. Her litter brother, Inveresk Count, was another to go to America, to the ownership of Ben Lewis. Dr Gifford already owned Horsford

Highness who, in 1921, had become the first Am. Ch. English Springer. L. J. Cherny of Platte River kennels, North Bend, Nebraska, also imported Inveresk stock. He brought in Int. Ch. Inveresk Chloe, Am. Ch. Inveresk Chairman and Inveresk Cheveley amongst others. He later used the Platte Inveresk affix for his kennels. This practice of using the affix of the founding stock, although useful in indicating the ancestry of the new kennel, is confusing to the researcher of later years. It should not happen nowadays with the reciprocal arrangements between Kennel Clubs concerning protection of affixes.

CRUFTS CHAMPIONS

In the first post-war decade, between Crufts resuming in 1921, and 1928, no fewer than five of the dog CC winners were exported (as Ch. Standard won two consecutive years this is effectively six). The 1921 winner was Horsford Hetman, who remained at home but made his mark abroad through his progeny. The winner in 1925, Bram of Duart Lodge, appears to have sunk almost without trace after his moment of glory. He did win another CC but he does not appear in any of the modern pedigrees that I have been able to trace. The expatriate five were: Dual Ch. Flint of Avendale (1922) and Tr. Int. Ch. Boghurst Rover (1924), who have both been mentioned previously; Int. Ch. Horsford Harbour (1923) who went to the US and helped to spread the blood of his sire, Ch. Little Brand; Ch. Standard (1926/27) who, as stated before, went to India; and, lastly, the 1928 winner, Ch. Nuthill Dignity, who also crossed the Atlantic and, like Boghurst Rover before him, would add Can. and Am. titles to his English one. Two years after his Crufts BoB he repeated the performance at Westminster. As far as I can trace, he is the only Springer to achieve this double. A son of his, imported from England, Am. Can. Ch. Norman of Hamsey, was the first English Springer to take the Sporting Group at Westminster. Fortunately, when David Macdonald decided to let E. de K. Leffingwell take Dignity to California he had already been used wisely by British breeders. Dignity was the kingpin of the breed in California and the Pacific seaboards, whilst the the influence of Recorder, some years later, was mostly felt in the Eastern States and the Mid-West.

In the late 1920s Wallace Larson of Anoka, Minnesota, purchased from H. S. Routley, of the Trent Valley kennels (who started in England but later settled in Canada), a dog called Trent Valley Lucky Strike, who was bred on Inveresk, Boghurst and Nuthill Dignity lines. He made his Am.

Int. Ch. Rufton Recorder.

title and sired about eight Champions, one of the most important being Am. Ch. Chancellor of Olmstead, who was bred from a daughter of Inveresk Chancellor and a bitch of Inveresk and Belmoss breeding. He figures in most pedigrees as the sire of Chancellor Lucky Dignity, who produced nine Champions for the Frejax outfit. During this period Lady Iris Portal had been successful with her Laverstokes, and her Hetman bitch Ch. L Pattern had produced a good litter to Dual Ch. Flint before his exportation. The pick of this litter was probably Ch. Laverstoke Pepper, who became the foundation for the Marmion kennel of The Hon. George Scott. Pepper was mated to an untitled dog named Buckshot Jock and this appears to be his only recorded litter. He was by Ch. N. Dignity out of a Jambok bitch, however, and the litter produced a dog that proved to be a prominent sire, Ch. Marmion of Marmion.

MAINTAINING UK STOCK

In spite of all these exports, and the ones to Australia and New Zealand detailed in a later chapter, sufficient numbers of the best progeny had been retained in the UK to keep the breed progressing satisfactorily. Warner Hill's second generation Beauchiefs by his Jambok son Nicholas had gained their titles, with Ch. Buchanan also winning Field Trial awards. His sister, Ch. Bonetta, reared a successful litter to Int. Ch. Nuthill Dignity before his emigration. This contained the great Ch. B. Benefactor. At this time, 1932, Warner Hill brought in a young winning dog from Ireland, sired by Int. Ch. Advent of Solway out of Reece of Solway – although he was all Scottish breeding – whom he renamed Beauchief Outcross. He

Ch. Beauchief Outcross.

was a full Champion within a year. Although, as his name implies, he was intended as an outcross to the rest of the Beauchief stud, he did, in fact, go back to Nicholas on his dam's side, and Jambok of Ware on his topline. As the sire of Showman and Speculation of Shotton he had a great influence on stock on both sides of the Atlantic, probably more so than some of the other dogs of Warner Hill's, such as Buchanan and Benefactor.

FIELD TRIAL BREEDERS

On the Field Trial side a new star, or rather galaxy of stars, had risen to shine beside the likes of the Banchorys and the Bryngarws, starting with Menaifron Jock in 1928. Tom Greatorex (usually known as Joe) handled Selwyn C. Jones' O'Vara dogs to a record number of FT Chs. Apart from Jock and FT Ch. Daud, they all bore the O'Vara suffix. Daud had, as parents, Nithsdale Speed and Coustray and was bred by John MacQueen Senior. Jock was by Foel Poncho ex Foel Letty. Most of the O'Vara stock by him were out of a bitch by FT Ch. Tedwyns Trump, called Flicker, selected as a potential brood by Joe Greatorex. History has proved Joe made a wise choice. Two of the FT Chs. from Jock and Flicker were Spy O'Vara and Pierpoint Splint. Another good producer was Molly O'Vara, by Dalshangan Dandy Boy out of Tedwyns Molly. She was owned by Miss A. M. Bickerton of the Thorneycroft kennels. A bitch called Judosa produced several trial winners to Spy O'Vara. O'Vara-bred stock were still winning at trials thirty years later. In the late 1930s Slice and Strike O'Vara went to New Zealand. Joe Greatorex also had his own dogs and used the affix

FT Ch. Peter O'Vara.

FT Ch. Style O'Vara.

FT Ch. Bee of Blair.

FT Ch. Spy O'Vara.

Corndean. One of his first dogs was Smashaway, by Flight out of Bunny of Aqualate. In later years, after the death of Selwyn Jones, he was bequeathed the O'Vara affix.

Tom Gaunt who handled for Lewis Wigan, the Duke of Hamilton and, latterly, Countess Howe, also had his own dogs. One was a bitch called Cheekie (by Horsford Humour) who, when mated to Cornwallis Cavalier, produced Rose of Avendale. Her son, by a brother of Dual Ch. Horsford Hetman, was Bob of Crombie, sire of Dual Ch. Flint of Avendale. Another famous Field Trial kennel to come into prominence at this time was that of George Clark and his Blair strain. FT Ch. Bee of Blair was one of a litter that contained two other FT Chs – Nithsdale Rover and Banchory

Rex. They were by Don of Avendale (Dalshangan Dandy Boy) out of Pomillion Meg, whose grandsires were Rivington Boatswain and Prince of Avendale. Bee produced a number of Trial Winners including FT Ch. Beeson of Blair, winner of the Spaniel Championship. Another litter was by FT Ch. Don O'Vara. George Clark died in 1938, the same year as the Maharajah of Patiala and Isaac Sharpe of the Stylish kennels. For many years the Blair dogs were trained and handled by John Forbes, who also handled for other owners as well as his own Glennewton dogs. He was still handling after the Second World War.

Another person whose career covered many years was John Kent. Apart from handling for other people, his own Chrishall affix became renowned worldwide. After the Second World, War Miss Francis used one of his FT Champions on her Champion bitch and the subsequent intermingling of the two strains produced many top Trial dogs successful on both sides of the Atlantic.

A personality who appeared on the trial scene in the late twenties was Mason Prime. His Wakefares prefix did not fully come into use until after World War Two, but he bred and owned many Trial winners in the thirties. His first winner was simply called Spanner. Another was Thrimley Joe, who just missed his FT Ch. title on a technicality – one of the stakes was a dog short. In 1935 Mason Prime's Wakefares Belle had a litter to FT Ch. Busy Podge of Ware, producing two dogs which became FT Chs., both in the ownership of the Maharajah of Patiala. One was Busy Lad of Ware and the other Wakes Wager.

Capt Onslow Traherne founded his Bryngarw strain on Banchory stock, as did Mrs Noreen Charlesworth with her Noranby kennel when she added English Springers to her already well-established Golden Retrievers. Originally the affix was Normanby, and some of Mrs Charlesworth's early Goldens bore this name, but a clerical error in one of the registrations led to the disqualification of her Crufts CC Winner in that breed and the Noranby prefix was settled on. Like Countess Howe, Mrs Charlesworth ended up leaving the ranks of Springers to concentrate on her Retrievers, but in her time with the breed she owned or bred several Trial Winners, including FT Chs. Noranby Pelican and Flatcatcher, owned by Capt Traherne, who both were exported and finished as Am. FT Chs. Mrs Charlesworth won several Field Trial awards with Porridge of Winscales, the dam of Pelican and Flatcatcher. Capt Traherne was honoured by the English Springer Field Trial Association in America when they asked him to judge their Annual Field Trial at Fisher Island, New York, in 1931. The Bryngarws were usually handled by W. Church. Another of the UK Field Trial personalities to be honoured with judging the Fisher Island Trials in 1933 was Dr J. Wilson, of the Solwyn prefix, from Scotland. He reversed the traffic flow of the day by taking Fisher's Island Phoebe back to Scotland with him – a present from the breeder Walton Ferguson. Phoebe was by Tedwyns Trex ex Chancefield Flight, so she did not bring any fresh bloodlines into the native stock.

FT Ch. Bryngarw Firearm.

AMERICAN SPORTINGS DOGS

Among the early sport-minded breeders of America's Mid-West was Arthur Moechner, of North Farnsworth, Aurora, Illinois. His Benno Bruning of Ashaba was a legend among Trial dogs of his day. Others were Dick Bruning of Ashaba and FT Ch. Busy Bruning of Ashaba. Busy was descended from Flint of Avendale. Some of the other Ashaba dogs went back through Am. FT Ch. Speed of Falcon Hill via Tedwyns Torch and T. Trump to Dalshangan Dandy Boy. As well as breeding winning dogs, Mr Moechner also founded the first two Breed Clubs in the Mid-West and, in 1932, had the far-sighted idea of organising the country's first-ever group training classes for the Breed.

In the spring of 1926, Bob Cornthwaite, in the UK, mated his Rufton Flirt to a son of FT Ch. Rex of Avendale out of a bitch by Beechgrove Mark'em called Vandoreen. This dog, Boss of Glasnevin, was a high-class Field Trial performer although he did not quite make his title. His brother, Rex of Glasnevin also performed well at Trials, and a bitch from the same litter, Breckonhill Vanlotta, was one of the early dogs owned by George Curle. The dog retained from this litter, Int. Ch. Rufton Recorder, was a late developer and did nothing spectacular, although he attained his Championship and qualified in the Field. As he was a year younger than Inveresk Chancellor and was also being shown against Nuthill Dignity in his prime, there was some good competition around. Other rivals included Ch. Standard and the early Beauchiefs.

RECORDER – THE GREAT FOUNDATION DOG

At the age of seven Recorder followed Chancellor and Dignity across the Atlantic – and probably had more influence eventually than either of them. He was originally purchased by Fred Hunt of the Green Valley dual-purpose kennels, Pennsylvania, as a potential dual-purpose stud dog. Most of the Green Valley matrons were by a dog called Tarke Freckles (apart from the fact that he came from the Okay kennels of George Morrison of Ohio, I am unable to trace any details of breeding of Freckles). On arrival it was soon realised that Recorder had by no means reached his "sell by" date and was, in fact, still at his peak. Just prior to this Fred Hunt had imported Rufton Rosita in whelp to Recorder. Recorder met with a mixed reception. Being better balanced and more compact he was different from the general type of Springer then being shown, but he made his American title fairly quickly and the more forward-thinking breeders soon realised his potential. Recorder arrived at the time when he was most needed, bringing more length of leg to the breed, along with a shorter back and better legs and feet.

I think in certain areas the breed was probably suffering from too much of the Flint of Avendale blood. Flint's pedigree on his bitch line was somewhat unorthodox. His mother, Helen of Crombie, was by Ch. Rivington Bobstay who was by Rivington Sam whose mother, as we have seen, was the Cocker R. Riband. Nothing unusual so far, Sam being in most pedigrees. However, coming to Helen's dam Answorth Bess we find she is by Fielding Blueboy, a Cocker, the same blue roan that sired Riband! He is the only dog that appears twice in her pedigree. Small wonder that in the magazine *American Dog World of 1943*, Dr W. B. S. Thomas, commenting on the clarity of markings on the Recorder-derived progeny, was asking whether any Springers had been registered as roan before the advent of Flint.

As Fred Hunt's kennel was by now rather strong in the Rufton blood (he had also imported Rufton Reveller) he started looking for a different bloodline to mate to the Recorder stock. He finally settled on a daughter of Nuthill Dignity, Ch. Woodelf of Breeze, and was able to lease her for a period. Mated to Recorder, she produced several Champions including Green Valley Merry, G. V. Judy and Dual Ch. G. V. Punch. There was also a bitch with rather badly shaped and placed eyes, and she was registered as Orientia without the kennel affix. Another dog in the kennels at

Am. Ch. Rodrique of Sandblown Acre.

Am. Ch. Cavalier of Cauliers.

this time was Int. Ch. Dunoon Donald Dhu, a son of Irvine of Avandale (Canada) and Dunoon Bonnie (Inveresk/Belmoss breeding), bred in Canada by Andy Dunn. From a mating between Donald and Orientia came the famous Ch. Rodrique of Sandblown Acre, foundation sire of Mr and Mrs W. Belleville's strain in Langhorne, Pennsylvania. In 1938 Orientia was mated to one of the Recorder/Rosita litter, Ch. G V Hercules, resulting in, among others, Tranquillity of Wellsweep, who was the foundation of the Melilotus strain.

The sister of Woodelf, Miss Dignity of Breeze, also produced some influential progeny to Recorder. Irvine was bred by E. Chevrier and was descended from Flint of Avendale on his sire's line and was a grandson of English FT Ch. Dan of Avendale through his dam. Dan carried the lines of Cornwallis Cavalier, Denne Jester and Rivington Bobstay. I have been unable to trace all the Canadian Avandales in the pedigree but no doubt Springbok of Ware and most of the other imports are there. Dunoon Bonnie was by Inveresk Cocksure out of a daughter of Inveresk Collyshot and Belmoss Fleur of Orford. The Rufton line was also the choice of Benjamin Newton of the Allegheny Park Kennels, Salamanca, NY. Apart from using his imported Recorder grandson R. Rogerson, he imported Rufton Rubicon (Rufton Ringleader–Maid of Honour). His early lines were descended from H Hetman via Am. Ch. Horsford Hazard. Maid of Honour had also found her way across the Atlantic and finished her American title. Rufton Roger (Recorder ex Rufton Rarity, a Dignity daughter) had been imported by the Clarion kennels of Charles Toy and, out of a daughter of Am. Ch. Horsford Historical, sired Am. Dual Ch. Fast who was in turn sire of Am. Ch. Amos of Melilotus (out of Tranquillity of Wellsweep). Prior to this Charles Toy had imported Rufton Trumpet and Tandy. Other Ruftons to go to the US were Rufton Pattern, who went as foundation for the Hunter's Hill kennels of Mrs E. Klokke in California, and her brother, Rufton Roberto, who joined the Greenfairs.

One of the many breeders to reap the benefit of the Green Valley breeding programme was Arthur Caulier of Canal Fulton, Ohio. His foundation was the great producer Cauliers Royal Maggie. She was by Prince Royal of Avalon (Int. Ch. Jamson of Ware ex Int. Ch. Belmoss Jacqueline) out of Oakdale Sally, who was the result of the father/daughter pairing of Trent Valley Luckystrike onto a sister of Chancellor of Olmstead. She thus carried a fair proportion of Inveresk blood. Her various matings to different Green Valley dogs laid the foundations for a strain that is behind many of the later top kennels. The kennel also owned G. V. Sandgirl, one of the

Recorder/Miss Dignity litter. Another kennel to be formed in this era was the Salilyns of Mrs Julia Gasow. Nancy of Salilyn when mated to Ch. Co-Pilot of Sandblown Acre (Rodrique mated to his daughter) produced the Ch. brothers Sir Lancelot and Sir Galahad of Salilyn. Nancy was descended from D. Ch. Green Valley Punch, Chancellor Lucky Dignity and Ch. Royal Flush of Avalon. Already the thoughtful breeding that would be instrumental in keeping the kennel in the top flight for the next 50 years or more was beginning to work. Lucky Dignity was the foundation of the Frejax line and was by Chancellor of Olmstead out of a bitch bred from the Canadian Avandale lines. Nancy carried two lines to her, through two of her grandparents, one of which, Frejax Tophole of Blighty, was by Green Valley Punch. It was this Recorder blood that Mrs Gasow intensified by the judicious use of the Rodrique descendants.

UK WINNERS OF THE 1930s

A grand-daughter of Recorder was born in England in December 1932, Ch. Roundwood Lass owned by Sam and Vera Till. For many years she held the record for the number of CCs won, including four in a row at Crufts from 1936 to '39. Lass was by a dog called Ellistene Elegant who came from a litter by Recorder out of Marville Queen. M. Queen was by Boghurst Bass, a brother of B. Bristle, out of a Little Brand daughter. Elegant had a brother called Bothering Boy, behind Boxer of Bramhope, and a sister, Chunal/Rufton Molly, dam of Am. Ch. Rufton Rogerson. The dam of Lass, Lady Gem, was a grand-daughter of Ch. Hemlington Kalgar. Apart from Lass, the Tills also owned her litter sister Pretty Wendy. These two, plus a son of Bothering Boy called Roundwood Remember, were the foundations of a strain that would last for more than thirty years. Wendy was mated to Rosslyn of Ranscombe and a daughter, R. Replica, was exported to Dana Knight of West Virginia. Replica was bred from before exportation and one of the litter (by her half-brother Rosslynson of Ranscombe), Roundwood Rapier, followed his dam across the Atlantic to the Clarion Kennels. (I was grateful for the kindness shown to me by Sam Till at my first Show in the summer of 1954 when he taught me how to pluck out the tops of my Springers' ears.)

In the late twenties Miss C. M. Francis had bought a son of Horsford Hetman called Higham Tan. His dam, Greenview Wundah, was by Horsford However out of Horsford Pixie. Tan was bred by William Humphrey and did some winning himself without actually getting his title, but his daughter, Higham Teal, became the first of the several Champions to carry the prefix. She won the

Sh. Ch. Whaddon Chase Robin.

Ch. Higham Tomtit.

CC and BoB at Crufts in 1933. Teal's dam was a bitch named Adcombe Clarice, bred by Colonel Badcock, by Thoughtful of Harting ex Juno of Harting. A brother to Juno was Adcombe Yakoob who, after getting his title in England, was exported to the US. Miss Francis mated Teal to Ch. Marmion of Marmion and from this litter came the well-known Higham Ticket, owned by Captain W. Selby-Lowndes, and Higham Tomtit, owned by his wife Angela (she was a member of the Arkwright family). Ticket won a CC and and was a good worker, but Tomtit not only gained his title but went on to have quite an influence on the breed. At one time the kennel also owned Higham Tug, a son of Higham Tan. Although he did not make much impact in England he did sire Am. Ch. Whaddon Chase Fanny.

Many of the bitches owned by Captain and Mrs Selby-Lowndes had only single-word names. Whaddon Chase prefix was solely in the name of the Captain. One such bitch was Tessca who gained her three CCs but was prevented from getting her FT qualifier by the outbreak of war. The same thing applied to her son Whaddon Chase Robin who had quite an effect on the post-war breeding programme. Tessca was by Beauchief Outcross, Robin being by Higham Ticket. An outcross to the main Whaddon Chase lines was W C Anthony, a son of Peter of Shotton ex Candy (Am. Ch. Stingo of Shotton (of Greenfair)–Shrew of Shotton).

THE SHOTTON KENNELS

The mid-1930s also saw the foundation of the Shotton kennels of Michael Withers. As he was not really interested in the family milling business, he decided to indulge his canine ambitions and had some modern boarding and breeding kennels built near Stratford-on-Avon. They were designed by Mrs Gwen Broadley, who became their first manageress. With her expertise the Shottons quickly became a top kennel. An early acquisition was a son of Ch. Dry Toast bred by Talbot Radcliffe. Originally called Saightons Saint, he became one of the kennel's well-known stud dogs under the name of Steady of Shotton. Many of the inmates were Beauchief derived and the kennel owned Ch. Beauchief Bahram. Bitches in the kennel included Ch. Jess of Shelcot, Ch. Fanshawe Fury, Ch. Speculation of Shotton, Sadie of Shotton and Sinful of Shotton. There were many others of course but these were the ones that have bred on. Fury was by Marmion ex a daughter of Boghurst Bristle and Carnfield Lucy; Speculation was a daughter of Beauchief Outcross. Sadie had as parents Beauchief Beaucoupe and Carnfield Betty. Sinful brought in some different blood through

Triple Int. Ch. Showman of Shotton.

Int. Ch. Speculation of Shotton of Greenfair.

Rosslinson of Ranscombe and Ch. Roundwood Lass. Sometime around 1937 Mrs Broadley bought a young dog called Highedge Benefactor. The following year he won four CCs and his FT qualifier after being renamed Showman of Shotton. Soon after this Showman left this country for the kennels of Paul Quay, of Chagrin Falls, Ohio. He quickly made his US and Canadian titles and was virtually invincible during his show career. He also sired around thirty champions. Showman was by B. Outcross out of a B. Benefactor bitch. His effect on the American stock was mixed. On the credit side he gave improved hindquarters, although his contribution to kind expressions and good feet was reputed to be detrimental. His son out of Sadie, Peter of Shotton, was one of the wartime stud dogs in England who had no show career to speak of, although his name appears in many pedigrees. After Ch. Speculation had produced a litter to Ch. B. Bahram she too crossed the Atlantic to Joseph Quirk of the Greenfairs kennels, soon to be joined by her son, Stingo, both achieving Champion status. Strangely, there does not seem to have much combining of the two Shotton imports by the American breeders, possibly because of the wartime conditions.

FORGOTTEN HEROES

Between the wars there were many dedicated breeders who did much for Springers without always receiving the credit due to them. One such was Mr J. Morell of Derbyshire with the Highedge Springers. As mentioned, his Benefactor became Showman of Shotton and his litter brother, known simply as Knighted, also won three CCs. Another person whose contribution to the breed does not always show up was Ernie Woodall of Rossendale, Lancashire. His Queen of Lumb was born in 1926 and started a line he carried on for over fifty years. Quite a lot of the dogs Mr Woodall bred or owned did not bear the Lumb suffix; Queen was by Carnfield King. Her litter to the Dual CC and FT winner Merlin Max contained Dolly of Lumb whose various litters produced some influential progeny, including the Field Trial and Bench Winner Merlin Mustard, and the well-known stud dog Bollinbroke Journalist, who was owned by Bob Cornthwaite of the Ruftons. Journalist was used quite extensively. In one litter he sired Sam of Shotton and R. D. Cank's Bench and Trial Winner Turbarry Trixie, grand-dam of Pasture Toddy, whose son was the top wartime winner Peter's Benefactor, sire of Boxer of Bramhope. He is also behind Confident Model, one of the first of the Whintonhill line of Bill Johnston. Sam of Shotton, although used at stud, does not seem to appear in any relevant modern pedigrees. Dolly, in her litter to Beauchief Nicholas, was the dam of Debonair Dinah, a CC Winner, who comes down through Roundwood Remember via Brookhill Tesscon to Boxer's maternal grand-dam, Lilac Beauty. Dolly's son by Ch. Timperley Gunmaster, Dolson of Lumb, was the grandsire of Ben of Lumb through his daughter Pasture Juliet. Ben was a son of Ch. Beauchief Benefactor and is behind several of the modern lines. Another grandson of Dolson was Am. Ch. Rufton Roberto of Greenfair.

DUAL-PURPOSE LINES

The Merlins of H. Ogden were a dual-purpose line well-known during the inter-war period. They were based on the Chancefields and J. Hulme's Withingtons. The Withington lines were descended from a double base: W. Kate by Rivington Sam ex Susan of the Cairnies and W. Duster by R. Bobstay out of a bitch called Airielands Bess. Airielands was an affix sometimes used by James Scott, trainer and handler of some of Lewis Wigan's Cairnies, especially FT Ch. Jed. The CC-winning Merlin Mytrusty went to the Walton Fergusons in the US. Trusty was by Chum of Chancefield out of Withington Dacia. Another of the prominent kennels of this era with dual-purpose ambitions was that of George Henriques. His Chunals won at Trials and on the Bench. As his Trial dogs were based on the Dalshangan and Tedwyns lines it was only natural for them to be trained and handled by the Dalshangan maestro, Mr A. L Trotter. Later his dogs were handled by

George Macqueen. Henriques' Bench aspirations were through Inveresk Caramond and Rufton (renamed Chunal) Molly. He later solely concentrated on Trials. Chunal Maidan was bred by Countess Howe from Dalshangan Loyal and FT Ch. Maida of Barnscleugh. She had Trial-winning progeny both sides of the Atlantic. Ben Newton's Am. Ch. Rufton Rogerson was out of Chunal Molly. The kennel's Chunal Peg O' My Heart, by Dalshangan Tan ex Tedwyns Tubs, achieved FT Ch. status.

THE START OF THE MODERN ERA

George Macqueen was a member of a family of trainers that includes the two Johns, father and son, and also Lawrence Macqueen, a cousin who became one of the top American trainers. John Sr. trialled some dogs in his own right and bred FT Ch. Daud, sire of so many of the O'Vara Trial Winners. John Jr. and his cousin Lawrence feature in the post-War period. For a period between the early and late thirties the Trevillis kennels of Mrs F. A. Santer amassed a large number of CCs. The inmates included Chs. Dry Toast, Nimble of Hamsey, Winning Number of Solway, Miss Amy of Solway, and Balgray Joy. There was also the CC Winner Trevillis Cuthie by Nimble out of Miss Amy. Dry Toast, Nimble, Winning Number and Joy also held their Irish titles. Dry Toast was by Marmion and was quite a heavily used stallion appearing behind all today's Show winners. The Solway pair were by Beauchief Benefactor out of different bitches and Nimble was by B. Outcross. Joy was a daughter of Inveresk Cameronian. When the kennel was dispersed Nimble went to J. Lee of Belfast for whom he won two further CCs. Trevillis Cuthie sired Stately Success who was quite a successful post-war stud dog. Winning Number had been acquired from Tom Meageen, when he gave up the breed for a short period, and already had his English and Irish titles. I am not

ABOVE: A.L. Trotter with Chunal Maidan (left) and Chunal Slick.

BELOW: Int. Ch. Dry Toast.

sure what connection S. J. Jackson had with the Trevillis kennels but he presented the Trevillis Trophy to the English Springer Club for the Crufts BoB winner.

At about the time Mrs Santer left the breed, a brother and sister by Dry Toast joined Mrs Nellie Howard's gundog kennels and founded the Chastleton dual-purpose line. These were Checkmate and Charming of Chastleton. June of Gerwn also joined the kennel and, apart from Charming's litter to a Shotton dog, scarcely any other blood was introduced. By means of selective line breeding to this trio for thirty years, a reputation as a dual-purpose strain was built up that was unrivalled. Field Trials and CCs were won and many of the Chastletons were exported.

The Canfordbourne kennels of J. Roster Latham achieved some distinction during the twenties and thirties. His Ch. Mediant of Canfordbourne by Roland of Harting (Marmion) out of Dream Girl of C., a daughter of Fop of Harting (Beauchief Buchanan), was the dam of Rostre of Ranscombe. The only bitch to win an open Field Trial stake and a CC on the Bench, she was sired by Ronald of Ranscombe. Mediant's litter to Ch. Higham Tomtit contained Allegro of C., who joined the string of Tom Meageen and was used quite a bit by the Irish breeders. Another of the Canfordbourne females was Leading Note, a black and white, by Nap Hand of C. (a Recorder grandson) out of Nesta of C., who was bred by D. Macdonald and was by Nuthill Dignity out of L'ile Mousie. Leading Note was mated to Whaddon Chase Anthony and a dog from this litter, Tony of C., was used quite extensively in the mid-forties. Another dog from this litter was Orpheus of Canfordbourne who went to Ireland. A daughter of his was dam to a litter born in August 1945 that had quite a strong influence on the early post-war English stock.

During the mid-thirties Mr and Mrs W. Travers started the Totonian dual-purpose line with Totonian Trigger, a daughter of Inveresk Caramond and Mollymus. Trigger, mated to a dog named Tan Spots, produced three winning dogs in one litter, but the most important of these was the dual CC winner Totonian Finder who sired many good ones during the early forties. Tan Spots' dam was Highedge Shedah, by Beauchief Buchanan out of Betty of Highedge. A reasonably successful owner at Trials during this pre-war period was Mrs W. R. Calvert with her Eromtew dogs. Her first dog was registered as Wetmore Sinner and was the sire of her son D. J. Calvert's FT Ch. Bobble. Her bloodlines had a strong influence on many of the post-World War Two FT stock. Eromtew Judge, through his litter out of a bitch called Florina, appears in many FT pedigrees. Eromtew Flash was used by the Boughey family and bred Downton Mischief. Her son, Longnor Splash, was grandsire of Lord Biddulph's Conygree Simon, sire of FT Ch. Willy of Barnacre and Hales Smut. The sister of Splash was Micklewood Sue, dam of FT Ch. Micklewood Scud. One of E. Flash's sisters, called Victory Vee, was dam to FT Ch. Ludlow Gyp, and Scud, mated to Gyp, produced FT Ch. Ludlovian Socks, sire of FT Ch. Pinehawk Sark, prominent in Trials lines both sides of the Atlantic. Gyp was also grandmother to FT Ch. Markdown Muffin. The dogs from this kennel were mostly trained and handled by Ronald Macdonald, who also had successes with Edgar Winter's Staindrops, and later trained many of the Chastletons for Trials.

In the late thirties Miss Dorothy Cupit began breeding her Ambergris Springers. Her foundation bitch was Meg of Amberside of all-Carnfield breeding. From her litter to Carnfield King Again came Ambergris, who was the dam of Sue of Amberside – one of the important post-war matrons. She was by the multiple CC Winner Knighted. Another to espouse the breed at this time was Mr A. Moncrieff Horsbrugh with his FT Winner Goldeneye Drake. His Strathblane prefix had been well-known in Cairns in the 1920s and he acquired some good dual-purpose stock in the early 1940s to lay the foundation of his Springers. He was a member of the English Springer Spaniel Club Field Trials Committee for about 15 years until his emigration to New Zealand in the early 1950s.

Captain R. Joyner was the owner of another small but successful Trials kennel of the latter half of the thirties. His Altskeiths won fairly well at the English Trials and some of them were exported to the US, where they were equally successful. He also owned Joburg of Chrishall, a Trial winner both sides of the Atlantic. Joburg was, in fact, by Hollingsworth's Dagnall Donald, a dog that was all show breeding going back to Chs. Pierpoint Perfection and Marmion and the two bitches Fullbrook Spring, who was the dam of many of the Hartings, and Render of Ranscombe. Mrs Broadley had left the Shotton kennels but, needless to say, when she added Springers to her

Sandylands Labrador kennels she founded her lines on the Shotton stock which she had been instrumental in building up and bringing to the fore.

Every so often a litter turns up that has an impact on the breed despite the fact that, individually, the dogs are not outstanding. One such litter was that by Stateley Success out of Staghorn Gorse. Success was the stud dog for the Staitley kennels of George Harwell of Edinburgh. Success was a son of Trevillis Cuthie and Meryle of Dellavaird who was sired by the litter brother of Ch. Dry Toast. Gorse was by Ch. Nimble out of L'ile Brown Lady. Two bitches from this litter were both mated to Tony of Canfordbourne: Juno of Fernie produced the quite useful stud dog Staghorn Jack Snipe, and Teithbank Teal was the dam of a bitch called Sweet Memory who, through her daughter, Sh. Ch. Deana of Glenbervie, was the grandmother of Glencora Tonga, the dam of so many winners of the fifties and sixties. Jack Snipe was born in 1945 and eventually joined the Crakemarsh string of Mrs R. Dawson. Among his progeny were Staghorn Pinkfoot, the foundation bitch of the Tillan line of Lady Belhaven (later Mrs Vale), and Crakemarsh Harley Teal, dam of Wollburn Wattle Honey, the beginning of the Scottish line of Mrs Heather Bell.

The Staitley Springers were basically a forties kennels, although Staitley Diana was shown once in 1939. She was by Ch. Beauchief Boreal out of a B. Benefactor bitch. Her progeny by Success included the sisters Sunrise and Sunbeam. Another bitch was Renrut Evon, a daughter of the FT Winner Roswal of Ranscombe. Evon produced a litter to Success which contained Staitley Sunshine and her brother Solo, the sire of Ch. Castlecary Cameronian who was bought and made up by Gwen Broadley and then sold to Galen Swaim of Oklahoma City, who finished his American title. On the death of Mr Swaim he became the property of Mr and Mrs Naylor of Tully, NY. S. Casket was by Success out of Falcon of Palmerston, a bitch from the Dorritys of Dublin. Mr Harwell also dipped into the Irish pot for his Ch. Staitley May Queen, which he campaigned in the late forties. She was sired by Velikie Lukie, a son of Allegro of Canfordbourne. Lukie was extensively used and figures quite strongly behind the Irish kennels of the period.

THE WAR YEARS

Canine affairs in Europe were quiescent during the Second World War for obvious reasons, although after a few months small shows were allowed to be held. These were known as Radius Shows and the catchment area was limited to a 25-mile radius (about 40km). Some kennels were disbanded and, naturally, breeding was restricted, although not as much as in the First World War. The Republic of Ireland, being a neutral agricultural country, was able to carry on a more extensive breeding programme and some of the stock was later brought over to the mainland to augment diminished bloodlines. The main strains still extant were the Shottons, whose stud dogs were kennelled out in various homes, Chastleton, Talbot Radcliffe's Saightons, the O'Varas and the Ranscombes. William Humphrey was still breeding the odd litter of Horsford Springers although, since moving to Shropshire in the 1920s he had concentrated on his falconry and trialling two separate strains of English Setters. Miss Francis had retained one or two working Springers although I am not sure whether she bred anything during the War.

Captain Selby-Lowndes had died and his wife re-married, but she carried on the Whaddon Chase line and the vintage Higham blood with the veterans Ch. Tomtit, Ticket, and the black and white Tristram, a son of Tomtit, who won two CCs as an eight-year-old after a belated show career. Tristram is also interesting from a pedigree point of view, as he is one of the few traceable links to Int. Ch. Crusader of Malwa. Tristram's dam, Higham Trusty, was bred by Mrs Ann Burge, who had the good luck to live fairly near the Ware kennels and thus had the pick of the stud dogs quartered there. She started with a daughter of FT Ch. Banchory Bosun, which she mated to Ch. Nutbrook Boy, with a bitch from the litter, Avenue Bess, going to Ch. Raider of Ware to produce

Ch. Nutbrook Boy.

the winning Wagger Beauty. Trusty was by Ch. Crusader out of Beauty. Mrs Burge later used the Gunsure prefix.

In the US the Salilyns, Melilotus and Greenfairs kennels among others had been steadily breeding to keep their strains going. One or two others had come into prominence; R. E. Allen of Provo, Utah, started his Timpanagos kennels on a daughter of Recorder and Clio of Avandale. This bitch, Am. Ch Timpanagos Bette, bred two Chs. to Showman of Shotton (T Radar and T Adonis). Fred Jackson had bred one last litter from Chancellor's Lucky Dignity by Showman of Shotton, one being Ch. Frejax Lilac Time, dam of the great Frejax Royal Salute. Salute's sire Ch. Sir Lancelot of Salilyn carried two lines of Lucky Dignity through his dam. Salute was born in 1945 and made his name both as a show dog and also as a sire. Fred Jackson, although an expatriate Englishman (he was born in Manchester), was, I believe, the first to trim his dogs in what is now known as the American Style. Although on the face of it Showman was an outcross to Lucky Dignity, he carried the same lines of Inveresk Chancellor and Jambok of Ware, back to Springbok more than once, just as she did.

THE IMPORTANT BOXER LINE
During the latter stages of World War Two one or two things of importance to the breed occurred. Mary Scott became interested in showing, and the Bramhope kennels came into prominence. Prior to this the family's dogs had been kept for shooting, from as far back as the late twenties when they owned Boghurst Berry, a litter sister of Ch. Boghurst Bristle. The 1940s Bramhope line was started with Tim of Chastleton, the sire of Bramhope Suzette, whose most prominent son was the immortal Boxer whose prepotency helped to stabilise the breed post-war. Boxer was picked out as an eight-week-old puppy by no less a personage than William Humphrey. Boxer was by one of the top winning wartime dogs, Peter's Benefactor, winner of some 500 first prizes at the local Radius Shows and reckoned to have been certain Championship material in better circumstances. His sire Ch. Pleasant Peter was by Beauchief Benefactor. Peter's Benefactor was bred by Thornel Browne of the Caerleon Kennels, although this was before he was granted the affix. Mr and Mrs Ian Hampton were given a Springer puppy as a wedding present from Michael Withers. This bitch, Pixie of Larkstoke, was the foundation of a line that is still in existence. She was by Sh. Ch. Starshine of Ide out of Solo of Shotton. Starshine had been added to Joe Braddon's gundog string

from the Shotton kennels and was by Peter of Shotton out of Ch. Jess of Shelcot. Solo was by Int. Ch. Showman ex a daughter of Ch. Roundwood Lass.

Another occurrence that had quite an impact on the post-war era was the breeding of a litter by Mr P. Hill. His bitch Butter was put to Ch. Higham Tomtit. Lady Lambe had two of the litter, Chs. Whaddon Chase Bonny Tom and Snipe. As Butter was by Ch. Dry Toast out of Ch. Balgray Joy, it is not surprising that these two produced a fair number of winning progeny. Like Peter's Benefactor, there were several dogs used at stud during this period that would probably have made their titles had peace-time conditions prevailed. The difficulties of travelling long distances made it expedient to use the nearest dogs, and this led to varying local types. Thoughtful breeders quite often used a dog owned by H. J. Price called Mountain Crest, by Tomtit out of a Dry Toast bitch. A son of his, called Hope Mountain Stronghold, went to South Africa. Miss Cupit was one to use him on Sue of Amberside. Two other Tomtit sons, Replica of Ranscombe and Northdown Maquis, who was owned by Bill Manin, were also popular stud dogs. Manin was another shooting man who turned to serious breeding, having owned Springers since 1931. This was also the case with Mr D. C. Hannah. After several years of shooting over various dogs he bought a bitch called Clintonhouse Elizabeth from Mrs G. Thomson of the Clintonhouse Springers – and founded the Stokeley dual-purpose line. Elizabeth was one of the Invincible George and Graceful Greta progeny. George and Greta were both out of a bitch called Hopeful Judy, Greta by Tomtit and George by Tan Spots. Hopeful Judy was another from Mollymus, this time by Inveresk Cameronian, thus the bloodlines were similar to the Totonian breeding. The first litter was born in January 1944 and contained as well as Elizabeth, C Janet and Judy of Hazeltong. Mrs Thomson repeated this mating more than once, leading George Taylor to resurrect his Carnfield kennel yet again. He acquired three of the first litter: Carnfield Monarch, CC Winner and Sh. Ch. Carnfield Field Marshall and Carnfield Laura. He also purchased what was one of the last from the L'ile kennels of David MacDonald. This bitch, known as Carnfield Tan Girl, was by Stately Success out of Staghorn Gorse, the litter that produced several influential matrons. George Taylor also took an option on the complete litter from a repeat mating of George and Greta.

An interesting cameo of the middle-war years was the purchase of one of the Mountain Crest–Sue of Amberside litter by an American serviceman, Lt A. L. Katz. This dog, Ambergris Cresta, was re-registered with his American affix, becoming Douglas of Doralan, and did some winning in the UK. At the same time, back home in the USA, Lt Katz's Denne of Doralan was winning his way to his American title. Denne was one of the litter out of Caulier's Royal Maggie by Ch. Green Valley the Feudist which produced C. Jonell (dam of Am. Ch. Rumak's King Cole) and Jakie Boy of C., both of whom appear behind Melilotus Shooting Star. On Lt. Katz's repatriation Douglas joined the Cocker kennel of W. Stordy and was the foundation stud of the Dhunean line which was based on various daughters of Mountain Breeze. Breeze was the dam of Mountain Crest and, besides the Tomtit litter, she had others to Whaddon Chase Anthony and Ch. Pleasant Peter.

Chapter Three

CHOOSING A PUPPY

The first thing to settle is your reason for owning a Springer, so that you will choose one from the most suitable stock for your purpose. With English Springers, as is the case with most of the gundog breeds, there are, nowadays, two different branches of the breed, the working and the show. If either of these options is your interest, then one of the Breed clubs will be able to point you in the direction of a suitable breeder in your area. If you just want a general family dog and companion, it would probably be better to acquire your puppy from show-bred lines rather than working lines. I say this because some of the working-bred dogs, especially the males, need something to occupy their minds, for they can quickly become bored. This is particularly the case where some of the more high-powered trial lines are close up in the pedigree. It is also a waste for a potentially good gundog not to be used for the purpose for which the dog was bred. Generally speaking, unless you have sufficient time and experience to get the best out of something from working stock, they are best left to the experts. Unfortunately, too many good dogs have been spoilt by novice owners taking on something which is beyond their capabilities.

DOG OR BITCH?
The second thing to decide is which sex to choose. This is purely a matter of personal preference, although local circumstances may dictate that one sex might be more convenient than the other. If you want something to show and have fun with, and intend only having one dog, then a male would probably be more suitable, being more showy, and would not miss shows through being in season. Oestrus is also the drawback to having a bitch for work, although females are usually slightly easier to train. For the family pet either gender is suitable, although if you live in a built-up area surrounded by males, it might not be prudent to own a bitch. I personally am not a great believer in spaying healthy females – in my view it leads to obesity and loss of correct coat texture so, if the inconvenience of the oestral cycle is a consideration, then a male is probably the best bet. Temperamentally, I have found little to choose between the sexes as companions. Usually it boils down to the relationship you build up with your dog.

CHECKING ON HEALTH
Whatever your final choice, your initial selection should be from sound, healthy stock. Some of the ophthalmic abnormalities such as PRA (in its various forms), cataract and retinal dysplasia have been found in English Springers, as have Hip Dysplasia and a condition called Fucosidosis. Most countries run schemes for eye tests and hip X-rays, as these are common to many breeds. Fucosidosis is not a very common condition. It is caused by an enzyme deficiency, and a simple blood test will determine whether or not the reading is within normal limits. This was originally

discovered in Australia. In some of the American lines the syndrome popularly known as "rage", correctly called Temporal Lobe Epilepsy, has become a problem. This is a different condition to the normal type of epilepsy found in dogs, which may or may not be genetic in origin. Many of those cases are the result of brain damage at birth, or from some causal agent later in life. TLE is apparently inherited and manifests itself at around four years of age, usually in the males, and the word "rage" is very descriptive of the condition, which so far has not been reported in the UK lines, although it has appeared in the British Cockers, mainly the reds or goldens. Other things that may crop up in all breeds are faulty jaws and dentition, entropion (in-turned eyelids), ectropion (out-turned eyelids) and also cryptorchidism – undescended testicles.

DOING YOUR RESEARCH

After deciding which type you are interested in, the next step is to research that particular branch. If possible try to attend Field Trials or Shows, or ideally both. A list of reputable breeders is a must. This can be got, as mentioned previously, from the Breed clubs, and an up-to-date list of these can be obtained on application to the Kennel Club. I am, of course, here referring to the English KC. The Kennel Club itself does, in fact, issue lists of people who have litters of puppies, but unfortunately these do not differentiate between show and work lines, or give any indication of any thoughtful breeding whatsoever. Puppy "factories" (or "mills" as they are known in the USA) are to be avoided at all costs, as are dealers who usually buy in stock for resale from these puppy farmers.

It is important to see the mother of the puppies, and any other close relatives, as this will give you an indication of how your puppy will develop.

Photo: Steve Nash.

Long-established and successful breeders will be only too pleased to show you their adults and young stock, and also to give advice. Again, it does no harm to visit both show and trial kennels – a broad-based appreciation of the breed as a whole will help you with your later breeding plans. Hopefully by now you will have seen enough dogs, and received sufficient advice – and, more important, *listened* to it – to be able to go home and mull things over in your mind, and decide what has impressed you most and what will be most suitable for you. Having made a carefully considered choice, contact the breeder you have decided upon and make arrangements to buy your puppy. A point to remember is that the breeder has bred the litter for his or her own use and the puppy of your choice may not be available. On the other hand, in the time I have been associated with the Breed, it has improved to such an extent that there is usually more than one choice worth having in a litter. It is also possible that the litter will not contain exactly what the breeder is looking for.

Remember, too, that a good-quality, well-reared, carefully-bred puppy has already had quite an amount of expense put into it. All puppies must now be KC registered by the breeder, most breeding stock is tested under the various Kennel Club/British Veterinary Association schemes, and many puppies nowadays have had a preliminary inoculation. An additional expense, that has arisen in the last year or so, is caused by the decision to ban docking by breeders, who now have to pay a vet to dock puppies. All these expenses are of comparatively recent origin, and are on top of the usual basics such as stud fees and feeding. Also modern, up-to-date broad-spectrum wormers and insecticides tend to be expensive. So, be prepared to pay a sensible price, but if you have visited enough of the right kennels in your researches, you should have a good idea whether the price you are asked for your eventual choice is reasonable or not.

MAKING A SELECTION

When looking at puppies you should be able to see at least one of the parents, if not both. Normally this will be the dam, but occasionally breeders have a "pick of litter" available by their stud dog, in which case you ought to be able to see the father. These "picks" are usually from selected bitches whose bloodlines the stud dog's owner is interested in acquiring, so they are quite often run on to assess their potential. Sometimes, however, the points hoped for did not materialise, or the wrong colour or sex turned up, and the P-O-L is for sale. Quite often, more than one generation is available for inspection, maybe even stock from an earlier litter of the same breeding. Whatever adults you see, you should be able to have some idea of what your pup will finish up like.

When making your selection, points to look out for are a bold, friendly temperament, a clean, glossy coat free from parasites, and the skin should be moderately loose and not stretched tightly over the body. A distended pot-belly is usually indicative of worms. The bone should be adequate, not too fine and certainly not too heavy, as these two extremes lead either to weedy specimens or an adult that is over-clumsy. The legs should be straight fore and aft, and the shoulders need to be fine and slope correctly. Also look out for a fairly well-pronounced forechest. At this age the fore-legs will have a reasonably pronounced carpal or knee joint. This will flatten as the puppy grows. If this "knobbly knee" is absent, usually the adult bone will be inadequate. In short, what you need in an eight-week-old puppy is what you would look for in an adult, and usually the pup at this stage will resemble the finished article, although the shape may change over the next few months as different parts develop at varying rates. Other points to watch out for are dark eyes, although these can darken with age in some strains; clean, tight eyes; and correct tail-set. The body ought to be sturdy and reasonably short-coupled. Picking out a good head can be more of a problem, as heads seem to vary with different strains. Some lines start off short and chubby, lengthening with

The puppy you choose should have a bold, friendly temperament, a glossy coat, and it should not be too slight or too heavy in build.

Photo: Steve Nash.

age, whereas others that look plain and snipey as puppies, will broaden and develop shape later on. In this you must be guided by the breeder's advice. With regard to selection for work, character must play an important part. Choose an alert, lively puppy, with an investigative nature. If the breeder is agreeable (and most of them will be), retrieving potential can be tested with a rolled-up handkerchief, or something similar.

FEEDING AND EXERCISE
Among the papers that you should receive with your puppy, in addition to the usual pedigree, registration and transfer forms, etc., will be a comprehensive diet sheet showing the basis, amount and frequency of meals for the pup. It is advisable to follow this as closely as possible. Do not be tempted to adjust it too much, too soon, as digestive upsets are almost certain to ensue. Quite often, the trauma of moving and settling into a new environment will also cause stomach upsets. Another point to remember is that the daily intake of food needs to be increased as the puppy grows. Beware of over-feeding the puppy, as this, apart from the above-mentioned stomach upsets, also causes, or aggravates, skeletal problems, such as HD or osteochondritis. The hip is a ball-and-socket joint and dysplasia takes various forms, ranging from a mis-shapen acetabular head, to a flattened socket, or a combination of both, and it is believed that over-feeding and too much exercise can have a worsening effect on these conditions. It may seem gratifying to have your puppy gain weight quickly, but too much weight for the bone structure, before it has gained the necessary strength, can cause bowing of the legs, slack pasterns and joint enlargement. The average daily weight gain for a Springer should be around two ounces per day for a Field Trial bred puppy expecting to make forty pounds as an adult. For a pup bred from heavier show lines, three ounces per day would be a reasonable gain. If your pup is blown out after being fed, you are probably overdoing things. Likewise exercise, if not treated with care, can cause problems with the bone structure. Too much muscle build-up in the wrong places can throw shoulders and other joints out of position.

ADVANCE PREPARATIONS

Assuming that you have gone about things in a sensible manner, and have booked and selected your puppy in advance, you will need to make some preparations for the time when you collect him or her. The type of food required should have been ascertained, and arrangements made for obtaining this. Most breeders give a few days supply to ensure continuity. Permanent items required will be a suitable bed (eventually), feeding and water bowls, collars and leads (I use the plural because the youngster will obviously grow out of these), and grooming equipment.

A useful item of equipment that has come on the market in recent years is the collapsible wire cage. This has many uses, not the least being its role as an indoor kennel. If one is purchased of a suitable size for an adult Springer, then it can be used as "home" for the growing pup. We find it best to put a cardboard box of a size suitable for the pup in one end of the cage as a bed, then line the remainder of the cage floor with newspaper, which aids house-training. The bedding can be an old piece of blanket or similar material – anything too smart is likely to be chewed. By the time the pup has grown too big for the box, usually an investigative analysis of its composition will have been completed and a new one needed anyway, and probably when this has happened a couple of times, the pup will be ready for a proper bed. If there is enough room, the water bowl can be put in the cage. While on the subject of bowls for water, it might be advisable to use the conically-shaped earthenware type, as these are heavy and awkwardly-enough shaped to discourage any attempts at carrying them about, and the narrow top stops any thoughts of paddling. Probably it would be best to feed the puppy closed in the cage, remembering that the times when young pups need to evacuate their bowels and/or bladder are after feeding and when they wake up. The cage can be left open most of the time and the puppy left to choose when it is time for rest. Being completely enclosed gives a greater sense of security and "belonging" than a normal bed, especially at night. If your floor is carpeted, it would be beneficial to have a sheet of plastic to stand the cage on, or if the floor is vinyl, or similar, then newspaper will be adequate. You will also find the cage is useful when travelling. The ingenuity of the car designers in developing the rear windows with heaters and washers means that the back door is now filled with wires and pipes behind a light-weight panel, which makes them very vulnerable to inquisitive Springers – although in my case it was a Cocker who did a demolition job. It is also convenient when you have wet adult dogs after shooting, or normal exercise, and keeps the car seats dry! A further advantage with some dogs is that, if they are travelling in their "home", it helps to allay the nervous type of travel sickness.

HOUSE TRAINING

I mentioned bowel and bladder function on waking and after meals. There are other times as well, and you will learn to recognise the signs heralding the need for this, one of the more usual ones being a fussy, bustling about with tail held up. Then, as with waking and post-feedings, is the time to put the pup out, preferably using the same place each time. Some form of command each time when the pup is about to perform will help to train the pup to "go" at the right time and in the right place. As with all training, the correct response should attract plenty of praise. I will leave you to choose what command to use, as I am sure you will find a suitable one. A late friend of mine, who used to board a few dogs, had all sorts of words of command left with the dogs, ranging from the ultra-twee to the downright earthy!

Some people use the paper training method, whereby the pup is initially taught to use a sheet of newspaper, which is gradually moved towards the door, eventually, after a few days, being put outside the door. This can have one or two drawbacks, one being it gives the dog the impression that "going" indoors is acceptable as long as it is on paper. When we are rearing puppies we put

Early socialisation will have started in the breeder's Home. These puppies are encountering a cat for the first time...

...but with experience a puppy learn to take things in its stride.

*Photos:
Steve Nash.*

newspaper down on the floor before putting the dishes down, and to them newspaper means "food, glorious food", after which the "tablecloth" goes through a ritual shredding! This is a fate that usually befalls paper that comes within reach of a Springer puppy's teeth, which is why I am not a devotee of the newspaper method. Mind you, with the outside method, and with young pups having a short length of concentration, by the time you have got them outside, they have forgotten what they were put out for, and the first reaction is to chase about, eat the heads of whatever is in the herbaceous border, chase butterflies, birds and generally take an interest in all forms of nature except the calls of! The quickest way to crystallise the concentration is to take the errant pup indoors – which induces instant recall and realisation that the matter is urgent! Seriously though, this does not always happen, and when it does it is soon overcome. Sometimes the problem is getting the puppy back inside afterwards. Most Springers are naturally clean and house training is relatively painless. As the pup grows up you should be able to gauge the length of time between feeding and bowel evacuation and thus estimate when the dog needs exercising. Different dogs have different metabolisms and, when you have calculated the digestion period of your dog, you can plan feeding times so that the pup will "go through the night".

SAFETY PRECAUTIONS

Other items to bear in mind prior to getting the puppy home include the name and address of a reliable veterinary surgeon, together with details of surgery times and out-of-hours arrangements, and also whether an appointments system is used. I mentioned earlier the wiring etc. in the car, and it is also worth checking whether any of your indoor electrical wiring or telephone cable is vulnerable. By the time the puppy is reasonably mobile, it will be necessary to ensure your garden, or at least part of it, is escape-proof. If you are fencing off part of the garden for free exercise, points to remember are that Springers like water and digging! So ponds and lawns are fair game.

When you get your puppy it is possible that the course of inoculations has already been started, and when registering with your vet ascertain whether he uses the same brand of vaccine, or one that is compatible. If not, he may have to order it specially. Otherwise, inform him of your new arrival and he will advise you when the puppy will need to have "shots". Our own practice now uses a vaccine which can be done at six weeks, with the second at twelve weeks. This protects against the usual distemper, hard-pad, leptospirosis, hepatitis and parvovirus, but also contains vaccine against two of the "bugs" causing kennel cough. An additional bonus is that the sixteen-week booster is no longer required.

WORMING

With the diet sheet that came with your puppy there should also have been a record of worming treatment carried out. Many of the old-type worming remedies in use and recommended in dog manuals were often more harmful than the worms. They usually entailed fasting the dog, and were only efficacious against one species, different preparations being needed for each type of worm. Not all of these were administered orally, treatment for hook/whipworms being by injection. Also, not all of the agents were efficient, especially those in tablet form. Happily, those in use today are safe, efficient and convenient to use. Of the modern wormers there are three main types that are used. Two different salts of Piperazine, either singly or compounded, are produced in either liquid or tablet form and marketed under various brand names. Piperazine is used for roundworms and is quite safe. The other two are broad-spectrum wormers, which are efficient against roundworms, tapeworms and some other species. They are reasonably safe, although more care has to be exercised against overdosage. There is also a paste on the market, which is again a broad-spectrum wormer, but I have no personal experience of this as yet. These modern worming compounds work in a different way to the old-fashioned remedies, inasmuch as they kill the parasites, and sometimes dissolve them, as well as dealing with the worm eggs, whereas many of the old remedies were straight vermifuges which flushed the worms out of the system as a live, wriggling mass.

Chapter Four

CARING FOR YOUR ENGLISH SPRINGER

If your new puppy comes from a reputable, well-organised breeder, such delights as worming, ear cleaning, nail trimming and parasitic washes or sprays should have already been experienced at least a couple of times. There is also a strong possibility that the vet will have been visited and the first inoculation done. If the pup is from a show kennel the breeder will have stood the pup in a show pose countless times, assessing possibilities; the work-oriented breeder will have doubtless played with the litter with dummies, gauging their working potential, so your new puppy has already had a certain amount of handling and it is important that this is continued.

BASIC GROOMING
At first there will not be much coat to groom, but it is important to go through the motions at least. Two or three times per week, brush with a softish brush all over, with the lie of the coat, and use a fine comb on any feathering and the ears. At every grooming session the puppy should be taught to lie on each side alternately while the underparts are groomed. This saves a lot of bother later on when you need to be able to comb and groom the long chest and belly feathering. Something else that should be introduced at an early age is the sound of – and I think that I had better spell this next word in a whisper in case there are still some purists about who would be offended – clippers. If these are switched on at periodic intervals during grooming, then, if and when it is necessary to use them, your pup will be accustomed to them. At weekly intervals the nails should be trimmed or filed taking care not to damage the quick. These first lessons should be designed to produce a laid-back attitude to, and an enjoyment of, the whole process. They, hopefully, will also bypass the "he's a mess but he won't let me comb him" syndrome so often encountered! During the grooming obviously checks will be made for parasites, and eyes and ears cleaned. You will also learn whether or not your pride and joy has any ticklish or sensitive spots. Some dogs are sensitive about the tail area, others seem diffident about having their feet done.

As the puppy grows, so will its coat, and more advanced grooming will be needed. Springer coats vary, and are dependent both on genetic and environmental influences. You should have some idea of the genetic makeup if you have seen the parents, and your pup should have a coat bearing some resemblance to those of its parents. However, this can be affected by outside factors such as diet and climate, especially as regards texture. Regular grooming with a deep stiff brush will usually stimulate growth of the feathering and will also help to keep the shorter parts of the coat healthy. Too low a ratio of fat in the diet will tend to give a dry coat, as can too much subjection to bright sunlight. Springers kept indoors in an artificially heated environment tend to have a permanent "summer" coat. Some of these variations in coat can be traced back to some of the alleged outcrosses used in the early days when the breed was being formed. These include a

This is what happened to a show Springer when there was a surprise snowstorm on a shooting day! In fact, some of the working dogs were nearly as badly affected. The snowballs had to be cut off with a pen-knife. Fortunately, the dog had not been entered for a show so his feathering had time to grow in again. On the credit side, his thick body-coat kept the rest of him warm and dry all day.
Photos: Shirley Deterding.

Poodle in the Aqualates by the Boughey family, and a Pointer by Sir Hugo FitzHerbert. During the adolescent stage, not much in the way of trimming is required, just a general tidying and shaping of the feet. At the same time the tail can be tidied.

Working gundogs need regular grooming especially during the shooting season. Briars and brambles help to pull out loose coat but they also get caught in the feathering, and this week's thorn will be next week's abscess. If the feet are kept trimmed fairly short, this will prevent them balling-up with snow or mud. The length should be balanced between that required for protection and that of convenience. This also applies to feathering. Although the coat is designed for protection, many of the completely working strains tend to have finer coats and less feathering.

TOOLS AND EQUIPMENT

These should be of as good a quality as possible and, in the case of some items such as scissors, which require periodic sharpening and servicing, a second back-up item is advisable. I have listed them in the order of most general usage. The items at the end of the list are normally only required for show presentation. The size of the "armoury" required will depend largely on the type of coat to be dealt with and the extent of your trimming ambitions. You will probably add to this selection later on, or find some other items more convenient.

(1) Combs: certainly a fine one for the shorter hair, a more open-toothed version for the feathering, and a medium one if necessary; those with handles are usually more convenient. A medium-toothed rake (with a central handle) is another handy tool, especially for teasing out tangles. A medium-toothed comb without a handle is useful to carry in your shooting pockets for "on-the-spot" use if required.

(2) Brushes: preferably bristle rather than wire, fairly open, with bristles of sufficient length to penetrate the coat. Pure bristle is preferable to nylon as the latter tends to create static electricity with a resultant "flyaway" effect, which is not a good idea when you are giving the final touches in the ring. A wire "slicker" is useful for dragging out dead coat and coping with slight to moderate tangles.

3) Scissors: one pair of seven or eight-inch straight pointed-end hairdressing scissors, one pair of similar size but round-ended and of the type known as "curved on flat", and, if your sights are set higher than just a general tidy up between visits to the grooming parlour, then a pair of 46-toothed single-blade thinning shears and a 30-tooth double-bladed pair of thinners can be added to the list.

(4) Other useful tools are: rubber thimbles to help make plucking easier, a stripping knife, a stripping block and a grooming glove. Ancillary items required are nail clippers and nail file, and a tooth scaler.

(5) A good pair of electric clippers. This item will be regarded with horror by the die-hards among us, but, let us be realistic about this, most exhibitors use them and their judicious use can save time and trouble.

TRIMMING

Trimming for the show ring is very much an individual thing, and has to be "tailored" to the animal concerned. Obviously, a heavy-coated dog is going to need far more attention and stripping-out than one with not enough coat. What and where you take off, or leave on, in the way of coat and feathering is going to make a difference to the general picture. In many cases feathering and excess coat may need to be shortened to give a balanced picture. Although profuse coat and feathering looks glamorous, in many cases it hides the good points of the dog. Trimming, like handling, should be done with the object of revealing the good points and minimising those that are not quite so good.

HEAD: The dead hair is plucked out using the finger-and-thumb method (here, rubber thimbles are useful). A stripping knife can be used to remove the excess hair. A stripping block can also be used for this. The best place to obtain these blocks is the pedicure section of the local pharmacy; the Scholl blocks for removing hard skin are ideal. The rough surface hikes out the loose hair. It is just used like a brush with the lie of the hair.

EARS: After pulling out dead and loose hair, comb out tidily, and then thin out gradually to achieve a soft effect. Too many expressions are spoilt by over-trimming of the ears, which gives a hard look to the whole head.

NECK AND THROAT: The throat is really the only place where clippers should be used. The area of use is from the chin down to a point approaching the breast bone. The clippers should be used with the lie of the hair. Use carefully under the ears, and combine with the thinners to gradually blend the hair from the clippered area into a smooth outline over the neck and shoulders.

BODY: Loose and dead hair should be combed, raked or plucked out. Judicious and careful use of the thinning shears to tidy and smooth coat where necessary.

LEGS AND FEET: Using straight-edged scissors, the feet should be trimmed into a round, compact shape. The unwanted hair underneath the foot should be trimmed off, and the surplus between the toes tidied up. Nails should also be clipped and filed to a sensible length.

TAIL: The feathering under the tail should be tidied and the whole trimmed to give a neat shape. When thinning the quarters and round the tail be careful not to remove too much coat at the rear of the pelvis, as this may lead to callousing at the pelvic points.

In the rough: An English Springer before trimming.

LEFT: The head prior to stripping.

RIGHT: The hair is fluffed up ready to pluck.

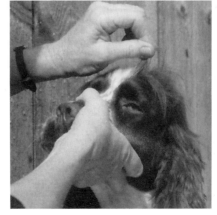

The finger and thumb method is used to pluck out the long hairs.

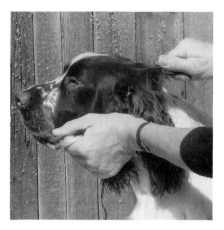

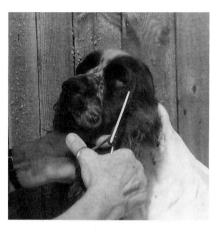

LEFT: Excess hair is removed with the aid of a stripping knife.

RIGHT: Thinning scissors are used to thin the hair on the ears.

LEFT: The clippers are used on the throat.

RIGHT: The hair under the ears is removed.

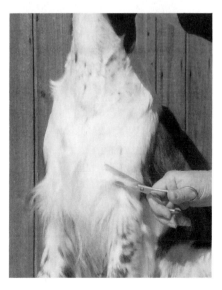

LEFT: Thinning scissors are used to blend the throat into the neck and shoulders.

RIGHT: The feathering on the chest and shoulders is thinned.

The finished effect on the head and neck.

LEFT: The foot prior to trimming.

RIGHT: The hair from the top of the foot is trimmed.

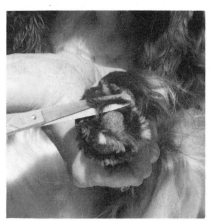

LEFT: The hair between the pads is trimmed.

RIGHT: The hind foot is trimmed on top.

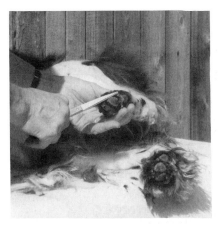

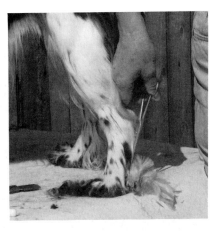

TOP LEFT: It is easier if the dog is lying on his side when trimming the hair between the pads on the hind feet.

TOP RIGHT: The hock joint is trimmed down to the pastern to give a smooth outline.

LEFT: The tail is tidied up.

RIGHT: Rear view showing trimmed and untrimmed hindquarters.

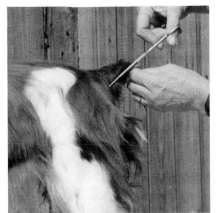

The finger and thumb method is used to pluck out the dead body coat.

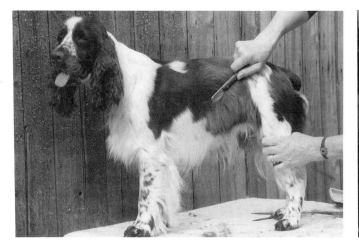
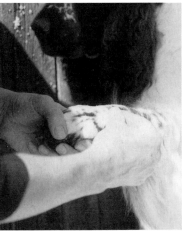

The stripper is used to rake out the dead body coat.

The long hair on the front of the legs is plucked out.

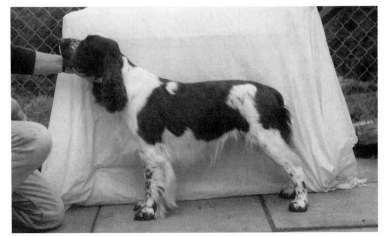

Basic Trim: The finished product.

CARE OF TEETH

This is something that is quite often neglected. In the past, when dogs were fed on hard biscuit, and had access to bones, the problem was not so prevalent, but nowadays modern convenience foods are more conducive to the building up of plaque, and to prevent any future dental problems, attention to the mouth should form part of the routine grooming procedure. There are now some canine tooth-pastes on the market (I shudder to think what gems of wisdom this would cause my old granny to utter – but, times change!). The system of brushing is the same as recommended for humans – away from the gums, to prevent forcing rubbish between the gums and the tooth. The pastes are flavoured to suit the dog, but I feel sure the old recipe of salt and bicarbonate of soda will do just as well. If, in spite of your efforts, tartar does build up, then this can be gently removed with a tooth scaler. Another aspect of mouth hygiene concerns the folds of skin found in the corners of the lips. These are more pronounced in some dogs than others, and food can get lodged in them, which becomes offensive. These folds should be cleaned with a mild solution of dilute hydrogen peroxide.

NAILS
The amount of attention that these will require depends on several factors. A tight, thickly-padded foot at the end of firm pasterns will have the nails set so that the tips are in contact with the ground, and are worn down naturally, especially if a good proportion of the exercise is on a hard surface. The nails on a thin, splayed, badly-knuckled foot are presented at a much more horizontal angle and less of the nail touches the ground, with a consequent reduction in wear. Over-long nails can spoil a good foot, while a certain amount of improvement can be achieved with poor ones by paying attention to the nails. Neglect, in extreme cases, can lead to the nails growing and curving round into the foot. If your Springer has been used to having the nails done from puppyhood, then there should be no problem. The nails can be kept at the proper length by regular filing. If clippers have to be used, care must be taken not to cut the quick. The guillotine type is better, and it is preferable to take off a little at a time, then smooth off with a file.

BATHING
Sometimes you will feel that your dog needs a bath, and this is sometimes necessary before a show, especially where you have a judge who is hot on presentation. Classically, bathing, if done, was never performed less than three days before a show, to give the coat time to settle down and regain the oils lost by the process. Nowadays with the wealth of modern shampoos available for different types of hair, this is not so necessary. A good-quality shampoo suitable for your dog's type of coat should be used. It should be rinsed out thoroughly, and the final rinse can have some glycerine added. Drying should be undertaken with care, towels being preferable to an electric drier which tends to dry out the coat, and make it brittle, if used too much. After the dog has shaken off the surplus water, drying can be started. Chamois leather is ideal, followed by the use of dry towels, remembering to go with the lie of the coat, encouraging it to lie flat. Combing while the coat is still slightly damp will assist in keeping it flat. Some people use jackets or towels to keep the coat flat while it is finishing drying.

HOUSING
Obviously if your Springer is solely a house pet, then housing is not a problem, and a suitably sized cage or bed is all that is necessary. With outdoor accommodation much depends on local conditions. The "kennel-house" of my Swedish friend Anna-Greta, for the obvious reason of climate, is constructed of double-skinned, thick walls with an insulatory sandwich, and double-glazing. Apart from the brick or stone-built kennels with wrought-iron fencing still to be found in many country houses, the classic method of housing dogs over the years has been in wooden kennels, with chain-link runs. The main considerations are that the housing should be warm, comfortably sized, draught-proof and capable of being kept hygienic and easily cleaned. It is essential to check any regulations which might apply when considering housing dogs in kennels. In the UK, for example, the Dog Breeders Act, applicable to Breeders with two or more breeding bitches, lists among its requirements the provision of an adequate-sized sleeping area, a play area and, if the kennel is attached to a grass or earth run, a paved section outside the door or entrance. If you are considering breeding, then a more specialised type of accommodation is needed. Rearing Springer litters indoors is hard work, although it has been done. Once the litter has had a week or so to get established, then moving to outside quarters will give you a chance to get the household

back to normality. This should be borne in mind when planning your kennel. Some form of heating and lighting will be necessary. Dull emitter infra-red lamps are quite efficient. These are also useful if you are nursing a sick dog.

DIET

Considering the fact that dogs, like jackals and other allied species, are basically scavengers, the volume and range of high-quality dog foods is amazing. The pet food industry has increased in volume enormously over the last two decades or so. This has much to do with the general increase in the standard of living of society as a whole, and the upgrading of the family pet from mongrel to pedigree dog. The advent of supermarkets and the purchasing of prepacked foods and other goods from them meant that families wanted to buy their canine foods with the rest of the family provisions. As with kennelling, the matter of feeding dogs has become beset with various rules and regulations, many of which have changed the time-honoured habits of feeding. In the UK hygiene rules emanating from the European Community have forced many of the smaller abattoirs to close, and the bulk purchasing of tripe etc., by the large manufacturers of pet foods, has curtailed the supply of raw flesh and offal.

But with so many proprietary dog foods on the market nowadays, this should pose very few problems. Ideally, you should carry on with whatever the breeder reared your pup on, or the next grade in the series. Sometimes, however, this is not always convenient, or possibly the feed is not available in your area, or perhaps the dog does not thrive on it. In these cases, one of the many other foods on offer will probably suit. Most of these all-in-one feeds are produced in several grades. Generally speaking, the higher grades are for the more active dogs, and the protein content ranges from around the 20% mark for the general maintenance grade, up to approximately 30% for working dogs. Find a brand and grade that suits your dog and stick to it, paying attention to the recommended amounts relevant to the size, and age, of your dog. Do not be tempted to feed too high a grade and remember, these foods are balanced, so do not use them as mixers with meat. No matter what the brand name, many of these all-in-one feeds are very similar in make-up and ingredients, and much of the supposed "superiority" of one brand over another is psychologically induced in the customer by the extent of the advertising. Like the "own brand" goods on supermarket shelves, some of the foods sold are, in fact, manufactured by one or more of the other firms and marketed under another name. The golden rule is, I repeat, find something that suits your Springer's stomach – and your pocket – then stick to it. One advantage of the prepared commercial foods is the effect on the incidence of worms. Feeding raw tripe and offal usually meant that various internal parasites, or their eggs, were transmitted from the host animal to the dog. Even cooking did not always remove the danger. Among the parasites transmitted were liver fluke from infected sheep's intestines, and tapeworms. The latter are now mainly passed between animals, fleas being the intermediary host. This means that a regular session with an efficient treatment against external parasites is essential.

EXERCISE

Like feeding, this is variable according to the needs of each individual. Most Springers will take as much or as little exercise as you care to give them. It should be balanced against the amount and quality of food consumed. When the puppy has learned to come when called, and you have access to safe areas, then a good proportion of the exercise should be free running. Exercise on the lead should be utilised to keep up work on obedience and general good behaviour.

Chapter Five

HEALTH CARE

Basic health care is part and parcel of general maintenance, such things as aural hygiene coming in with regular grooming. However, other regular treatments, like worming and so on, need to be part of a longer-term regime. Anything serious is obviously the province of a qualified vet, and I am not proposing to encroach on their field. However, many of the old-fashioned remedies for minor problems, or first aid, which fell into disuse with the discovery of modern alternatives, are now coming back into favour, for various reasons. Some of the newer treatments produced long-term side-effects and were withdrawn, while others, although safe in usage, proved uneconomical to produce purely for small animal use, when new regulations, for example those regarding testing, were introduced. Some items are still available in the versions used for human treatment, although naturally some adjustment to dosages would be necessary. For general cleaning of wounds, a solution of common salt in warm water is preferable to any proprietary brands of antiseptic, as it does not affect any antibiotic ointments which may be prescribed.

An avenue worth exploring, which is now gaining popularity, both in human and veterinary medicine, is Homoeopathy, and access to a vet who is interested in this field can be very useful. Alternative medicine can be especially important where allergies are concerned. One of the problems that seems to affect some bitches nowadays is irregular or abnormal seasons, or even, in extreme cases, anoestrus. For these a course of Pulsatilla or Sepia can prove beneficial, without recourse to hormone treatment which can have unwelcome side-effects. An allied form of alternative aids to health is Herbal medicine. Probably the herb most widely used by dog owners generally is garlic, which has properties as an internal disinfectant and also has a reputation for keeping dogs worm-free. Another widely-used herbal extract is raspberry leaf, useful as an aid to easy pregnancy and whelping. Its equivalent in Homoeopathy is Caulophylum. Vitamin supplements should not be necessary if a properly balanced diet is fed. Indeed, over-feeding of some vitamins can be as harmful as a shortage of them.

Among the conditions found in English Springers, which are generally supposed to be genetic in origin, are Hip Dysplasia, some eye disorders, Fucosidosis and epilepsy. I say 'supposed', because sometimes these defects occur inexplicably in an apparently clear line, and appear to be caused, or exacerbated, by outside influences. Some of these are congenital (the puppy is born with the condition) and some non-congenital (that means it is not present at birth but appears later in life). I would like to make the point here that many people confuse the term 'congenital' with 'genetic' and think that a congenital condition means hereditary. This is not necessarily so. Many of the congenital disorders are caused by malign influences during gestation. These can range from wrong dosage or timing when worming the pregnant bitch, or an infection at the wrong stage of pregnancy. Conversely, some of the non-congenital 'nasties' such as PRA are inherited.

Feorlig A Dream Lives On, bred and owned by Don and Jenny Miller.
The English Springer is a hardy breed and should experience few major health problems.

ANAL GLANDS

Like some parts of your car, these are things you don't know exist until they cause trouble. They are a pair of glands situated either side of, and just inside, the rectum. Their main purpose appears to be the provision of lubrication to assist the expulsion of faeces, although some authorities incline to the belief that the fluid is used in the marking of territorial rights. With normal firm motions the pressure on the glands means that this secretion is expressed quite easily, and no problem is experienced. However, prolonged periods where the stools are not firm enough to activate the glands leads to a blockage of them resulting in a build-up of the contents, with discomfort to the dog and necessitating manual evacuation of the fluid before it becomes septic and forms an abscess. The first time you suspect that you (or, rather, your dog) have this problem, it is as well to check it with your vet and learn how to clear the glands yourself. Actually this is quite a simple procedure to perform, if you are not too squeamish to carry it out. Basically, it consists of holding the dog with one hand, and squeezing the sides of the anus between the thumb and forefinger of the other hand. Points to remember are: to wear surgical gloves; to work from above; and to treat the problem as you would a loaded shotgun – stay out of the line of fire! With a fully-grown Springer, put the dog between your knees, facing behind you. Have the rear end facing into open space! The amount and viscosity of the fluid emitted depends on the length of time the problem has been developing. It is not a dangerous condition, except in extreme cases, but like most low-grade conditions which nag at you over a period, a general malaise is felt, and relief from it usually engenders a general lift in spirits and condition. Some breeds appear more prone to gland problems than do others, but this may be because of different lifestyles and diets. Prevention of any recurrence of the problem is by dietary control of the texture of the motions.

ANAL ABSCESS

If the above condition results in a septic condition, then professional treatment is necessary. If conservative treatment with medication is unsuccessful, then surgical intervention is the only alternative. The glands can be removed, often with no ill effects.

ANAL PROLAPSE

More correctly known as rectal prolapse, this is caused by prolonged excessive straining to pass a motion, and a portion of the rectum is forced through the anal sphincter. A common cause is chronic constipation, especially in older dogs where the sphincter has become weak through old age. Professional treatment is obviously needed, and usually consists of the protruding portion of the intestine being replaced and secured by purse-string suturing of the anus. To prevent repetition, an anticostive diet is recommended.

ANAL TUMOURS

These sometimes occur, but are usually benign and once the vet has removed them, they do not often recur.

AURAL PROBLEMS

Externally Spaniels' ears are susceptible to damage by knocks, causing haemotomas. The leathers bleed very easily, and it is not too easy to stem the flow if they are cut or bitten. With a knock, the blood forms a blood-filled sac under the skin. This needs to be lanced to allow the fluid to drain away, and the flap is usually anchored to the head to complete the process. Needless to say, like all surgery, this should be done professionally. Internally, ear troubles can crop up, and like skin problems, can have several causes. Basic hygiene during grooming will help to keep any problems at bay. Trimming of the hair round the entrance to the canal will aid ventilation of the inner ear. A routine cleaning inside the ears with Benzyl Benzoate will keep them free from earmites. If the lotion is poured down into the canal, the ear plugged with cotton wool and the dog allowed to shake its head, adequate penetration of most of the nooks and crannies inside the ear is achieved without the need for any poking about, which really should be avoided. Gentle external massage of the base of the ear, just behind the jaw, will help to loosen any waxy deposits which may be present. If the plugs have not been shaken out by the dog, they should be removed and the inside of the earflaps wiped dry with clean cotton wool. If trouble does occur, then the cause must be sought and unless it is immediately obvious, such as a grass seed, or the dog has been in water and got an earful of pondlife, then it would be prudent to get your vet to do an auriscopic inspection. My bugbears when I lived on the coast, and exercised my dogs on the beach and cliffs, were sand and seawater.

COPROPHAGIA AND DEPRAVED APPETITES

Dung-eating among dogs has increased very much over recent times. The theories advanced for this are many and varied. When this was a relatively rare phenomenon, the reason most popularly given was lack of vitamins. But with all the vitamins etc. in modern foods the problem has increased, so that idea hardly seems tenable. Worms have also been blamed but, here again, dogs that are regularly treated and are worm-free do it. Why? This is a question often asked and as yet nobody has come up with a watertight answer. My own idea is that it is probably a deep psychological throw-back to the days when dogs ate the entrails of other species and were generally scavengers. Many other items that get swallowed, such as stones etc., are often the result of misplaced play, or sheer mischief.

DENTAL PROBLEMS

These should be few, if dental hygiene is routinely carried out. Many years ago, scarring of the enamel and brown staining were commonplace, as a result of distemper. But this is rarely encountered nowadays. Probably the most usual problem encountered is damaged, or broken teeth, due to chewing hard items such as stones or metal partitions. We had a Smooth Fox Terrier who wore such grooves in his canines, through chewing the fencing, that they finally broke off level with his premolars. Anything serious should obviously have professional care.

EPILEPSY

The causes of fits in dogs are, like the causes of many other conditions, manifold. In some strains the cause can be genetic, a true epilepsy. This is not very common. Epileptic-type episodes can occur through brain damage. Many years ago this, and chorea, were the result of distemper, but this cause is very rare since the development of modern vaccines, although there is an extremely remote chance of the vaccine causing an adverse reaction. Other causes that used to precipitate attacks, but with modern rearing methods are seldom encountered nowadays, were teething, worms and food allergies. A related condition, Hysteria, was prevalent in the late 1930s and was eventually traced to the bleaching agent used in the flour. I would assume, although without any evidence, that the nervous impulses of the brain could be stimulated, in susceptible subjects, by flashing lights etc. in the same way that those used in discos can trigger off attacks in humans.

FUCOSIDOSIS

This is found in human beings as well as dogs. It has been noted in Springers, and the breed appears to be the only one to recognise and monitor the condition, although it must occur in other breeds. The disease was first isolated and identified in 1981 following autopsies on three English Springers at Sydney University. Abnormalities in their nervous systems led to further research. Simply explained, it is an enzyme deficiency. The enzyme is required to break down compounds for the body to use. Its absence leads to these compounds building up in various tissues, the deposits in the brain and nerves being most important, giving rise to temperament changes, lack of co-ordination in movement, loss of hearing and sight. The transmission is believed to be by a simple recessive gene. The level of the enzyme in the blood can be identified by a blood test showing whether the animal is a carrier or not. This can be done at a fairly early age, so prospective breeding stock can be cleared. On the downside, the reading can fluctuate depending on the health of the subject, and the levels vary with different dogs. Thus in some cases a dog whose normal level is at the lower end of the scale could give a false picture if it were off-colour, and show up as a possible carrier. In these cases a second test, at a later date, would either confirm or contradict the original finds. Fortunately two clear parents should not, theoretically, produce affected progeny.

OPHTHALMIC DISORDERS
There are ten inherited conditions recognised as affecting the canine race, only three of which are so far known to affect English Springers. Five of these are congenital: Collie Eye Anomaly (CEA), Retinal Dysplasia (RD), Congenital Hereditary Cataract (CHC), Persistent Hyperplastic Primary Vitreous (PHPV), and Persistent Pupillary Membrane (PPM). Of these, only RD need concern us. Likewise, of the non-congenital items, only the two forms of Progressive Retinal Atrophy (PRA), Central (CPRA) and Generalised (GPRA) are tested for in ESS. The others, Hereditary Cataract (HC), Primary Lens Luxation (PLL) and Goniodysgensis (G), have so far not been found to be such a problem in the breed as to warrant inclusion in the testing schemes. Theoretically, PLL, being present in Border Collies, a breed which has been used as an illicit outcross in the past, could turn up in English Springer Spaniels; but as this would entail two carriers from the outcross combining after many generations, this would be a very remote possibility, even supposing the original "bar sinister" was affected. The conditions listed are tested for by retinal examination with an ophthalmoscope. RD testing can be done at a fairly early age and, being congenital, is present at birth and only one examination is necessary. The two forms of PRA, as their name indicates, are progressive, and although early testing can be done, annual checks are recommended. One worrying aspect of PRA is the fact that it was previously thought that, at about five or six years of age, a dog was presumed clear, and permanent certificates were issued. However, recent cases in some breeds have been diagnosed in previously clear dogs as late as ten years of age. This being well past the age to start a breeding career, these dogs will have already been used in good faith, and possibly have children and grandchildren incorporated in breeding programmes.

I will also include in this sub-section Ectropion and Entropion, although, in my opinion (admittedly as a layman) they are more to do with a poor relationship between the soft tissues of the skull and the bone structure. In the past, the loose, droopy eyes showing the inner membranes of the dog with the Ectropic condition were a feature of many Spaniels, and were mistakenly thought to be a desirable point. When common-sense prevailed and it was realised that this type of eye was nothing but a rubbish trap, breeders started breeding for a tighter, cleaner eye. The result of their labours was reasonably satisfactory, and the everted lower eyelids are rarely seen nowadays, unless the dog is off-colour, when the "hung-over" look is sometimes present. Breeding for a smaller, tighter eye-rim has in fact produced the opposite condition, Entropion, where the rims are too tight and roll inwards, making the lashes and hair rub against the eyeball. This condition can be hereditary in certain bloodlines, in which case it is permanent, and can only be remedied by surgery. In a minority of cases the condition can be temporary, some youngsters going through a phase which corrects itself as the skull grows. Other pseudo-entropic conditions can be caused by infections of the eye, causing the dog to screw up the eye with the irritation, and the muscles to go into spasm. General debility causing shrinkage of the fatty pads supporting the eyeball firmly in the orbit will also produce a similar effect. In these cases, treatment of the underlying cause will cure the condition. True entropion is usually present in both eyes.

PARASITES, EXTERNAL

Of the various "guests" to which the dog plays host, the most common are fleas and lice. Less frequently encountered are ticks, although these can be picked up quite often in certain locations, where sheep have been. Another parasite that is met with fairly regularly is the rabbit mite, the so-called "creeping dandruff". Most people are familiar with the highly mobile flea; unlike the others mentioned, these do not spend much time on the dog, only arriving at meal times, but they breed and live in the bedding and environs, so as well as treating the host, the living quarters also need attention. Signs of the presence of fleas are dried blood and the dark specks of excrement. Lice and ticks both attach themselves to the dog and spend their time sucking blood from the host. Lice are much smaller than ticks, and are found in colonies almost anywhere on the dog. They are greyish in colour and about the size of a pinhead. The most usual place is on the earflaps. They attach their eggs to the dog's hair. Ticks are similar in shape and colour, but when fully engorged with blood are about the size of a grain of sweet corn. They are usually found singly and they resemble a smooth wart. Rabbit mite, as might be guessed from its nickname, looks like a bad case of scurf. When this is brushed or combed out on to a dark surface and examined, if it moves, you've got rabbit mite. Any good insecticidal spray, powder or shampoo, will help to keep the parasites in check, although the best ones are probably only obtainable from your vet.

PARASITES, INTERNAL

This term is used to refer to the various types of worms that dogs are prone to. Confirmatory signs of infestation are the presence of worms in the stools. Roundworms are the most common and look like pieces of string, size depending on their state of maturity. The various species of tapeworm are chain-like in structure with the head attached to the intestines in a similar manner to ticks: portions of the worm are expelled and can be recognised by their resemblance to flattish grains of rice. The other types of worm are not often of a size to be recognised except via microscopic examination. Fortunately these are fairly uncommon. Most of the modern wormers are now broad-spectrum and are efficacious against more than one variety of worm.

SKELETAL PROBLEMS

The main problem found in the Springer is Hip Dysplasia. This occurs in all breeds to a greater or lesser degree and is diagnosed by radiography, the X-rays being read and assessed by one of a panel of experts. The hip is a ball and socket joint where the almost spherical head of the femur should fit snugly into a similarly shaped socket. As with most things pertaining to living organisms, nature does not always produce the perfection that scientists would like to see, and defects in the joint occur. These can range from something fairly minor, such as a slight flattening of the femoral head, to a really serious condition where the acetabular cup is so shallow that it cannot retain the head. To read the film, the joint is divided into segments which are assessed and given a points value according to the degree of seriousness. This is done for each hip and the result given as a double figure e.g. RH3/LH4, total 7. Perfection is zero for both hips and the maximum is 53 each side, giving a total of 106. In the UK the KC/BVA scheme keeps records of the scores and periodically the mean score for each breed is published, the eventual aim being to reduce the averages to as low a score as possible. The average for English Springers is about 12. Obviously the radiography cannot be carried out until the dog is fully developed and the bone structure set. Theoretically, one should not breed from afflicted animals, in the hope of eradicating HD. Practically, this is not completely feasible. In some breeds this would mean discarding most of the breed. A variety of anomalies crop up – dogs with virtually perfect hip scores moving like cripples all their lives, whereas some with a much higher score will move soundly and continue working until very late in life. Sometimes a litter bred from parents and grandparents with very low hip scores will produce stock with well over the average for the breed. At other times the reverse happens. In one breed the top stud dog of the day had the absolute maximum score, but the breed average remains about the same. Perhaps one day something positive will come from the research, and we shall learn the cause of the problem (which incidentally is also found in humans) and how to deal with it.

SKIN DISORDERS
Various forms of skin trouble are quite common and the cures and treatments recommended for them are legion. These can range from old wives' cures such as dunking in a bath of sheep dip three times daily after meals, to modern remedies such as cortisone. The former might be successful if the problem is parasitic in origin, but what if the cause is an allergy to irritants such as sheep dip? The point I am making is that there are so many similar symptoms with differing causes that, unless the reason is obvious, such as an infected abrasion or reaction to parasite activity, when a typical remedy such as a medicated bath is indicated, then a veterinary opinion will probably save a lot of time and trouble. The most difficult causes to diagnose are the allergies, both external and dietary. One item that causes a certain amount of grief and hassle is the nylon carpet. An allergic reaction to this can look very nasty round the legs and feet. Grass seeds, of the type similar to barley heads, can penetrate the skin, especially of the forelegs, and migrate, causing ulcers in a different site. Interdigital cysts between the toes, usually the front feet, appear to have no specific cause, some dogs suffering from them more than others. Infected pricks from thorns have been blamed, but this does not explain a multiple outbreak in both feet. Bathing with hot salt water and gently squeezing out the contents is a help. Other conditions can be fungal in origin. Homoeopathic sulphur tablets are useful.

Chapter Six

TRAINING YOUR ENGLISH SPRINGER

BASIC OBEDIENCE

This chapter is meant to give a general explanation and grounding in good behaviour to enable you to get your dog past the preliminary stages, ready to progress to the higher standards in whichever sphere of competition you choose to embark. The main idea behind this early education is to get the necessary response to commands instilled in your dog. These rules for harmonious living, variously known in different quarters as "yard breaking" by gundog trainers, "discipline" by those of a military or educational bent, or, in modern psychological jargon, as "bonding", are a must for any Springer – even the household pet. This "learning-to-live-with" technique is actually begun by the dam who will educate the pups into sundry minor "Do's and Don'ts" and, if you have more than one dog, the older members of the kennel will do their share in teaching the young ones their manners. Your job is to carry on from this elementary introduction to civilised behaviour, and channel it from an animal basis to that required by a human society. All dogs of whatever colour, race, religious persuasion or any other label used for differentiation, should have a certain amount of obedience instilled into them. This is necessary for their safety, and also for your peace of mind.

TRAINING RULES

1. Training should be a pleasure for both you and your Springer.
2. As Springer temperaments, like those of human beings, can vary from the sensitive, thoughtful types to the arrogant, pig-headed "know-alls", so a different approach is needed for each one. Springers generally, however, are highly intelligent creatures and usually any failures are down to the owner giving out the wrong vibrations.
3. Commands should be kept simple and given in a firm tone. The important thing is to make sure your Springer knows what you are asking to be done. This means that you should have the undivided attention of the pupil.
4. Always use the same command for the same exercise. Similarly, use different words for different things; "down" is a command that is frequently used to mean more than one thing by people, but can cause confusion to the dog.
5. Try not to confuse your dog by giving involuntary gestures that apparently contradict your vocal commands.
6. Repetition helps to fix the commands in the dog's mind, but do not carry this to the point of boredom, either for you or your Springer.
7. Vary the time and place of your training slightly so that the idea doesn't become fixed that we only do certain things at specific times, and in the same place. Obedience is all the time and everywhere.

Irish Coffee (Field Trial bred) pictured in Holland. The English Springer is a highly intelligent dog and will respond well to the stimulation of training.

8. If the subject under instruction carries out the lessons well for a few times give lots of praise, reward with a tidbit and quit while you are ahead. While composing this section on training, I suddenly realised how many of the relevant words began with P – Patience, Perseverance and Praise. With the next two it is imperative to get them in the right order as, if the first is successful, the second is unnecessary – Prevention and Punishment. Any Punishment should be Pianissimo, so of course, the Praise should be Phortissimo! Physical Punishment should only be used in extreme circumstances. The key phrase in training is Practice makes Perfect.

WORDS OF COMMAND
The commands for the different exercises can vary, according to personal preferences. In Obedience circles the words of command are virtually standard, whereas in gundog training the orders sometimes differ. The command SIT is universal throughout the Obedience world, but many gundog trainers use the word HUP (a corruption of SIT UP) or sometimes DOWN. Of the three, I prefer the SIT as, by stressing the sibilant, you can progress easily via a long hiss to a soft whistle and eventually to a proper whistle for distance work. The DOWN is a separate exercise in Obedience and means Lie Down, although some instructors use the term FLAT. It is also useful to reserve the word UP for when you need your Springer to jump up on to something such as the grooming table or the gamecart. I think I am safe in saying the word HEEL means the same in both Obedience and Gundog disciplines. It is one of the basic skills necessary for the comfort of both dog and handler. It is especially important for the pet dog. The STAY as an Obedience exercise is taught at both SIT and DOWN for varying periods. With Field work it is imperative that the dog should remain in position until the command to move is given. The STAND is part of the Obedience routine in advanced tests and, obviously, is an integral part of Show ring technique. It is superfluous in Gundog work, as it is usually better for the dog to be taught to sit or down when the bird is flushed, to ensure steadiness.

The Stay exercise can be taught from the Sit and the Down position.

Photo: Steve Nash.

LEARNING THE SIT COMMAND

Training can begin in the nest if you have bred your own litter. At feeding time, raising the dish usually brings the instinctive reaction from the dog of lifting the head, and sitting at the same time. When this happens, give the command SIT and thus begin the association of the command and the action of sitting. This early combination of the raised hand and the SIT comes in useful for later distance work in either obedience or gundog training. If the action does not occur instinctively, then a gentle push down on the rump while giving the command should soon produce the desired effect. It also helps to build up the essential relationship between you and your dog that is so important. If the pup can be encouraged to stay at the sit for a few seconds before being allowed to approach the food, this can help to instil steadiness to game later on. Anyone who has experienced the Springer's affinity for food will know that this is probably a bigger achievement than it sounds. The period at sit can be extended gradually. The raised hand association with the SIT is further extended later on when the SIT order is given while Heeling on the lead. The right hand pulls the lead upwards at the same time as the rump is pushed down and the command given. Once the hand signal is assimilated, you can experiment with omitting the verbal order and substituting a whistle command or, occasionally, try using the hand signal only. Later, when the whistle and the hand signals have been perfected, you can practise dropping the dog at a distance.

COLLAR AND LEAD TRAINING

At an early age, your pup can be accustomed to the collar, a lightweight item at first, then a lead can be attached after a few sessions, and the pup allowed to drag it along for a moment or two, to get the feel of it. When you pick up the end of the lead there are two probable reactions: either "I'm a tree rooted to this spot", or "Watch my impression of a kite in a hurricane". Hopefully this phase will soon pass, and you will be able to teach the pup to walk sedately. The lead should be held in the right hand and the dog should be on your left side, leaving the left hand free to control the lead. Actually, once the puppy is used to having something round the neck, it is preferable, for training purposes, to transfer to an item such as a choke chain, loose-running show lead or check cord. Of the three, I think a light-weight, one-piece show lead, made of flat material, is better for young pups to start with, as a choke chain can be a bit harsh for first lessons. Likewise, the check cords used for training gundogs are usually made of heavy-duty cord and are a bit thick for puppies' necks. Do bear in mind the need to walk at a sensible pace to suit the pup – your legs are much longer than those of a ten-week-old Springer. Softish shoes are also recommended and, if you are a lady embarking on a training session, most puppies, if they are confronted with a billowing skirt, will either shy away from it or, more likely, proceed to grab it and hang on for dear life. Once the dog has mastered the walking on a lead in a sensible manner, you can progress to walking to heel on a lead. With all these elementary lessons, remember the cardinal rules: keep it short; keep it fun.

HEELWORK

Teaching heel work at a reasonably early age should be undertaken with care, and in easy stages, but a few short, gentle lessons now and again, while Junior is still walking more slowly than you, will implant in the pup's mind the general idea of trotting beside you. Take the lead in your right hand as before and have the pup on your left. With the lead as loose as possible, walk slightly in front of the pup, at the same time patting your left leg and giving the order "Heel". To start with some encouragement may be necessary, possibly edible, or something to hold the attention at the required position, not darting forward. Naturally, as with all education, progress is variable; some dogs learn some things quicker than others, and their concentration varies from day to day.

When you feel you have achieved an adequate standard of heelwork on the lead, the next step is to try Heel Free. You should be able to assess the possible results by the reaction when the lead is slackened. If the pup lurches forward and needs checking too much, then more work is required. On the other hand, if the puppy trots along in the correct position on a loose lead, then the next progression is to drop the lead completely while continuing the command and patting your leg. If the pup does the natural thing and takes off, hopefully you will be able to stand on the lead while shouting "Heel". When the dog is reasonably steady when dragging the lead, the next step is to wind the lead loosely round the pup's neck in a suitable state to grab if the need arises. Eventually, you will reach that happy situation where you can have your dog at heel with just the choke chain.

RETRIEVING

Many Springers are natural retrievers and love carrying things. However, not all of them are, and those that aren't need to be taught and encouraged. Quite often these diffident retrievers come from powerful hunting lines and are more interested in flushing live birds than in picking up inanimate objects. This apparent anomaly is not really surprising, bearing in mind that the original job of the Spaniel group was flushing the game, and teams of retrievers were kept for picking up. The "maid-of-all-work" mantle is of comparatively recent origin. The classic dummy is usually an old sock stuffed with straw, or a similar soft filling, starting off with something small enough for the eight to ten-week-old pup to manage. Dummies should be firm, but not too hard, as certain items such as wood seem like an invitation for some puppies to bite, especially if they are teething. An ideal starting dummy is a rolled-up knotted handkerchief. When the pup is six to seven weeks old, make sure you have the pup's attention fixed on the dummy, and throw it gently, about four to five feet away. The normal reaction of most pups will be to investigate, pick it up and take it away to bed, so make sure you are between the puppy and the puppy's bed when you throw the dummy.

When the dummy has been picked up, call the puppy. When the pup reaches you, take the dummy and give plenty of praise. Repeat the exercise once or twice, stopping before the pup gets bored, finishing off with a tidbit as a reward. After a day or two of "games", commands can be introduced. When throwing the dummy I tend to use "fetch it" when the dummy is in view, and "hie lost" when the dummy is hidden, and "give" when taking it. Dummies of varying shapes and textures can be gradually introduced to condition the pup to the feel of different items and prevent

Young puppies will respond to the dummy from an early age.   Photo: Steve Nash.

a fixation with one object. The eventual idea is to retrieve anything and everything on command.

For those diffident or reluctant retrievers, it may be that you will have to resort to the method used by Obedience Trainers for non-retrieving breeds. This is to open the dog's jaws gently, place the dummy in its mouth and hold it there for a time, telling the dog to "Hold" in an encouraging tone and stroking the dog's underjaw. If the dog drops the article when you release your hold, try again and continue until you have made some progress. When the object has been held for period, take it, and reward the pup with a tidbit and plenty of praise. Then, after a minute or two, try again, only this time offer the dummy first. If it is taken then perhaps you can encourage the dog to walk about with you for a time while holding the dummy. If the dummy is not readily taken, then the first exercise should be repeated until it is satisfactorily accomplished. The article used in this exercise should be of a comfortable size and weight until the desired objective is reached.

Everything concerning retrieving should be done gently, otherwise the end result could be a hard-mouthed dog. Taking the dummy should be done one-handed – this becomes important in the field if you are already carrying game or a gun – and you should bend to the dog to take it. I noticed, when I dabbled in Obedience years ago, that the dogs with the teeth marks on their dumb-bells were usually those that came in close and held their heads back for a tall handler to take the article retrieved, and I came to the conclusion that the action of putting the head back led to an involuntary tightening of the jaw muscles, which is not good in a gundog breed.

The converse problem, with regard to retrieving, is the exhibitionist who will pick up and carry, but feels the need to show off, and so prances around showing the world and his wife how clever he is – I say "he" because this syndrome is usually associated with young males. The remedy usually recommended, if the facilities are available, is to use a long, narrow passage, or a lane, enclosed on both sides and shut off at one end, with the handler standing at the open end, thus leaving the dog with one option. On no account should you make any movement towards the dog, as this will be taken as an invitation to play and chase. It is, of course, just a natural extension of the games played with siblings in the nest. Sometimes an attitude of complete indifference to the performance will have the effect of making the star bring his act down centre-stage into the spotlight, hoping for some reaction. As he approaches, the best thing to do is turn and walk slowly away, calling him in to Heel. There is a slim chance that this might work and the dummy will be brought in to your side. If this happens, reach down and take the dummy calmly, giving plenty of praise and a tidbit. There is a possibility that, when you turn and call Heel, the dog will drop the dummy and come in without it, in which case he should be put on his lead, and taken back to the dummy, encouraged to pick up again, given some heelwork on the lead carrying the dummy, and then have the dummy taken from him as above. If a suitable passage or lane is not available, it may be that the problem can be cured by using a longer-length lead and giving retrieves on the lead until the desired effect is achieved. The idea is to persuade the pup that sharing your game of bringing the dummy straight back to you is more exciting than his solo performance.

GOOD CITIZEN DOG SCHEME

Recognising that there is a world-wide anti-dog lobby, the UK Kennel Club, in 1992, instituted their Good Citizen Dog Scheme. This is a very basic set of exercises designed for all pet owners and, really, is what most responsible owners have been doing for years. However, any attempt to make sure all dogs are well-behaved and under control is to be commended. The test is in eight Parts which are as follows:

1. Put on collar and lead.
2. Walk on lead without distractions.
3. Walk on lead through door/gate.
4. Walk on lead passing people and dogs.
5. Lie down and stay on command, on lead.
6. Groom.
7. Present for examination on lead, including mouth, teeth, throat, eyes, ears and feet.
8. Release from lead, play with or without toy, recall and attach lead.

This makes the obvious assumption that the dog has a name, knows it and, more important, will respond to it when called. The scheme is administered by the KC but is co-ordinated by local training Clubs etc., the tests being incorporated as part of their normal classes. The tests are assessed by various people such as Dog Wardens, Police Dog Handlers, or similar suitably qualified persons. On successfully passing all eight sections (in one session) an Official KC Certificate and Rosette are awarded. It is too early yet to gauge the success of the scheme. Groomers and vets will obviously appreciate sections 6 and 7. Your puppy will still need some preliminary lessons before commencing this course. The Kennel Club is underwriting the scheme, but has had generous support from many of the dog food manufacturers and insurance firms.

FIELD TRAINING

This section is mainly concerned with the rough-shooter, the beater, or the acquisition of the Show Gundogs Working Certificate. Hopefully, with luck, it will enable you to educate your Springer sufficiently to give both of you pleasure when working. The production of a reasonable working gundog is dependent on two sets of characteristics – those that are taught or acquired, and those that are inborn basic instincts. With regard to training your Springer for the field, many local Gundog training clubs have started in recent years, and these can be very useful. The expertise passed on from the instructors, and the training with other dogs in the classes, are all helpful experiences. Many of the training manuals published in the past have been geared to training for trials and have made the assumption that such niceties as rabbit pens and space for a "retrieving passage" were on tap. Nowadays the acre or so I have seen airily recommended as an ideal size for a rabbit pen would probably have been sold as building land and covered with a mini housing estate.

With the increase of interest in shooting and training gundogs, coupled with people living in smaller properties, the Gundog training clubs have, to a large extent, taken the place of individual training. In the absence of any nearby gundog classes, as a means to an end, your nearest Obedience club can prove an adequate substitute up to a point. On the credit side you are building up that essential sense of rapport with your dog and providing the required Obedience schooling.

THE RETRIEVE
Photos: Steve Nash.

The Springer is commanded to "Wait".

It is important to stay in position when the dummy is thrown.

The Springer is sent out to retrieve the dummy. As the dog becomes more experienced, it will learn to retrieve from thick cover.

The dummy is brought back to the handler.

The sitting and heelwork in the company of other dogs is beneficial. Later on, the more advanced exercises, such as the timed stays, especially those with the handler out of sight which help to promote steadiness, and the distant control exercises which include dropping at a distance to command and, possibly, hand signals, are basically what you need in a gundog anyway.

You may have to come to an arrangement with the Obedience instructor with regard to one or two small matters. Gundogs generally are not switched on to the preciseness in work on which Obedience exercises are marked – not for them the pristine pose of the German Shepherd Dog, sitting as upright as a Guardsman hard into the handler's leg, or the almost obsequious "wrap-around" technique of the Border Collies. Instead, the average Labrador will, more than likely, loll over on one buttock stolidly awaiting the next command, while Spaniels are prone to slew round so that they can watch your face. Similarly with heelwork: working gundogs are not the tight "muzzle into back of the knee" type. They usually walk with their shoulder level with the knee. This scrupulous accuracy can be achieved with Springers in the training hall but, hopefully, you are thinking about giving your dog some real Spaniel work, and a muddy field of sugarbeet, heavy cover such as brambles, or pheasant cover and feed such as maize, are not the places to worry about crooked sits or tight heeling.

Another point where you may have to compromise with the Obedience trainer is over the matter of retrieving articles. The normal dumbbell used in Obedience in its basic form is not really suitable for field training. The centre dowel connecting the ends, being fairly narrow in diameter and also being wood, is tempting to mouth, which means the dog will grip over it tightly and leave teeth marks. One advantage, however, is the fact that the ends hold the connecting bar up from the floor, making early experience of picking-up simpler. Also, because the ends are heavier, this assists in teaching the pupil to get a balanced grip. To get over the disadvantage I have mentioned, the connecting bar should be wrapped with foam rubber, or something similar, to a suitable thickness and secured. Once the initial art of picking-up has been achieved, the dumbbell can be dispensed with and other, more orthodox, gundog dummies substituted. Manufacturers of gundog training equipment make various sizes and weights of canvas dummies, some of the larger ones being limp and equating to a hare. Needless to say these larger ones are not suitable for too young puppies.

At a very much later stage of training, these dummies can have rabbit skins or pheasant wings wrapped round them and secured by elastic bands. Some of the old countrymen could skin rabbits without gutting them, peel them off inside out, and finish up with a complete skin in the form of a tube. The skin side could then be scraped clean of fat etc., rubbed with salt to cure it, turned back the correct way and stuffed with whatever was to hand. Result – one realistic dummy. However, in the preliminary stages of training it is as well to avoid anything that arouses the hunting instinct until the Obedience side has been fully mastered, and that is why a stuffed sock, or a canvas dummy is recommended as a starting point.

I cannot emphasise too much the need for the initial Obedience and dummy training to be well instilled before introducing the pupil to actual game. Too often I have seen promising youngsters spoilt by over-keenness on the part of the handler, possibly with his first Springer, bred from the top bloodlines, and probably a bit too "hot" for a novice to cope with. A typical scenario I have imagined features such a case. In previous seasons he has possibly been beating in his spare time, without a dog. Possibly with the chance of some rough shooting and extra opportunities for beating, he purchases a puppy from a litter whose parents he had seen working when on holiday. Good thinking up to a point – but the mistake was in buying a pup from two or three hundred miles away, where the advice and help from the breeder is not so readily to hand.

The next mistake is impatience. The pup comes from a spring-born litter, so there is all summer

RETRIEVING FEATHER
Photos: Steve Nash.

When your Springer is proficient at retrieving dummies, you must progress to the type of retrieve required in the field. This Springer is retrieving a pheasant.

The Springer's physique is supremely well adapted to carrying heavy weights as it moves at a reasonable speed.

A soft mouth is essential so that the dog does not damage the bird.

to deal with the preliminary training and socialising. However, come mid-October, our Joe presents himself at the first shoot of the season complete with new pup – training, if any, minimal. The pup is now seven months old, and obviously from a keen working line. Our friend now learns the hard way that to try and school a young Springer from scratch, in a field full of reared game, is well-nigh impossible. I should explain that, at the start of the season, reared game are young birds that have not fully developed the strength in their wings for a quick take-off and, still being used to the keeper feeding them, have not yet learned to be shy. The consequence is that they are slow to fly and will rather run. In these circumstances, it is pointless to try to teach the dog to sit with all those distractions. Had the dog had an adequate amount of education prior to this, the situation would have been ideal to help instil steadiness. Very often puppies like this, introduced too soon to live game, turn out to be "squeakers", whining with frustration when there are birds about.

BASIC INSTINCTS

Your Springer has already got inbuilt working instincts to some degree or other. These cannot be taught. You can, however, train your dog to use them to the best advantage, i.e. yours. The basic Obedience such as sit, stay, walking to heel, has already been covered, and the degree to which this is incorporated in the preliminary field work will depend on the temperament of the individual puppy. It may be advisable to allow more laxity in this respect with a backward puppy, whereas a pup that is a "hard-goer" will probably need sitting on from the word go. The basic instincts are:

Nose: the sense of smell is well developed in most breeds, not only gundogs, (even the show strains) and cannot be put there. This is evident in the scent discrimination test in advanced Obedience. The best you can do is teach your dog to use it for your benefit and load the dog's memory with those scents on which you wish to concentrate.

Game sense: some dogs seem to possess a sixth sense and know intuitively from an early age where the birds etc., will be, and how they will break, even when they are some distance away and the wrong way of the wind.

Biddability: often referred to as kindness, this desire to do anything to please you is of great importance in a gundog. I believe this to be more important in a normal working dog than the speed and style needed for competitions and trials. This often develops into an almost telepathic state, where the Springer knows what is needed almost before the handler.

These traits are nearer the surface in some dogs than they are in others, and you will discover how long your individual dog needs in order to develop them.

IMPROVING THE RETRIEVE

Following on from the general Obedience the next step can be improvement of the retrieve. When the SIT has been taught, and the rudiments of retrieving achieved, it remains to combine the two, and make the pup stay at the SIT until sent for the dummy. We started off by letting the pup run in to the thrown dummy. The next step is to restrain the puppy at the SIT for a while after the dummy has been thrown, then to send the pup for the dummy, with the command you intend to use for the retrieve. At first there may be a little confusion in the pup's mind about whether to sit or go for the dummy, but this is usually sorted out fairly easily. When steadiness at the SIT is mastered, further refinements can be attempted, such as moving some distance from the pupil before sending for the dummy. This can be done both before and after throwing the dummy, but you should be prepared for the possibility of breaking when you are out of reach. Later exercises can involve the above, but from the STAND position, where there obviously is more temptation to break. A further aid to steadiness is to occasionally give the SIT command halfway to the pick-up – but, I would stress, NOT after the pick-up has been made, as the retrieve should then be made with as much speed and efficiency as possible.

As soon as the pup has learned to retrieve the seen dummy fairly efficiently, then education must be started to find hidden dummies. This is achieved by a series of progressions, starting with a dropped dummy in long grass fairly near the pup, who should see it drop. The pup is then taken a few yards away and, after sitting, is sent for the dummy with a hand signal in the direction of the dummy and a simultaneous verbal command, HIE LOST. If this exercise is successful, the distance can be extended gradually up to about 100 or 150 yards. Following on from this, the dummy should be dropped without the dog seeing where it is, and the exercise repeated as before, remembering the hand signals to indicate the general direction of the hidden dummy. Later on the dummies can be planted without the presence of the dog, before attempting the exercise.

INTRODUCTION TO GUNFIRE

At some point the education of a gundog will need to include becoming accustomed to the sound of gunshots. Of all training aspects, this is the one needing most care. Too loud a bang, too close to a young puppy, can cause a distaste for the sound, which then becomes a long-term problem to eradicate. Like most training, it needs to be taught a step at a time. Gentle hand-claps at feeding time make a useful lead-in to getting the pupil used to sharpish noises, as does bursting blown-up paper bags – but this is not so easy now that the plastic-bag age is upon us. The next stage used to be the child's cap pistol, but since Cowboys and Indians have been superseded by Space Age and computer games, these are more likely to be found in curio, rather than toy, shops. Starter pistols firing blanks are useful, usually the same type as is used in the dummy launcher, but without the distraction of the dummy, to start with. These small calibre blanks have a rather sharp-sounding crack which can upset some dogs, so care is advocated in their use. As soon as possible the sound of a proper shot-gun needs to be phased in. One useful tip I learned a year or two back – from a show person, believe it or not – was that, if you have a clay pigeon club fairly near, then walk your dog as near to it as is possible. This gets a dog used to gunfire at no cost!

The location of your schooling should be selected with some care. The ground chosen should be as open as possible, to allow the dissipation of most of the sound of the shot. I once landed myself with a problem by firing a shotgun in a semi-enclosed yard. The resultant re-echoing from all sides left me with a very confused and gun-nervous dog. Fortunately, he was a retrieving addict and, once out in the shooting field, quickly associated the bangs with the fall of those lovely birds to be picked up, and the damage was soon repaired. But the outcome could have been catastrophic with a dog of different inclinations. A gradual increase in the loudness of the bang, coupled with a decrease in the distance from the pupil, will gradually accustom the dog to the sound. Combining this with the retrieve will need the help of an assistant and a dummy launcher. Making the dog Sit or Hup, either by verbal or whistle command when the dummy is launched, will encourage "dropping to shot".

WHISTLE SIGNALS

At some stage of training whistle signals should be introduced and gradually substituted for the verbal commands. What type of whistle you use is a matter of preference, but you should try and get one that is as individual as possible. As most keepers tend to use police-type, or Acme Thunderer, whistles, for starting and ending drives, these are best avoided. Some trainers in fact use two. The usual signal for the SIT is a short single blast. As I said before, I prefer to use the command SIT as this is easily converted to whistle-like sound, and the proper thing is easier to introduce, especially when combined with hand signals. Most people use two quick "pips" as a recall signal. Later in the training you will probably need to stop your dog, when hunting, in order to give some directional hand signals. A longer drawn-out whistle is often used to attract the dog's attention long enough to give the relevant hand signal.

QUARTERING AND COLD GAME

Quartering to a certain degree comes naturally to the Springer but, like most of the natural instincts, this ability varies with individual dogs. The development of this follows on from the previous exercise with hidden dummies. Diffident students will need to be encouraged, but for a hard-ranging dog you will probably have quite a lot of recourse to the Sit/Stop whistle. All of the exercises should be done on cords in the early stages, short ones at first, gradually lengthening as proficiency increases, until you feel sure enough to try them without a lead. Teaching to follow a line, e.g. for wounded game, is achieved by dragging a dummy some distance on the end of a cord and then hiding it. The usual methods recommended are either to lay the trail with the dummy attached to two cords equidistant between two people, or with one trail-layer using one cord on a pole, similar to a fishing rod. This stops the pup following the scent of the trail-layer. Sooner or later comes the time to introduce cold game in place of the dummies. Sometimes this is easy, and at other times snags occur. I once had to ruin my rabbit skin dummy when training a Sussex who would retrieve fur but not feather. I wrapped it round a partridge and gradually, with each successive retrieve, cut pieces off the fur until the dog was retrieving the partridge.

In recent years there has been introduced a piece of training equipment, the use of which is controversial. I refer to the electric collar, used either to stop dogs at a distance or, in other instances, to speed them up. To give a dog an electric shock for some error of training on the part of the handler seemed, at first, to my mind, barbaric, and far worse than some of the rough handling of the days when the job was called "dog breaking". I think in the early days, with the more primitive versions, this was probably true. With the more sophisticated models now on the market, and a more sensitive control of the current, I consider that possibly it may have a place as a piece of training equipment if used carefully in the right hands. The people I would term the "right hands" would probably not need to use the item anyway, having made the correct choice for training initially, and having discarded any failures before reaching the stage where the collar was needed. However, on a recent shoot I discussed this with a police dog handler, and subsequently I must confess to moderating my views a bit. In point of fact I suppose, in my own case, I now have an ideal situation in which to try one out. This arose by a combination of circumstances I had not encountered before. I have a young dog that I had been taking just to get the feel of things. At first his nose and brain were not completely synchronised and he was cautious about going too far away from me.

With encouragement, he was beginning to flush and sit – no thoughts of chase when the birds flew. All was going to plan. Then came disaster day! By some mischance, various members of the beating team were missing and, apart from the 'keeper's dog, he was the only dog there, which meant, in effect, the only one available to work a deep ditch on one of the drives. With visions of my pup staying in the field, and the ditch getting neglected, I set off to do my best. He did potter about at the start of the ditch where there were brambles and, with encouragement, flushed a few birds. The trouble started when the brambles gave way to blackthorn, so the ditch now resembled a tunnel, the birds became visible, and scent and sight fused with my previous exhortations of "get in" and "good boy". Everything clicked in his brain and he went to flush the birds. Unfortunately, due to the tunnel effect of the ditch and shrubs, the birds could not fly and the flush became a chase. I think perhaps a collar might have been more use than my whistle at that moment. Normally, however, he would not have been in that precise situation.

In contrast to modern technology I include, from about a century ago, a series of quotes from *I Walked by Night,* the autobiography of Rawle, the King of the Norfolk Poachers. On training, he says: "Pacence and a lot of trubble – I have trained a lot of breeds of dogs and I have always found that Kindness have been much better than the wipp."

"I have trained a lot of Spanells but they are class of dog that if you get one that will do as he is told you will get others that are verry wilfull."

"It is a long Job and take a rare lot of Patence, but of corse some are much easier than others."

"Some are born teachable, some are verry stubben – they are the worst to train and come in most for the wipp."

"If you have a stubben one try him first with kindness. If that fail you and its not often that it do, you must try Punishment, but kindness mostly win in the end."

"At the age of four months he may begin his lerning. First get a rabbitt skin and stuff it with some thing soft, wading is the best. Take the pup out and throw the skin for him to bring to you. He will soon lern that. Wen he bring it to you reward him with a piece of sugar, but on no account alow him to play with it. If he is that way inclined punish him but not severely. As sone as you find he will bring the skin to you hide it up in the Hedge and let him find it, that will lern him to seek for his game later on. Do not let him run game."

On picking a puppy he advocates: "The pup must have a broad head across the eyes, as that is were he keep his brains, deep chest and sturdy legs."

POINTS TO REMEMBER

During training you will have, no doubt, accustomed your dog to a certain amount of cover with your hidden retrieves etc. However, unless you are very fortunate in your neighbourhood, the cover will probably be a bit on the sparse side and, moreover, your dog will soon become used to the same ground every time. Be warned – the battlefield will be far worse that the parade ground! An ideal follow-up to your training sessions, should you be able to find an amenable keeper, is walking up partridges. The dogs usually have to be kept on leads, but for a youngster, being able to polish the obedience side of the training "on the job" is an advantage. A further plus is the fact that partridges, being shy birds, rise some hundred yards away and not straight under the dog's nose. This gives a gradual introduction to warm scents without too much temptation close at hand. Also, being field or open country birds, rather than woodland ones, you will be walking stubble and roots, which is another bonus for the first time out. On some shoots the beaters are sometimes asked to help "pick up" at the end of the drive. This is useful experience if you are so lucky. Even helping to carry the "bag" helps to get the feel of things.

On the debit side, the autumn crop of nettles seems to possess particularly vicious stings which can affect some dogs more than others, until they get used to them. They also smell very strong and rank which, on poor scenting days, makes finding birds very difficult, even for older, highly experienced dogs. The same applies, in a lesser degree, to turnip fields. Sugar beet poses a different problem. Spaniels hunting with their heads down in the roots often do not hear the whistle, as the sound is drowned by the rattle of the beet leaves in their ears. Hopefully, you will have got your Springer working to hand signals as well as the whistle. Too much noise and shouting is frowned upon on some shoots, as it disturbs the birds. It is also a practice that is not too popular at Trials.

At the end of the day you will have a better idea of the points where you need to go back to the schoolroom. You will often find that the items you thought you had perfected in training have gone overboard in a different environment and your supposed weak points have posed no problem. Nil desperandum! So long as your dog has committed no unforgivable crime such as eating half the bag, or biting the guv'nor (The Shoot Captain, if we are being posh), there is always the next time. A few lessons between shoots will add polish, and experience will come with each day out. The metamorphosis from the shy young puppy cautiously sniffing the strange new scents, nose wrinkling as they are savoured, through to the gradual awareness that these aromas belong to the game we are after, to the eventual product hunting the ground with enthusiasm, or driving into thick cover with courage, flushing game, finding lost birds or runners, and generally doing the job for which the dog was bred – filling the game bag – does bring quiet satisfaction.

WATER-WORK AND FENCES
With regard to water work, this should be introduced gradually, starting in shallow water, preferably in summertime when getting wet is more pleasurable – keeping in mind the fact that you will more than likely get as wet as the dog. Playing with a stick is probably as good a way as any of introducing water. Good floating dummies can be made from plastic detergent or soft-drinks bottles wrapped around with some padding and an old sock. Another lesson that has to be instilled at some time is the art of negotiating fences, with and without the retrieved article. Care must be taken with barbed wire and sheep netting. Another creation of the last few years is the electrified plastic sheep or rabbit fence.

THE FIRST DAY OUT
Coming to your first day out on the proper job, you will undoubtedly come across new experiences for your dog. If you are beating on an organised shoot, you will possibly encounter various forms of farm livestock. A recent animal that is on the increase on some of our local shoots is the Muntjac deer, which tends to flash past in the middle of a drive and provide temptation to the beaters' dogs. The transport provided for beaters is also extremely variable, and your dog is likely to be in close proximity with upwards of a dozen humans and several other dogs. The steps up into cart can also be awkward until the dog has learned to cope with them. Your dog may, at times and for various reasons, travel in a truck with the bag – very tempting! When the actual work starts your dog will, no doubt, be overawed at the amount of scent to be found, and may need to be kept on a lead until the initial excitement has worn off. In any case the keeper will tell you when dogs should be kept on a lead for certain drives.

SHOW AND RING TRAINING
I am assuming that, if you are interested in this section, you possess a reasonably sound, well-constructed and fairly typical Springer. These attributes, plus general fitness and good presentation, are basic requirements for the show ring. To them need to be added the ring technique required for the judge to appreciate these virtues. The ideal in this direction should be a natural stance and a free-moving exhibit at the end of a loose lead, as has been the norm for the exhibits from the Ware Kennels for many years. It is also the recognised method of showing two of my other breeds, Border Terriers and Cavaliers. Fashion, however, at the present time, has pushed the breed into the "top and tail" camp when posed. While on the move the dogs are strung up on a tight lead and gaited round the ring at an excessive pace, undignified to both dog and handler. One particularly grotesque method of "stringing up" involves pulling the lead up tight behind the ear nearest the handler. This cannot really be necessary. This flashy, over-fast movement is untypical of the Breed, but seems to find favour with inexperienced judges or those with a superficial knowledge of it.

THE SHOW STANCE

You will probably have stood your puppy up numerous times while grooming, or when assessing potential, so the budding star should be fairly conversant with the show stance. If you are using photographs in publications as a guide to standing your pup, a point to remember is that many of these are posed and possibly retouched. Youngsters will obviously have their very early training on a table, and should be encouraged to stand in as near to the show stance as possible. Some puppies seem to do this naturally. Quite often though, especially with a heavier type of puppy, the hind legs do not develop the muscular strength in the early stages to support the rear section in the required position. If this is the case, do not be in too much of a hurry to get the pose exactly right. When the muscles harden as the pup grows, this will come. If space allows, when assessing the pup on the table, try to spend some time facing your dog so that, when you come to free-standing on the floor, the pup will automatically look up at you. Many pups are diffident at first about standing up. Stroking the tummy underneath will help with this. The main thing is to get the dog to stand in a comfortable position and, hopefully, to assume this when required. One of the main reasons for fidgety dogs in the ring is that the handler is posing them uncomfortably.

The pup while growing and developing can be taught to stand on the floor, both free-standing and "topped and tailed", or "stacked" as it is sometimes called. Teaching the free stance initially means placing the dog in the desired position, encouraging the dog to stay, then moving to the front, still encouraging the dog to stay. Then stand a few paces away facing your dog with a loose lead, and attract your dog's attention with talk and by "baiting" with a tidbit. The goal is to get the exhibit standing in an alert pose with a wagging tail. Probably, at first, the pup will move forward, in which case the original position must be resumed and the exercise started again. Some dogs may require more time and patience spent on this exercise than others. When it is necessary to "top and tail", the pose should be practised with the exhibit facing each way. The value of this will be found when one is asked to "face your dog the other way, please". At outdoor shows it is usually advantageous to face the dog uphill. If you have access to a large mirror, you can practise standing your exhibit in front of it and assess the best pose.

MOVEMENT

When the rudiments of lead training have been mastered, a little gentle instruction in moving for the show ring can be started. The exact pace is immaterial at first, the primary considerations are to educate the pup to walk up and down in a straight line, around in a circle and also a triangle. The straight up and down moving should be practised with the dog on either side: although moving on the left side of the handler is the norm, there are occasions when it is necessary to change hands. In all cases, moving on a loose lead should be encouraged. The movement can be speeded up gradually once the initial education for the ring has been taught; the eventual aim being a brisk walk, bordering on a trot. Later on, when moving sensibly has been mastered, the pup can be similarly encouraged to move with a high, proudly-held head carriage by means of a tidbit held in front and just above the nose. Some people advocate starting off by walking backwards from the free-standing position, with a loose lead, when teaching this. You will need to enlist the help of a knowledgeable friend to watch you moving your dog at different speeds and help you select the best speed to get the best out of your individual animal.

RING TRAINING CLASSES

Many clubs now hold ring training classes and these are useful for experience and for socialising your puppy. Usually there are several instructors who work on a rota basis, so that the pup becomes accustomed to being judged and handled by all sorts of strangers.

SHOW EQUIPMENT
Items you will need for showing your dog should include:
1. A show lead of whatever pattern you have decided you prefer.
2. A card clip to hold your ring number.
3. Your grooming tools, or some of them at least.
4. If the show is benched, then a strong collar and a sensible-length bench chain, and also a blanket for the bench.
5. If the show is unbenched, most exhibitors now use collapsible cages where the show executive permits their use and there is sufficient space. The top of the cage can double as a grooming table.
6. Food and drink for canines and humans.

AT THE SHOW
Do remember to try and show your dog to the best advantage. Minimising faults is a combination of careful handling and judicious trimming. This comes with experience. Wear non-slip shoes, and sensible clothes that your dog will show up against. Arrive at the show in sufficient time to allow you and your dog to get settled, and to give plenty of time for a final grooming, especially if the weather is unkind.

Chapter Seven

BREEDING AND REARING A LITTER

Having made your decision and selected your foundation, do remember that all breeding must be for the improvement of the breed. Exaggeration in any form should be avoided. It is very easy, when trying to improve a feature, to cross the line that represents the ideal and to finish up with a fault. This applies to working points as well as physical attributes.

BREEDING FOR QUALITY

Presumably, if you are thinking about breeding, you have started with a bitch – although some kennels have commenced with a dog with the female side added later, but for this to succeed is uncommon. There is much talk about "planned breeding programmes". This has always puzzled me slightly, as I have usually found nature reluctant to conform to a plan. It is difficult to try to breed out faults until you know what they are. As your pup grows you will be learning what points need improving in the next generation. Over the eighteen months to two years that will have elapsed before your bitch is ready for breeding, you will have assessed where you need to improve the next generation. You should have a good idea of which stud dogs are suitable to correct any shortcomings in your bitch's make-up. Select a dog that is perfect in the point you are seeking to improve and, more important, one who sires stock that is good for that point. Do not be tempted to go to the extreme to correct it. "Too little" mated to "too much" does not give you "just right". More often than not you get a lot of each and, in trying to eliminate one fault, you bring in another – or, even worse, a combination of the two that makes a third. It is usually better to try and stay in the same bloodlines, unless the fault you are trying to lose is endemic to that line. In that case, you are wasting your time, and a suitable outcross is indicated, again using a dog that excels in the required point. Actually, the first litter out of any bitch is a bit of a lottery, as some will "throw to the dog", and produce puppies of a quality relevant to the class of sire used. Others, unfortunately, will often breed to themselves, no matter how good a sire is selected. This makes eliminating faults that much harder, although, if the faults are too serious, you should consider whether the bitch should be bred from anyway.

One thing to take into account, which is often not considered, is whether the shortcomings are in the breeding or in the rearing. If the latter is the case, then the faults will not be passed on to the puppies. This especially applies to cases where, for example, a traumatic experience at an early show has resulted in a dislike of shows. In referring to faults I am talking about deviations from the standard, not current fads and fashion. Naturally, when talking about things to be improved, I am including the mental side and temperament. A further point to be considered is that some faults are harder to get rid of than others, especially if they are deeply ingrained in a strain or, even worse, the breed as a whole. There are, of course, some unexplained things that crop up. One

A group of Hazelwood Springers in Sweden: The aim of a breeding programme is to produce dogs with good conformation, sound temperament and of similar type.

example I know of is the dog who, out of four Champion brothers, was the only one to sire bad mouths, whereas the other three appeared to be clear of the fault, as were the females from the same breeding.

TIMING THE MATING

For your first litter from a maiden bitch it is best to go to a breeder who is experienced in stud work. The oestrus, on average, lasts approximately twenty-one days and consists of three stages. The first is when the vulva swells and hardens and there is a discharge, pale-coloured at first, then gradually becoming more profuse and darkening through to a pinkish shade until, by the eighth or ninth day, it has become almost pure blood. In the secondary stage the colour reverts to a colourless fluid, and the vulva softens although it remains enlarged. This is usually considered the optimum time for mating, and it lasts from about the tenth day until about the fourteenth. From then on the tumescence gradually decreases until, by the end of the third week, things are back to normal.

The whole process is accompanied by a strong scent attractive to the male. This is a point not always made in text books on canine physiology. The time-scale quoted above is the average for all breeds, but can be very elastic, varying with individual bitches. As you should not be breeding from your bitch before the second or third season, you should be able to gauge whether she conforms to the average or not. Whether your bitch is one of the exceptions that has a short oestrus, or perhaps hangs things out for a month, the same basic rules apply. Mating should take place roughly half to two-thirds through the heat when the vulva has softened and she has stopped showing colour. The scent is also variable, being much stronger in some cases than in others. Arrangements should be made with the stud dog owner well in advance, and a date fixed for the mating. If all goes well the normal gestation period is about sixty-three days. The bitch should have been wormed some weeks before she was due to come into season and, if she has been regularly wormed anyway, it should not be necessary to risk further dosing during her pregnancy. This, however, is a point on which you should take your vet's advice. I, personally, am loath to push too much medication down an expectant mother, especially in the first third of the pregnancy when many of the important bits and pieces are being formed.

THE MATING PROCESS

Having decided the optimum time for mating your bitch, and made the necessary arrangements with the owner of the stud dog, we now come to the actual deed. Although the basic requirement of the deposition of the sperm into the female by the male is the same in most mammals, when we get to the canine race there are several differences in the performance of the act. As with other animals, an erection is required for copulation, but with dogs, once penetration of the vaginal sphincter has taken place, a secondary stage occurs in which the penis becomes further engorged with blood, locking the bulb of the glans penis behind the sphincter, which also tightens in order to hold the dog. This "tie" can last from a few minutes to an hour, or possibly more. This experience is often disconcerting to a novice. Another interesting part of the dog's mating is the practice of turning back-to-back during coition. This again can be slightly disturbing the first time it is encountered, but it is perfectly normal and quite harmless. After ejaculation has taken place, the penis gradually subsides, the sphincter relaxes and the "happy couple" part.

By now you will have had sufficient experience of dogs to realise that, no matter how simple the basic technicalities seem, complications will arise. This is the time you learn the truth of the old saying – "the course of true love ne'er did run smooth"! There is always the chance that, in spite of your plans with a carefully chosen stud dog, there is not the same idea on the part of the dogs. This may be because, although all the outward signs look right, the bitch is not ready. On the other hand, some dogs and bitches just do not take to teach other. On introducing the pair, a certain amount of play and flirtation takes place and normally, after a few minutes of this, they get down to serious business. If the bitch is ready, her scent should be enough to excite the dog, and usually she will be keen to accept him. Things then proceed to take a fairly normal course. Sometimes the female has little, or no scent, which does not affect a keen or experienced dog very much, but a young or diffident dog may be reluctant to start the courtship. This is especially likely where the bitch is also on the shy and retiring side. In cases like these a lot of patience and encouragement is called for. It also helps, in this circumstance, if you have access to another bitch in season and can transfer her scent by means of a pad of cotton wool. Some keen stud dogs can be overpowering and put the bitch off to start with. A bitch that will not stand for one dog will be perfectly amenable with another. As well as this mental incompatibility, physical difficulties can be encountered. When the bitch is ready and fully ripe for mating, her vulva should be full and standing proud to present a better "target" for the dog. This ideal is rarely met for various reasons. Some of these are due to our desire to "improve" conformation. Using animals of differing heights to try and correct size can pose problems. We are fortunate in having a building with an uneven floor and we can usually manage to find a spot to suit. Some females, when they feel the dog mounting them, brace themselves, which can move the vulva out of reach. The opposite can also happen and the bitch will sag under the dog's weight, with the same result. A good stud dog, who is experienced and knows his job will, when he mounts and clasps the bitch round the waist, pull her into the correct position with no problems. At other times all manner of manoeuvring and manipulation may be needed. A useful trick that sometimes works with a fidgety bitch is to hold one of her forelegs off the ground, thus putting most of the weight onto the hind legs. Among other things which make mating difficult can be tightness of the vaginal passage. This is sometimes due to tension on the part of the female and disappears when she relaxes. Another cause is a stricture or obstruction in the passage. This calls for veterinary advice. An over-excited stud dog sometimes swells up before he has completely penetrated the bitch and the tie terminates prematurely when the dog turns. When this occurs he should be taken away until the tumescence subsides. This sometimes happens quite quickly. On other occasions, if the prepuce is tight, then retraction takes a little longer and the dog can become uncomfortable, especially if the soft tissues begin to dry. In such cases, the careful application of liquid paraffin will ease things back to normal and ensure no damage is done. After a short rest, most dogs will be ready to try again, and usually the second time, his ardour will be less, and with a more relaxed approach he will make a more efficient job.

FEEDING THE PREGNANT BITCH

As we give our main feed in the morning, one sign of pregnancy that we have noticed over the years is that, with some bitches, during the first week or two after mating, they are slow in eating in the morning. This is usually a sign that things are progressing in the right way – presumably this equates with "morning sickness" in humans. Another sign, which happened with one of our bitches, was a personality change if the mating was successful. Normally good-tempered, she became aggressive during the early days of the pregnancy. The bitch should be well-fed but not fat and, as the pregnancy progresses, the quantity stepped up slightly. As the abdominal cavity fills with the ensuing litter, she will feel much more comfortable if the daily ration is fed in two or, if she looks like having a large litter, even three meals. At about five weeks, she will usually show signs of a successful mating. The part behind her rib cage will start swelling, and the nipples will enlarge and become red rather than pink. Once you are sure she is in pup, you can change her diet to include more protein and, possibly, vitamins. If you feed one of the all-in-one balanced foods on the market this might mean just using one of the higher grade foods produced by the same firm. Basically, for her comfort, improve quality rather than quantity.

PREPARATIONS FOR WHELPING

At any time after eight weeks she will, probably, start to show signs of "nesting". Some bitches will do this several days before they actually whelp. We always use a corner of the kitchen as the "Maternity Ward" and have the prospective mother in at night, from about seven and a half weeks, to get used to the idea. The kitchen is an ideal place, being in close proximity to hot water, heat, light and the other items needed at the appointed time. Obviously a bed is needed and, after numerous experiments over the years, we now use one of the large oval-shaped, moulded fibre-glass beds. This has the merit of being scrubbable with disinfectant, quickly dried, and cosy. Being in one piece, there are no gaps to let fluids leak through or to trap germs for future trouble. For bedding, during the actual birth, plenty of newspaper is ideal, being warm, absorbent and easily disposed of. The dam will usually dig it up into shreds when the process actually starts and – be warned – with some births there is likely to be copious amounts of fluid, and the paper will need frequent changing.

Some form of artificial heat is desirable, although some bitches resent this, despite the fact that their body temperature drops prior to giving birth. The pups need to acclimatise to the outside world, having been used to a temperature of over 100F (38C+), for several weeks, and they should not be exposed to a drastic temperature drop when they are born. This chill factor is possibly the cause of more puppy mortality than is generally realised. A temperature of around 80F(27C), is necessary for the first few days, gradually decreasing to the normal outside temperature by about three weeks. There are various forms of artificial heating available. We use a dull emitter infra-red lamp (of the type used for poultry) in the early stages when the litter is indoors. This is useful for drying off newly-born puppies. Later on, when we put the litter in their outside quarters, we use a heater designed for pigs, complete with a thermostat. Both these items can be obtained through agricultural merchants, although possibly some of the larger suppliers of kennel ware might stock something suitable, if possibly more fancy and expensive. These heaters are of the overhead type and have the merit that they can be raised, which adjusts the heat and also keeps them away from inquisitive noses. There are several forms of heated underpads available, but I have no experience of these, as we became used to the other heaters before these pads were marketed.

THE BIRTH

When the first pup is imminent the bitch will normally start panting and show increased restlessness, tear up the bedding, and eventually start straining and will push the pup out. Sometime during the contractions the cervical plug is ejected; this is a thickish fluid that has sealed the mouth of the womb during the pregnancy. The puppies are encased in a bag attached to the placenta by a tube. The reaction of a maiden bitch to her first puppy can vary from sheer panic to a very laid-back outlook. Most Springer bitches are sensible and down-to-earth in their attitude, but there are those who, having produced a pup, look round and wonder what to do next. They should, of course, open the sac, bite off the umbilical cord, and lick the puppy into life.

You may have to assist at this point and, in fact, do everything until the dam has got the idea of what to do. The sac should be broken as soon as possible and the umbilical cord cut about four or five centimetres from where it joins the body. We usually leave this to dry and drop off naturally, but some people tie it with a nylon thread. The puppy should be rubbed dry with a clean, warm, dry towel, the rougher the better. The mouth and nostrils will need to be cleaned of mucus. This can be done with warm, wet cotton wool. The drying and stimulation of the new-born pup should be done holding the pup with its head hanging down. Your vet may prescribe some drops to help clear the mucus. Some pups respond straightaway and start struggling and yelling, others will perhaps take several minutes. What you do with the "after birth" or placenta is up to you. In the natural state it is a source of nourishment for the bitch for the first few days after parturition, when she is loath to leave her litter to go seeking food. The placenta resembles a piece of liver and, during pregnancy, has been responsible for channelling nutrients to the foetus. It is thus very rich and, if the mother is allowed to eat too many of them at birth, the result, for two or three days after whelping, is the passing of shapeless, tarry-like motions. Some components of the placenta break down at birth and turn a greenish colour, which looks awful but is perfectly normal.

It may sound rather far-fetched but you might possibly have to teach the new arrival how to feed! If the dam will let you, after you have got the pup going, and replaced the wet paper, you can try the pup on one of the nipples. Some puppies will plug in immediately, but others may need their mouth gently opened and the teat placed in, at the same time having a drop of milk squeezed into their mouth. It is important to try and make sure that all the puppies get some of this first drawing of the milk, because this primary flow, known as the colostrum, is richer in nutrients for the first few hours than the later milk. It also contains antibodies and other substances to stimulate the working of the gut, as this has been a non-working organ prior to birth because the umbilical cord acts in the manner of an intravenous drip. The intervals between puppies can vary, and are not necessarily regular. A common sequence is two very quickly following each other, then a longer space and then another pair. It is best to keep the puppies away from the nest, in somewhere warm and dry, during each successive birth, otherwise they get wet and cold. We have a polystyrene box in which we put a hot-water bottle and cover this with a piece of blanket. The box we use actually contained frozen fish, but it is just the right size to take a hot-water bottle and some puppies, but any suitable container will do, as long as it is deep enough. The bottle should be well-covered to prevent the puppies getting burnt. If the bitch is fretful, it may be necessary to put the puppies back with her between births, removing them to the box when the next puppy is imminent.

ESSENTIAL WHELPING EQUIPMENT

By now you will have realised that you need rather more than just a bed and the bitch. You will need a clean, sharp pair of sterilised scissors to cut the umbilical cord, plus a plentiful supply of clean towels for drying the puppies and quite often the dam, some large bags to put the soiled paper in after each birth, cotton wool, and a plentiful supply of hot water for washing your hands and, possibly, for cleaning up the bitch's "trousers" between each birth. The bitch will not normally take food during her star performance, but a drink of milk, warm usually, although some

The English Springer mother will care for all her puppies' needs in the first couple of weeks

prefer it cold, is appreciated, not after every pup, but every second or third on average. As far as the midwife is concerned, the necessities are plenty of black coffee, a comfortable chair, probably a cushion if there is much kneeling entailed, reading matter, and an endless supply of patience, fortitude and common-sense. If you are so inclined, you could have scales and writing materials to hand to record sex, colour, times and weights of each pup as it is born. It is a good idea to warn your vet about the forthcoming birth, and ascertain any out-of-hours arrangements, in case of problems. When all the pups have arrived, the paper bedding can be changed for something softer and more comfortable, such as one of the synthetic fur fabrics which are washable. Often this will get scraped up into a heap, and some means of fastening it down will have to be employed. We have a removable base to the nest, and wrap the blanket etc. round it and secure it on the underside. Making the covering into the form of a bag would be ideal. Many mothers prefer the bedding in the form of a nest, with a hollow in the centre down to the bare bed. The main drawback to this is that the puppies cannot get sufficient purchase on the hard surface when they are feeding.

PROBLEM WHELPINGS
Springers are not usually prone to whelping problems, but if you have any misgivings, with anything, call the vet sooner rather than later. The breeder of your bitch should be able to advise you if there is any record of difficulties in the bloodline. Snags that can crop up include uterine inertia, when the bitch produces few or no contractions, or a transversely placed pup that cannot clear the canal. Both of these require professional attention: the first is treated by a simple injection, but the second will need a cæsarean section. These are urgent cases. Eclampsia rarely occurs as early as this, being a calcium deficiency condition that builds up over two or three weeks, the symptoms being an anxiety state and panting, accompanied by spasmodic shaking. *Urgent* treatment is necessary, but relief is immediate with a massive injection of calcium. The usual cause is insufficient intake of calcium to balance the output through the "milkbar". More rarely, there may be some reason why the calcium is ingested in suitable quantities but not absorbed properly.

EXAMINING THE LITTER
When the dust has settled and things are as normal as they are likely to be for the next eight or nine weeks, you should examine the litter for any signs of abnormalities, Springers generally do not have many, but you should be able to spot harelips just by looking at the muzzle. If you gently open the mouth and feel the roof of the mouth with your finger (clean, naturally) you can detect

cleft palate. Other defects do not show up until later on. From here on in, the main consideration is to make sure that enough nourishment is going into the mother to keep her in good condition, and ensuring the supply of milk is being produced in enough quantities to satisfy the demands of the pups.

THE EARLY DAYS

Following on from the birth of the litter, except for feeding and administering to the dam, probably the most time-consuming job you will have to deal with will be changing the bedding. For the first few days newspaper is ideal, being cheap and easily disposed of when soiled. Later on, depending on how soon the bitch dries up and the bedding stays clean for longer periods, some other form of bedding can be substituted. We use shredded paper but, as I mentioned before, other materials can be used. Many bitches will dig the bedding about and seem to prefer lying on the bare floor of the bed. For the first two or three weeks, apart from having the tails docked at about two or three days old, there is really nothing much to do except monitor the progress of the litter and dam. During this period, depending on the time of year and the weather conditions, any heating should gradually be reduced. As long as the pups are warm, dry, full and thriving, things are pretty well OK. At regular intervals the puppies' nails will require careful tipping with a sharp pair of scissors, otherwise they will scratch the mother when they are feeding.

Now, the text-books will tell you the pups will open their eyes at ten days; in our experience fourteen is nearer the average. At around the three-week mark they will be getting on their legs and tottering about in the bed. After this, progress speeds up, and by the time they have reached a month old they will be walking, attempting to run, playing with each other and becoming vocal, especially if there are signs that food is on the way. We have found that each litter varies, some being more forward than others. If we have any of our FT outcrosses fairly close up in the pedigree the litter will be a day or two ahead of the average.

WEANING

When the pups have started to get on their feet, they can be tried with some sloppy food, either puppy milk mixed according to the manufacturer's instructions, or some tinned puppy meat mashed down with some warm water. You may have to try both, as we have found over the years that some puppies do not like milk, while others are not in a mind to experiment with meat at first. The normal pattern of learning to feed is for the puppies to totter blindly through the dish, get in an almighty mess, and then wash each other clean. The penny then drops as to what the dish was put there for. The next time, possibly, they will sample the contents before bathing in it. We put down a newspaper 'tablecloth' and this is soon associated with the idea of food. Gradually, as the pups get used to feeding themselves, the number of meals can be increased, until they are on four meals per day. At this stage, in addition to food, they will need a supply of clean water available. This, for safety's sake, should be in a flat, shallow dish that they are capable of managing, without falling into mother's larger one.

In most cases, the mother needs to be removed before putting the food down for the family. I had one odd case when a litter of Cavalier pups flatly refused to have anything to do with the food that they were given, but always tried to help the bitch to eat her food. So from there on in, mother got fed "slops", the pups joined in and, after a few days, weaning was able to proceed normally. Usually, however, one of two things happens. Either the dam eats the puppies' food or, if they approach her dish, she warns them to go away. So, when starting weaning, separate the mother from her pups. And I repeat: beware of overfeeding – this can lead to stomach upsets.

WORMING

When the litter has got used to the introduction of feeding, it will need to be wormed. It is best to seek your vet's advice over this as new ideas about worming are constantly being put forward. Liquid wormers are obviously required for young pups; we do ours at three, six and eight weeks. Regular treatment with a parasiticide that is recognised as being safe for use on young puppies is also necessary. Like the wormers, these should be used in strict accordance with the manufacturer's instructions.

As the pups grow, various aspects of their personalities will emerge, not least the element of hooliganism. Each succeeding litter seems to find a new item of mischief. One trick that appears common to most of them, however, comes at about seven weeks, when they are strong enough to rear up on their hind legs. Just as you are putting the dishes down some of them will "help" by putting their front feet in the dish and pushing down the last few inches. This game is usually invented at about the same time as they discover the joys of riding on the "scooper", invariably when it is full. As they get older, you must allow more time for each job, unless you have somewhere to put the puppies while you are cleaning out, changing bedding, etc. Putting six pups to bed feels like somewhere between ten and fifteen of them – it is usually one in, two out, unless you have a low-sided pen where they can be put over the top.

ABNORMALITIES

The foregoing assumes that everything has gone smoothly, with no problems. However, problems do sometimes occur, for various reasons, some of which are not always obvious. In a fair proportion of cases mother and offspring are off-colour together, and it is not always easy to assess whether mother's indisposition is affecting the litter, or her fretfulness is caused by the knowledge that things are not quite right with her babies. Sometimes the answer is quite simple, such as too much artificial heat being supplied, or more usually, too little. Very often the cause is a minor infection, usually associated with the gut. Other causes can be related to the dam's milk, the supply being insufficient in quantity or quality. Normal puppies are usually quiet most of the time. Experienced breeders can usually tell the difference between the noise made by healthy puppies and that produced by a sickly or off-colour puppy. The latter sound is a very plaintive wailing note reminiscent of a cat miaowing. At any abnormal sign, such as the litter not thriving or the dam showing any unusual behaviour, it would be advisable to get veterinary advice – again, sooner rather than later.

A useful addition to the diet when weaning first takes place is plain yoghurt, which has the merit of containing bacteria similar to those naturally occurring in the gut. This is especially useful if, for some reason, oral antibiotics have been prescribed. These destroy the natural bacteria and yoghurt helps to restore the balance faster than would normally be the case. One problem that occurs quite frequently is when the dam's nipples are too big for some of the puppies to manoeuvre and simple malnutrition occurs, usually of a gradual nature. However, if the puppies are checked fairly often to make sure they are all feeding and, if necessary, they are held onto the nipple to ensure an adequate supply of milk, then this should be avoided. After two or three days of this treatment any suffering puppy should have grown sufficiently to feed naturally.

PICK OF THE LITTER

By this time you have probably become switched on to one of the litter, usually the one that does everything first, and shows the most personality. Quite often this one may not be the best constructed one, however, or have the best head, so be prepared to make an objective assessment, enlisting the advice of other breeders if necessary. If you are selecting for work, probably the

As the puppies get bigger, they will want to explore the outside world.
Photo: Steve Nash.

Play is an essential ingredient of the rearing process, aiding mental and physical development.
Photo: Steve Nash.

personality pup will be the one to pick, although I like the ones that sit back and look up at you with a thoughtful expression. This usually goes with that "I'd do anything for you" temperament. As regards shows, if the construction is right, the flamboyant character could be the difference between a good winner and a top performer in group and variety competition.

SELLING PUPPIES

In the UK it is now mandatory to register all the litter and you should have had a signed certificate of mating from the stud dog owner, on the relevant KC form. This incorporates the necessary section on which to register the litter. This should be completed as soon as you have got the litter past the stage where any puppies are likely to die. Any disasters usually have occurred during the first three weeks, and if the litter is registered at about this time, the registrations are normally back in time to be given out when the puppies are ready to go to the new owners. On the back of the registration is the requisite form to transfer the pup to the new owner, and this needs to be signed by the breeder. This is important, as the KC gives a period of free insurance to the new owner, so you need to have the registrations to hand. You will also need an adequate supply of pedigree forms. Care is required in completing these: they need to be legible and accurate. Some form of receipt is desirable, preferably one of the special books supplied by a specialist canine publishing firm. Last, and by no means least, a comprehensive diet and rearing sheet should be provided, together with a few days' supply of food. If the puppies have been inoculated, then obviously, you will also need to include the relevant certificates with the "luggage".

You should always come to an arrangement concerning anything that might entail the new owner having to part with the pup. As the breeder, for the first few months it would be better if the pup was returned to you with any refund mutually agreed upon, depending on the circumstances. Later on, it would still be courtesy for the new owner to tell you, and you could probably help with rehoming. Usually, these mishaps are caused by families splitting up, or moving to an unsuitable area or some other change of circumstances.

Chapter Eight

BREED STANDARDS AND INTERPRETATIONS

THE BRITISH BREED STANDARD

GENERAL APPEARANCE Symmetrically built, compact, strong, merry, active. Highest on the leg and raciest in build of all British land spaniels.

CHARACTERISTICS Breed is of ancient and pure origins. Oldest of sporting gundogs; original purpose was finding and springing game for net, falcon or greyhound. Now used to find, flush and retrieve game for gun.

TEMPERAMENT Friendly, happy disposition, biddable. Timidity or aggression highly undesirable.

HEAD AND SKULL Skull of medium length, fairly broad, slightly rounded, rising from the fore face, making a brow or stop, divided by fluting between the eyes, dying away along forehead towards occipital bone which should not be prominent. Cheeks flat. Fore face of proportionate length to skull, fairly broad and deep, well-chiselled below eyes, fairly deep and square in flew. Nostrils well developed.

EYES Medium size, almond-shaped, not prominent nor sunken, well set in (not showing haw), alert, kind expression. Dark hazel. Light eyes undesirable.

EARS Lobular, good length and width, fairly close to head, set in line with eye. Nicely feathered.

MOUTH Jaws strong, with a perfect, regular and complete scissor bite, i.e. upper teeth closely overlapping lower teeth and set square to the jaws.

NECK Good length, strong, muscular, free from throatiness, slightly arched, tapering towards head.

FOREQUARTERS Forelegs straight and well boned. Shoulders sloping and well laid. Elbows set well to body. Strong, flexible pasterns.

BODY Strong, neither too long nor too short. Chest deep, well developed. Well sprung ribs. Loin muscular, strong with slight arch and well coupled.

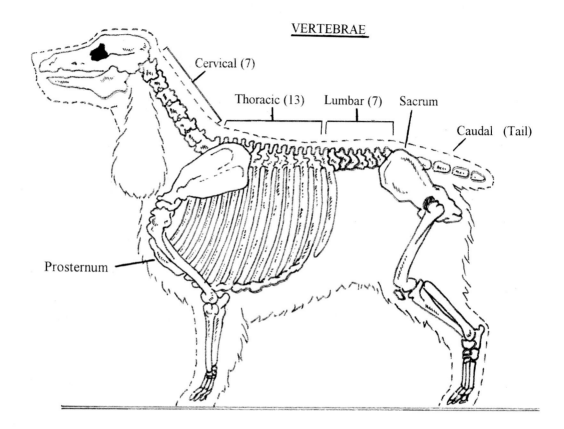

VERTEBRAE

Cervical (7)

Thoracic (13)   Lumbar (7)   Sacrum

Caudal (Tail)

Prosternum

This drawing shows the position and number of the various components of the spine and ribs. Also shown are the shape and relative positions of the parts of the fore and hind limbs. At the front these consist of the large, flat scapula leading down to the point of the shoulder where it joins the top end of the humerus, near the breastbone. The lower end of the humerus meets the top of the foreleg at the elbow. The pair of bones forming the front leg are the radius and the ulna. These fade down into the phalangeal group of small bones which form the wrist of front pastern.

The rear assembly consists of the pelvic girdle (sacrum, ilium, etc.) linking both hind legs (unlike the forelimbs which are separate from each other), the femur, which is joined to the pelvis via the acetabular socket, and which at its bottom end it meets the tibia and fibula at the knee or stifle joint. These, in turn, lead down to the hock joint where they connect with the tarsal group of bones. These, like the phalanges etc. in the foreleg, are several small, multi-articulated bones which give greater flexibility to the front and rear pasterns.

HINDQUARTERS Hindlegs well let down. Stifles and hocks moderately bent. Thighs broad, muscular, well developed. Coarse hocks undesirable.

FEET Tight, compact, well rounded, with strong, full pads.

TAIL Set low, never carried above level of back. Well feathered, with lively action. Customarily docked.

GAIT/MOVEMENT Strictly his own. Forelegs swing straight forward from shoulder, throwing feet well forward in an easy, free, manner. Hocks driving well under body, following in line with forelegs. At slow movement may have a pacing stride typical of this breed.

COAT Close, straight, and weather-resisting, never coarse. Moderate feathering on ears, forelegs, body and hindquarters.

COLOUR Liver and white, black and white, or either of these colours with tan markings.

SIZE Approximate height: 51cms. (20ins).

FAULTS Any departure from the foregoing points should be considered a fault and the seriousness with which the fault should be regarded should be in exact proportion to its degree.

NOTE Male animals should have two apparently normal testicles fully descended into the scrotum.

Reproduced by kind permission of the English Kennel Club.

THE AMERICAN BREED STANDARD

PROPOSED REVISION: 1993 FINAL DRAFT
OFFICIAL STANDARD FOR THE ENGLISH SPRINGER SPANIEL.

GENERAL APPEARANCE The English Springer Spaniel is a medium-sized sporting dog, with a compact body and a docked tail. His coat is moderately long, with feathering on his legs, ears, chest and brisket. His pendulous ears, soft gentle expression, sturdy build and friendly wagging tail proclaim him unmistakably a member of the ancient family of Spaniels. He is above all a well-proportioned dog, nicely balanced in every part. His carriage is proud and upstanding, body deep, legs strong and muscular, with enough length to carry him with ease. Taken as a whole, the English Springer Spaniel suggests power, endurance and agility. He looks the part of a dog that can go, and keep going, under difficult hunting conditions. At his best, he is endowed with style, symmetry, balance and enthusiasm, and is every inch a sporting dog of distinct Spaniel character, combining beauty and utility.

SIZE, PROPORTION, SUBSTANCE The Springer is built to cover rough ground with agility and reasonable speed. His structure suggests the capacity for endurance. He is to be kept to medium size. Ideal height at the shoulder for dogs is 20 inches; for bitches it is 19 inches. Those more than one inch under or over the breed ideal are to be faulted. A 20 inch dog, well-proportioned and in good condition, will weigh approximately 50 pounds; a 19 inch bitch will weigh approximately 40 pounds. The length of the body (measured from point of shoulder to point of buttocks) is slightly greater than the height at the withers. The dog too long in body, especially when long in loin, tires easily and lacks the compact outline characteristic of the breed. A dog too short in body for the length of his legs, a condition which destroys balance and restricts gait, is equally undesirable. A Springer with correct substance appears well-knit and sturdy with good bone; however, he is never coarse or ponderous.

HEAD The head is impressive without being heavy. Its beauty lies in a combination of strength and refinement. It is important that its size and proportion be in balance with the rest of the dog. Viewed in profile, the head appears approximately the same length as the neck and blends with the body in substance. The stop, eyebrows and chiselling of the bony structure around the eye sockets contribute to the Springer's beautiful and characteristic expression, which is alert, kindly and trusting.

EYES The eyes, more than any other feature, are the essence of the Springer's appeal. Correct size, shape, placement and color influence expression and attractiveness. The eyes are of medium size, and oval in shape, set rather well-apart and fairly deep in their sockets. The color of the iris harmonizes with the color of the coat, preferably dark hazel in the liver and white dogs and black or deep brown in the black and white dogs. Eye rims are fully pigmented and match the coat in color. Lids are tight with little or no haw showing. Eyes that are small, round or protruding, as well as eyes that are yellow or brassy in color, are highly undesirable.

EARS Ears are long and fairly wide, hanging close to the cheeks with no tendency to stand up or out. The ear leather is thin and approximately long enough to reach the tip of the nose. Correct ear set is on a level with the eye and not too far back on the skull.

SKULL The skull is medium-length and fairly broad, flat on top and slightly rounded at the sides and back. The occiput bone is inconspicuous. As the skull rises from the foreface, it makes a stop, divided by a groove, or fluting, between the eyes. The groove disappears as it reaches the middle of the forehead. The amount of stop is moderate. It must not be a pronounced feature; rather it is a subtle rise where the muzzle joins the upper head. It is emphasised by the groove and by the position and shape of the eyebrows, which are well-developed. The muzzle is approximately the same length as the skull and approximately one half the width of the skull. Viewed in profile, the toplines of the skull and muzzle lie in approximately parallel planes. The nasal bone is straight, with no inclination downward toward the tip of the nose, the latter giving an undesirable downfaced look. Neither is the nasal bone concave, resulting in a "dish-faced" profile; nor convex, giving the dog a Roman nose. The cheeks are flat, and the face is well-chiselled under the eyes. Jaws are of sufficient length to allow the dog to carry game easily; fairly square, lean and strong. The upper lips come down full and rather square to cover the line of the lower jaw, however the lips are never pendulous or exaggerated. The nose is full-pigmented, liver or black in color, depending on the color of the coat. The nostrils are well-opened and broad. Teeth are strong, clean, of good size and ideally meet in a close scissors bite. An even bite or one or two incisors slightly out of line are minor faults. Undershot, overshot and wry jaws are serious faults and should be severely penalized.

NECK, TOPLINE, BODY The neck is moderately long, muscular, clean and slightly arched at the crest. It blends gradually and smoothly into sloping shoulders. The portion of the topline from withers to tail is firm and slopes very gently. The body is short-coupled, strong and compact. The chest is deep, reaching the level of the elbows, with well-developed forechest; however, it is not so wide or round as to interfere with the action of the front legs. Ribs are fairly long, springing gradually to the middle of the body, then tapering as they approach the end of the ribbed section. The underline stays level with the elbows to a slight up-curve at the flank. The back is straight, strong and essentially level. Loins are strong, short and slightly arched. Hips are nicely-rounded, blending smoothly into the hind legs. The croup slopes gently to the set of the tail, and tail-set follows the natural line of the croup. The tail is carried horizontally or slightly elevated and displays a characteristic lively, merry action, particularly when the dog is on game. A clamped tail (indicating timidity or undependable temperament) is to be faulted, as is a tail carried at right angles to the backline in Terrier fashion.

FOREQUARTERS Efficient movement in front calls for proper forequarter assembly. The shoulder blades are flat and fairly close together at the tips, molding smoothly into the contour of the body. Ideally, when measured from the top of the withers, to the point of the shoulder, to the elbow, the shoulder blade and upper arm are of apparent equal length, forming an angle of nearly 90 degrees; this sets the front legs well under the body and places the elbows directly beneath the tips of the shoulder blades. Elbows lie close to the body. Forelegs are straight with the same degree of size continuing to the foot. Bone is strong, slightly flattened, not too round or too heavy. Pasterns are short, strong and slightly sloping, with no suspicion of weakness. Dewclaws are usually removed. Feet are round or slightly oval. They are compact and well-arched, of medium size with thick pads, and well-feathered between the toes.

HINDQUARTERS The Springer should be worked and shown in hard, muscular condition with well-developed hips and thighs. His whole rear assembly suggests strength and driving power. Thighs are broad and muscular. Stifle joints are strong. For functional efficiency, the angulation of the hindquarter is never greater than that of the forequarter, and not appreciably less. The hock joints are somewhat rounded, not small and sharp in contour. Rear pasterns are short (about 1/3 the distance from the hip joint to the foot) and strong, with good bone. When viewed from behind, the rear pasterns are parallel. The feet are the same as in front, except they are smaller and often more compact.

COAT The Springer has an outer coat and an undercoat. On the body, the outer coat is of medium length, flat or wavy, and is easily distinguishable from the undercoat, which is short, soft and dense. The quantity of undercoat is affected by climate and season. When in combination, outer coat and undercoat serve to make the dog substantially waterproof, weatherproof and thornproof. On ears, chest, legs and belly the Springer is nicely furnished with a fringe of feathering of moderate length and heaviness. On the head, front of the forelegs and below the hock joints on the front of the hind legs, the hair is short and fine. The coat has the clean, glossy, "live" appearance indicative of good health. It is legitimate to trim about the head, ears, neck and feet, to remove dead undercoat and to thin and shorten excess feathering as required to enhance a smart, functional appearance. The tail may be trimmed, or well fringed with wavy feathering. Above all, the appearance should be natural. Overtrimming, especially of the body coat, or any chopped, barbered or artificial effect is to be penalized in the show ring, as is excessive feathering that destroys the clean outline desirable in a sporting dog. Correct quality and condition of coat is to take precedence over quantity of coat.

COLOR All of the following combinations of colors and markings are equally acceptable; (1) Black or liver with white markings or predominantly white with black or liver markings; (2) Blue or liver roan; (3) Tricolor: black and white or liver and white with tan markings, usually found on eyebrows, cheeks, inside of ears and under the tail. Any white portion of the coat may be flecked with ticking. Off colors such as lemon, red or orange are not to place.

GAIT The final test of the Springer's conformation and soundness is proper movement. Balance is a prerequisite to good movement. The front and rear assemblies must be equivalent in angulation and muscular development for the gait to be smooth and effortless. Shoulders which are well laid-back to permit a long stride are just as essential as the excellent rear quarters that provide driving power. Seen from the side, the Springer exhibits a long, ground-covering stride and carries a firm back, with no tendency to dip, roach or roll from side to side. From the front the legs swing forward in a free and easy manner. Elbows have free action from the shoulders, and the legs show no tendency to cross or interfere. From behind, the rear legs reach well under the body, following on a line with forelegs. As speed increases, there is a natural tendency for the lines to converge toward a center line of travel. Movement faults include high-stepping, wasted motion; short, choppy stride; crabbing; and moving with the feet wide, the latter giving roll or swing to the body.

TEMPERAMENT The typical Springer is friendly, eager to please, quick to learn and willing to obey. Such traits are conducive to tractability, which is essential for appropriate handler control in the field. In the show ring, he should exhibit poise and attentiveness and permit himself to be examined by the judge without resentment or cringing. Aggression toward people and aggression toward other dogs is not in keeping with sporting dog character and is not acceptable. Excessive timidity, with due allowance for puppies and novice exhibits, is to be equally penalized.

SUMMARY In evaluating the English Springer Spaniel, the overall picture is a primary consideration. One should look for type, which includes general appearance and outline, and also for soundness, which includes movement and temperament. Inasmuch as a dog with a smooth easy gait must be reasonably sound and well-balanced, he is to be highly regarded – however, not to the extent of forgiving him for not looking like an English Springer Spaniel. An atypical dog, too short or long in leg length or foreign in head or expression, may move well, but he is not to be preferred over a good all-round specimen that has a minor fault in movement. It must be remembered that the English Springer Spaniel is first and foremost a sporting member of the Spaniel family, and he must look, behave and move in character.

Reproduced by kind permission of the American Kennel Club.

FCI: THIS STANDARD DOES NOT DIFFER FROM THE U K STANDARD.

COMPARISON BETWEEN THE STANDARDS

As can be seen, the American Standard is very much fuller and more descriptive, whereas the English version gives a fair imitation of a cablegram. Having said that, a detailed analysis, with one or two minor exceptions, gives a picture of the same basic dog. Any deviations between the two that have arisen over the years are mainly due to fashion, and the importance attached to different virtues. The greater ratio of all-rounders over specialist breed judges in the US means that more weight is given to things such as general balance, presentation and stylish movement, whereas some UK judges can be faddy over minor breed points. One omission from the American Standard is the mandatory footnote to all UK Standards calling for both testicles to be present in the scrotum. The US Standard is commendable in giving the reasons for many of the points.

General Appearance: Notwithstanding the difference in length of the two descriptions, the salient points are the same, namely balance, merry personality, compact build, strength and activity.

Temperament: Here again the only difference is the economy of the UK Standard.

Head and Skull: Although these are split in the US Standard, when taken together and compared with that of the UK, it is much the same, one difference being that the American Standard gives the relationship of the head to the balance of the complete dog. Another point mentioned in the fuller version is the pigmentation of the nose, the English version making no requirement for full pigmentation, a "butterfly" (partially coloured) nose apparently being permissible, although this has always been regarded as highly undesirable. Another subtle, but important, nuance is in the matter of the mouth. The UK Standard carries the official English KC paragraph as a separate entity, whereas the US Standard puts the dentition in the section under Skull and, much more sensibly, allows a certain amount of leniency in the matter of the odd misplaced tooth.

Eyes: Again the two Standards are more or less in parallel, except that the UK clause makes no mention of eye rim pigmentation, and gives the colour as dark hazel (the iris, I presume; it does not say). The US Standard asks for fully pigmented eye rims to match the coat colour and also allows for darker irises in black and whites. The two descriptions of the shape of the eye are intended to mean the same, although I understand these were not exactly the words mooted by the Breed Clubs when the Standards were recently reformulated, but were suggested by the respective Kennel Clubs.

Ears: Here the two Standards almost equate – the US version just gives an approximation of length.

Neck: Although in the American version this is included with the topline and body, the essential requirements are the same, but the US Standard, by taking the three parts together, permits of a description of the set-on of the neck, and its relationship with the shoulders etc.

Forequarters: Once more the American version gives a better guide to requirements.

Body: The essential differences here are that the UK makes no mention of the length of the rib cage, and the US Standard indicates a slight slope on the topline.

Hindquarters: Here the two Standards call basically for the same things, although again the American section has more definition.

Feet: Both Standards require round, compact feet with thick pads.

Tail: There is a subtle difference here, inasmuch as the English version categorically states "never carried above the level of the back", whereas the American requirement is for a horizontal carriage or *slightly elevated*, although clamped or terrier tails are equally faults.

Gait/Movement: Basic requirements correspond, although the US Standard makes no mention of the pacing at slow speed permitted in the English description.

Coat: No real difference between the Standards in the desired coat.

Colour: The rather austere wording of the English Standard would appear to indicate that roaning or flecking were not desired (although this is not the intention) but, in spite of the full description of roans in the American Standard, the dictates of fashion in the show ring have, in the main, led to Springers being shown with the white being absolutely devoid of any freckling.

Size: No difference.

Faults: In the American Standard these are numerated under the various headings and are rather more specific. The bald statement contained in that of the UK – "any departure from the foregoing points should be considered a fault" – leaves quite a lot to personal choice, especially in view of the fact that some of the sections are rather nebulous.

INTERPRETATION

The breed Standard was originally formulated to provide a blueprint for breeding the ideal conformation for an efficient working dog. The originators of the Standard were mainly breeders who were interested in both working and showing their dogs. Unfortunately, in all walks of life, competition leads to excesses and dog breeding is no exception. On the exhibition side, what should be virtues are usually exaggerated to the point of becoming faults, while the quest for the extra style and speed needed to win Field Trials all too often leads to the sacrifice of conformation,

Sh. Ch. Hawkhill Connaught: Winner of 50CCs.   Photo: Anne Roslin-Williams.

Ch. Mompesson Remember Me: Winner of 55CCs to date.   Photo: Jackson.

and sometimes size and stamina. The Standard indicates a medium-sized Spaniel, capable of doing a hard day's work, and therefore the dog should be free of all exaggerations.

All breeds are the same in that they have the same number of bones, and these are all in the same positions, thus loosely giving, admittedly within fairly wide parameters, the same basic structure. No amount of selective breeding can alter this. What can be done, however, by making use of individual deviations that occur naturally, is to change the relative lengths and angles of the various bones, thus producing different types. The number of muscles and other soft tissues is also Standard issue, although diet and exercise can influence these. The outer wrapping of skin and coat is much more amenable to external influences, such as diet, grooming and cosmetic items like shampoos and trimming.

ABOVE: Correct: This head has the desired strength of muzzle, both in depth and length, with good width of nostril. The balance between the length of the skull and the foreface is approximately equal; the frontal bones are not too pronounced, but sufficient to give an adequate stop. The eye-shape and ear-shape are correct – all adding up to a good English Springer head. The same attributes are shown from a frontal view. (ABOVE RIGHT).

Incorrect: The muzzle and skull are in balance, which conforms to the Breed standard. However, the whole structure is too short (although the muzzle is of a good depth and width) and this allied with too much stop gives an untypical aspect to the head. The ears are also incorrectly high-set.

Incorrect: The muzzle and skull are in balance, the length is correct, but the foreface is too narrow and lacks depth. This fault is masked somewhat by a shallow, sloping stop – which is another fault. A deep stop would have accentuated the faults of the foreface.

HEAD AND SKULL

During the evolution of canine species, two basic types of head seem to have emerged, the long-headed and the shorter-faced round-headed type. The Springer belongs to the former group. The difference is mainly caused by the arched bones forming the eye socket and also the length of the nasal bones. In the case of the English Springer, the bowing of the arch just below the eye is not so pronounced, giving the desired quality in the head. The lower jaw is attached to this bone by the cheek muscle and, if the arch is too pronounced, there is a resultant bulge of this muscle, and the chiselling below the eyes is lost. The rear ends of the nasal bones join the cranium by way of the frontal bones, a pair of triangular bones between the eyes. The amount of stop is governed by the angle of these frontal bones. This,

Aust. Ch. Wongan Dynasty. ACK Photo.

in turn, is regulated by the amount of upward curvature of the cheekbone. The two sides of the skull are joined down the centre by a raised ridge of bone which ends at the rear of the skull, at the occiput. This crest anchors some of the cheek muscles and is more prominent in some breeds than others. It should only be moderately raised in the Springer, otherwise the head becomes too domed. Correct skull shape is essential to the desired eye shape and placement.

The stop should be equidistant from occiput to tip of nose and should not be too pronounced. It should be deep enough to provide adequate protection to the eyes while working thick cover, but not so deep as to give a heavy look to the skull. There is a widely held belief that Springers with coarse heads are less easy to train. I, personally, have no experience of this as we have never kept anything with that type of head, so I cannot make any comment on the matter. The fluting takes away any tendency to a dish-faced "Pointery" look and also any plainness, as does the chiselling called for under eyes. The bottom jaw should be slightly broader than the top of the muzzle, giving a triangular look to the muzzle when viewed from the front. This gives a strong base for retrieving. The skull should be of a reasonable width, slightly rounded in section, giving adequate brain room, although it should not be apple-headed.

EYES

The actual description of the eye shape has been added to the Standard in the recent update. Previous versions only mentioned size. The late Dorothy Hooper explained to me many years ago that the desired shape was an oval, veering on the triangular. Technically speaking, normal eyeballs are all the same shape and virtually the same size within each breed. The apparent differences in size and shape are in the aperture, in the soft tissues which hold the eyeball in the socket. The size, shape and position of this slot is governed by the shape of the skull. The desired shape is dependent on the correct relationship between the arch forming the cheeks and the stop. The curvature of this arch alters the position of the outer corner of the eye – the greater the curve, the further forward the corner is placed, and the eye is subtly widened. The amount of stop also affects this width. The effects of these different combinations can best be seen by comparing the two varieties of the Cocker Spaniel. The chubby-headed American Cocker, with its wide cheeks and deep stop, has full, round, forward-looking eyes, whereas the English Cocker, with a more refined stop and flatter cheekbones, has an eye shape entirely different and nearer to what is required in the Springer. The eye colour should tone with the coat shade. What would pass as dark in a dog whose coat is one of the paler varieties of liver would, perhaps, be adequate in a darker dog, and stand out like a beacon in a black and white. It depends on your definition of hazel – I knew an exhibitor many years ago who opined that hazel nuts were green. Loose eyes are a trap for dust and other foreign bodies while working. The expression should be kind and should give an indication of the dog's character.

EARS These should be of a sensible length and width; too long can be a hindrance when working and can get damaged; too narrow at the top often impairs the ventilation to the ear cavity, giving rise to ear problems. Too low a set gives a "cockery" appearance to the whole head.

NECK
Over the years careful breeding has succeeded in lengthening the cervical vertebrae to produce a neck with a sensible length and arching. The short, upright neck-set known as the 'ewe-neck' is rarely encountered today. The neck should be of a good length, sufficient for comfortable retrieving, but not so long as to lose its strength. It should be set at a sensible angle into well-laid shoulders, to give a streamlined look. A neckset to give a high head carriage like a setter is foreign to the breed.

BODY
This should be long enough to give the necessary athleticism, but not of such a length as to develop weakness. The chest should be deep enough to reach the elbows, the ribs should be fairly well-sprung and carried well back to a short, well-coupled loin, which is very slightly arched. There should be adequate space between the forelegs, and the breastbone (prosternum) should be well in evidence. Most of the length in the body should be contained in the dorsal area of the spine. Each of the vertebral bones in this section carries a pair of ribs and they should be of an adequate length to give the long rib cage necessary to house and protect the vital organs. At the top end the ribs are attached to the vertebrae and project laterally for a distance, before curving downwards and eventually inwards. This curvature is the "spring of rib" and a well-sprung rib stands out further from the spine before curving downwards. Too narrow a curve results in a herring-butted animal, more suited for going down an earth or drain like a terrier, than doing the type of work a gundog is expected to perform. The bottom ends of the ribs are gristle for a proportion of their length, and the forward ten of them join together at the breastbone, which is somewhat curved along its length. The deepest point is just behind and level with the elbow. The front end, the prosternum, comes out between the front legs, approximately level with the point of the shoulder, but rather more pronounced. This acts in the manner of a ship's bow when the dog is swimming. A hollow chest is to be avoided. Behind the elbows, the breastbone gradually curves upwards along its length towards the abdomen. This tapering of the ribcage is carried on by the next two ribs which, although not connected to the breastbone, are joined to each other by gristle which anchors them partway down rib ten. The last rib is free. This long, well-rounded shape to the ribcage is necessary to provide as much volume as possible, the so-called "heart room", although in fact it is the lungs which need this lebensraum when fully inflated with air. Thinking back to the days when some poor unfortunate tried to teach me maths, a completely circular section to the cage would give a greater capacity, but this would throw out the shoulder girdle in the fashion of a Bulldog, impeding free action and certainly spoiling the aesthetic aspect of the forehand. The seven bones that form the lumbar section of the spine are somewhat shorter, which

gives the short, strong couplings required. They should not, however, be so short as to lose flexibility. Another reason for a sensible length in this section which houses the abdomen is the need for adequate space for bitches to accommodate any litters. The next few vertebrae linking with the tail are, in fact, fused together to form a triangular bone, the sacrum. This forms the part of the pelvis which connects the hindquarters with the rest of the dog.

FOREQUARTERS AND HINDQUARTERS

These are taken together because, to use a motoring analogy, they comprise the "suspension" of the dog. Correct angulation of these components gives the conformation for the true movement of the breed. Basically, they are a simple arrangement of hinges and levers. Like the modern mechanical products based on these principles, there is a point in their relationship where maximum efficiency is obtained. Generally speaking, the dog is in "rear wheel drive", deriving most of its propulsion from the hindquarters. The front is usually only used for balancing, unless the dog is clambering over something and the rear is not in a good position. Balanced relationships between the angles and lengths of the relevant bones, allied to a correct length of leg and flexible pasterns – these act as shock absorbers – are essential to the correct effortless easy stride of the English Springer. Any deviation from the ideal in angulation, or length of components, will result in untypical movement. For instance, a short humerus will give a hackney action, or a straight back end will result in a loss of drive.

The forequarters and hindquarters differ in that the forequarters are a separate entity from the

FOREHANDS

 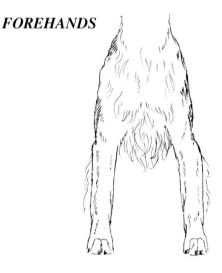 

Correct: A good front with straight forelegs and adequate width of chest allowing plenty of room for the essential organs.

Incorrect: Out at elbow, a condition allied to an oversprung ribcage, and the limbs are often bowed in an attempt to bring the feet under the body.

Incorrect: Tied-in elbows, and weak, splayed pasterns. The narrow chest is often coupled with a mincing, front action.

Correct: The pasterns from hock joint to foot are straight and parallel, set perpendicularly.

Incorrect: The hock points turn outwards and the toes turn inwards. This condition is often associated with curvature of the femur and tibia/fibula, making the hindquarters look like a tunnel.

Incorrect: Cow hocks – the points of the hock turn inwards and the toes turn outward.

rest of the skeleton, only being joined by muscle and ligaments to the body. This means that an excess of muscle or fat can build up between the scapula and the ribs, giving a loaded shoulder, so correct exercise and diet are imperative. The sloping shoulders called for actually refer to the shoulder blade (scapula), a flat, triangular-shaped bone connected at the lower end to the humerus at the point of the shoulder. The upper end is anchored to the spine at the fore end of the ribs, and the top edge is formed of gristle. As well as being set at an angle from the horizontal, the scapulae are also inclined inwards at their top ends. The corners of the front edges of the blades stand higher than those of the rear edges, and form what are usually known as the withers, which is the point where the height is measured. The gap between the blades at the withers should be relatively narrow, although care should be taken that this is not too close for efficient retrieving – as the dog lowers its head, the scapulae alter position and the blades close at the withers, so if they are already too fine, they have nowhere to go. The humerus, or upper arm bone, which joins the scapula at the point of shoulder, linking it to the foreleg at the elbow, should be of proportionate length to the scapula to bring the foreleg virtually under the withers. When the dog is standing normally, the angle between the humerus and the scapula is ideally about ninety degrees, and this angulation is usually present. The fault commonly found in Springers is the short humerus. With correct angulation this fault has either of two effects. If the shoulder placement is right then the upper arm becomes steep, and the forelegs are thrown too far forward. The result with a more upright shoulder is to bring the humerus at a better angle and the forelegs are set further back, but

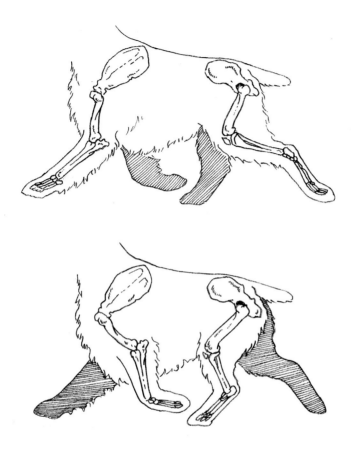

Correct movement: These drawings show the changes in angles when a dog is in motion. The shoulder blades and the pelvis move very little, leaving the lower part of the limbs to do most of the work.

the neckset and topline are wrong. Therefore, to get the ideal forequarters, the scapula and humerus should be of a similar length.

The hindquarters are linked to the spine and the rest of the skeleton at the pelvis. The pelvis is basically three bones fused to make a framework; the top end is the sacrum, the bottom bone being the ilium, and this contains a socket into which the head of the thigh bone fits to form the hip joint. The pelvis needs to be relatively wide, to promote strong hindquarters, and should be set at an angle somewhere between thirty and thirty-five degrees from the horizontal. Too upright an angle here results in loss of drive. If the set of the pelvic girdle is too flat, however, not only are the nicely-rounded hindquarters frequently absent, but the resultant tail set is too high. The femur (thighbone) at its bottom end is jointed with the tibia (and fibula) at the stifle which equates with the human knee. These in turn connect to the tarsals at the hock, and thence to the ground. Like the forequarters, a sensible ratio of length and angles between the relevant bones is desirable. Lack of angulation will produce a stilted action, with no drive, while an over-angulated dog (especially if ultra-short in back) will over-reach on the forward stride and, to avoid the backward reaching foreleg, will move crabwise. The hock joint should be reasonably close to the ground, and the tarsals perpendicular, set a little distance behind the rear point of the ilium. The section between hock and stifle, comprising the tibia/fibula and the attendant musculature, is usually known as the second thigh, and like its counterpart in the front assembly, the humerus, is quite often too short in

FORE AND HIND LIMBS WITH APPROXIMATE ANGLES

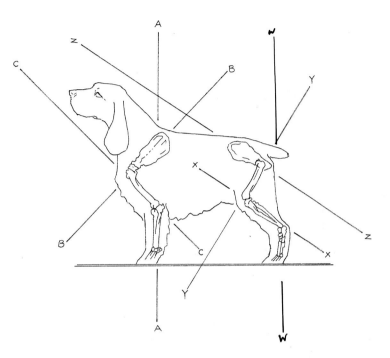

The angles given are those that have been agreed, over the years, as being the optimum for efficiency. They are, naturally, evaluated when the dog is standing, and also in a free stance and not held in a rigid pose.

Line A-A: Perpendicular down from withers through forelegs.

Line B-B: From point of shoulder through the median line of scapula.

Line C-C: From elbow to point of shoulder.

The preferred lie of both scapula and humerus is 45 degrees from the horizontal. If this is achieved, these two bones are set virtually at right angles (internal angle BB-CC). This in turn, contingent on a correct length of humerus, gives an exterior angle AA-CC of about 135 degrees.

Line W-W: Perpendicular through rear pastern.

Line X-X: Through tibia/fibula.

Line Y-Y: Through femur.

Line Z-Z: Through median line of pelvis. This should be between 30 and 35 degrees inclination from the horizontal to give a reasonable shape to the hindquarters.

The external angle between the tibia/fibula and the pastern, i.e. WW-XX, ought to be about 125 degrees. A reasonable internal angle between the femur and tibia/fibula (XX-YY) would be approximately 110 degrees.

the Springer. The femur and tibia should be balanced in length and well-muscled to provide the powerhouse required.

FEET
The reason for the type of foot described in the Standard is that a flat, spreading foot would expose the tender skin between the pads to too much danger of damage.

TAIL
The first sentence referring to set and carriage is relatively simple to achieve when the breed is docked. The question that will face many judges as more undocked animals get shown is what to do with the dog that has a good set and carriage for the first half of the tail, and then lifts the second part.

GAIT/MOVEMENT
Although the Standard allows for pacing at a slow gait, this is usually penalised by judges.

COAT
It is ironic that the Standard calls for a weatherproof coat when many of the working dogs have much less coat, which generally seems much less protective, than that of the show lines.

Chapter Nine

FIELD TRIALS AND SHOWS

This Chapter gives an outline of the rules and protocols governing the organisation and judging of shows, field trials and working tests internationally.

UNITED KINGDOM

The main governing body for canine affairs in the UK is the English Kennel Club. The exceptions are the International Sheepdog League and the Greyhound Racing Association. These are specialist organisations with their own separate Stud Books. They are recognised by the KC, and in certain spheres there is mutual co-operation, as in the British Veterinary Association's hip and eye schemes. The KC, although it is a Social Club with a maximum membership of 750 members, is also an autonomous body, issuing rules and regulations governing all aspects of canine affairs, with the exception of those mentioned above. The Breed Standards are the copyright of the KC and any change to them that Breed Clubs wish to make must be ratified by the KC.

The KC is responsible for the registration of all pedigree dogs in the UK and, recently, has made it obligatory for breeders to register all the puppies in a litter within a specified time. All dogs must be registered with the KC in the relevant breed register before they can take part in any KC event. There is a special Obedience register for dogs from unregistered stock specifically for competition dogs. There is at present no provision for transfer to the relevant Breed Register even after several generations. The KC also maintains the official KC Stud Book. This is issued annually and is a record of the top winners at shows and trials during the year. Entry to the KCSB is restricted to the winners of certain awards at Championship shows in limit and open classes and to awards above a certain grade at Field Trials. A permanent number is allocated to each dog entered, coded by years, the entry consists of a three generation pedigree (or back to the nearest KCSB reference). Another part of the KC's duties is that of licensing the various grades of show and the different trials. These are, mostly, organised by various clubs, either breed or general, which have to be registered with the KC.

SHOWS
The different grades are:
(a) Championship Shows: these are shows at which the KC Challenge Certificates are on offer. They can range from the single breed club show, through the group or sub-group shows, to the general Championship shows. They are open to all exhibitors except in cases where an entry qualification has been granted by the KC General Committee – a case in point being Crufts.
(b) Open shows: as their title implies, these are open to all, like the Championship shows. However, there is no award at Open shows which can count towards the title of Champion.

(c) Limited shows: these are restricted to certain exhibitors, the restrictions being approved by the KC General Committee. The usual limitation is to members of the organising club, but it can be restricted to owners within a certain radius – during wartime it was twenty-five miles, and they were the only types of show permitted.

(d) Sanction shows: restricted to members, and the highest class permitted is post-graduate.

(e) Primary shows: restricted to members with a maximum of eight classes. First prize winners are ineligible.

(f) Matches: usually held between clubs, these differ from the ordinary type of show. As may be inferred from the name, the dogs are matched head-to-head in pairs, one being declared the winner; sometimes run on a knockout basis and, at others, on a round robin system.

(g) Exemption shows: at which the KC has granted exemption from many of its regulations. Unregistered dogs may compete. Pedigree classes restricted to four any-variety classes for pedigree dogs plus any number of novelty classes.

Categories (f) and (g) are usually held as social and fund-raising occasions, not normally by breed clubs unless, as has been done with the English Springer Spaniel Club, an exemption show has been held in conjunction with simple working tests at a "Fun Day" to bring the working and show sides together. Primary shows are a comparatively recent innovation by the KC and have not really taken off. They were originally started to provide a training ground for young stock, but in most areas the regular weekly Ring training clubs are too firmly entrenched and most societies already run their quota of shows. Sanction shows are not normally run by breed clubs and are not too numerous with general clubs.

Most of the English Springer Clubs used to hold limited shows and an open show, but with the re-allocation of CCs the norm now is a Championship show and an Open show. The Challenge Certificates are allocated to shows by the KC, one for each sex. The total number allocated annually is based on the average number of entries at Championship shows over a certain period previously and it is reviewed periodically. The KC try to keep a balance between Breed and Championship Shows when they make their allocation, and also try to spread them evenly geographically. Under the UK system, three CCs, under three different judges, are needed to become a Champion, or in the case of gundogs, Show Champion. To become a "full" Champion a gundog must gain an award at a trial, or, more commonly, get the Show Gundogs Working Certificate. Unlike some systems the Challenge Certificates all have the same value, and the number of entries is irrelevant. Judges are empowered by the KC to withhold the award of the CC if the dog is not considered to be of sufficient merit to be a Champion. Classes at Championship shows are usually Puppy, Junior, Novice, Postgraduate, Limit and Open. Occasionally these are mixed sexes, but not very often nowadays, since the Crufts qualification came into being. At Crufts and Club shows there are usually extra classes to the above. There is, of course, a Reserve CC awarded in each sex. The two CC winners meet for Best of Breed, the victor going on to Challenge in the Gundog Group. There are six groups in the UK, and the eventual Best in Show winner is selected from the six winners of these. Unlike some countries, there is no obligation for the BOB winner to stay and Challenge for the Best in Group award.

There is also a Kennel Club award called a Junior Warrant; this is based on a points system. These are gained at Open and Championship shows. The points are awarded for breed classes only and are restricted to first placings. Three points are given for Championship show wins where CCs are on offer, and one point for open shows and Championship shows where there are no CCs offered. Twenty-five points are needed for the Warrant, and they must be gained between the ages of twelve and eighteen months. The award is not automatic, but must be claimed by the owner on a special form, so it is essential to keep accurate records of wins. The JW does not count towards the title of Champion, or anything else for that matter; it is not even permitted to be placed after the dog's name.

FIELD TRIALS

The official KC definition of a Field Trial is: "A meeting for the purpose of holding competitions to assess the work of gundogs in the field, with dogs working on live unhandled game and where game may be shot." Game that has been handled, either dead or alive, is not permitted at a full Field Trial although its use is allowed at water tests or in a test for the award of a Show Gundog Working Certificate. Societies which are registered with the KC and have been authorised to do so may organise Field Trials. Like Shows, each Trial is individually licensed by the KC and they are conducted under the KC Field Trial regulations. Clubs which are authorised to hold Trials would normally be those which include in their constitution under "Objects of the Society" some mention concerning the improvement of working ability and the promotion of Trials and Working tests. These are usually Breed Clubs and various general Gundog Clubs, together with the many societies formed with the sole object of organising Field Trials and Working Tests.

A Field Trial can be made up of one or more stakes, which are separate competitions in themselves, much like the various classes at a Show. Unlike Shows, however, the stake winners do not meet for an overall winner. In view of the differing work requirements of the various breeds, the gundog group is divided into four sub-groups for the purpose of assessing their abilities. Stakes are run for the sub-groups under slightly different Regulations according to the relevant needs of that sub-group. Springers come under the umbrella of "Sporting Spaniels other than Irish Water Spaniels". With the need for fresh ground for each dog to have two runs, and the amount of game required, coupled with the time used up giving each competitor an adequate testing, during the short days of winter stakes are limited to a certain number of runners. This is usually a maximum of sixteen. As most stakes are over-subscribed, this necessitates a draw for places sometimes, with preference given to members of the society in accordance with certain KC guidelines.

The Stakes usually run for Spaniels are:
(a) Open. This is the stake in which the winner qualifies towards the title of FT Ch. or towards entry in the relevant Championships or Champion Stakes. In the case of Springers this is the Spaniel Championship. Entry is open to all dogs of the specified breed(s).
(b) All-aged. This stake is open to all dogs of any age in the specified breed(s); however, it carries no qualification for any title or Championship entry.
(c) Novice. The restrictions for entry in this stake are as follows: dogs which have won first, second or third in an Open stake or first in an All-aged stake are ineligible.

The basic Spaniel requirements for an award at a Trial are: to quarter the ground in quest of game, to be steady to flush, shot, and fall, and on command to retrieve tenderly from land or water. Certain faults carry the penalty of elimination. These are: hard mouth, being noisy, running over game when hunting, giving chase, running in to a falling bird, being out of control, changing game on a retrieve and not entering water. Other faults which do not necessarily carry the mandatory elimination, but are considered major faults, and putting out is at the discretion of the judges, are: failing to find dead or wounded game, failing to quarter properly and not going back to cover ground missed, failing to stop to shot or on flushing game, pegging live game, not being under full control, trespassing on ground that is not part of the dog's "beat" and – this last is not strictly the dog's fault – noisy handling.

In the competition the dogs are numbered and are run in pairs, one under each judge, and in the

The British Show scene: Sh. Ch. Teesview Transcontinental (left) and Sh. Ch. Cleavehill Hunting Melody.

second round any dogs not eliminated run under the other judge. The title of FT Ch is awarded to a dog which has won two Open Stakes at different Trials, or won the Spaniel Championship. In addition, a water test pass is also required. For the stake to count there must be at least fourteen dogs running. The Show Gundog Working Certificate is, in effect, a watered-down version of a Trial, and is designed to test that the basic working qualities are still alive and well. Dogs are worked in the line under the direction of the judges; noise in the line renders the dog ineligible for the certificate. The basic tests are: testing hunting ability, checking for gun-shyness – the dog must be off the lead when the gun is fired – cover must also be faced, and a retrieve is required (obviously tenderly). Absolute steadiness is not essential, although anything running riot is not likely to gain a SGWC. Sh. Ch. or CC winners may run for the SGWC at a Field Trial provided that one of the judges is on the A list, and the organising Club is one recognised for the Championship. The Midland English Springer Spaniel Society organises, in conjunction with other Spaniel Clubs, a Specialist SGW Trial, popularly known as "The Field Day". Conditions are the same as above, but the organisation is more on the lines of a full trial. Whereas the dog going for its certificate at a proper Trial will probably be on its own, and be tested at a convenient lull in the morning proceedings by both judges at once, at the Field Day the dogs are run in pairs, once under each judge. There is a more competitive atmosphere, as the participating Clubs donate numerous specials. Entries at the Field Day are permitted from first prize winners at a Championship show. If a SGWC is awarded it must be signed by both judges. The Field Day judges are both normally from the A list.

UNITED STATES

SHOWS
Canine competitions in the USA come under the administration of the American Kennel Club. This organisation is, in fact, a club of clubs and not of individual members. There are some 500

clubs with full membership and voting rights, but there are getting on for ten times this number of clubs holding events licensed by the AKC. The member clubs largely consist of the Parent breed clubs, and some All-breed clubs, together with some Obedience and Field trial clubs. The AKC is non-profit making. It registers all dogs, maintains a Stud Book and issues licences for any competitions, of which there over 10,000 held annually. Unlike the English KC, the AKC does not issue Breed Standards. They are the responsibility of the Parent Club of each breed. The AKC was inaugurated in 1884, and was chartered by the State of New York in 1910.

Regular classes
The progression from class winner to the Challenge for best of sex and then on to Best of Breed, through to the group (the relevant group for gundogs being the Sporting Group, as there is no separate group for Gundogs) and then Best in Show, is similar to that in the UK. The differences in the classifications start after the novice class. Up to this class the age classes are roughly similar to those in the UK – 6-9 months, 9-12 months, 12-18 months, although there is no overlap as in the UK and exhibits can only enter in the relevant class. After novice the classes are: bred by exhibitor, American bred, and Open. These classes are barred to Champions. From these classes the winners come forward for the Challenge for best of sex, and reserve best of sex. The winner of the Challenge is known as Winners Dog or Winners Bitch, as the case may be, and these two are awarded Championship points, which are based on a sliding scale dependent on the actual number of exhibits beaten. There are no mixed classes, except for Specials only: this is the class where the Champions appear, and the winner of this competes with Winners Dog and Winners Bitch for Best of Breed. The schedule of points available is determined by the AKC based on the popularity of the breed and the district concerned. The stipulated minimum number of dogs judged might range from three or four to attract a one point Winners Dog, to over twenty to gain a five point "major". Fifteen points are required for the title, and the total must include at least two majors (three points or more). If a dog that only wins two or three points in the breed wins Best of Breed and then goes on to win the Sporting group, it is possible to convert to the score of the highest winner the dog has defeated in the group. In Specialty shows there are other classes such as Sweepstakes, which are usually under another judge, and are not eligible for "points". Once a "pointed" dog is "finished" it becomes ineligible for the regular classes and has to go into the Specials Class.

FIELD TRIALS
The US Field Trials are run basically along the same lines as those in the UK. The dogs are numbered and run in pairs under two judges, odd numbers under the first judge, and evens under the other, in parallel beats as in the UK. The crucial difference is that, whereas in the UK trials dogs are tested on natural game, in their American counterparts planted game is used to give greater equality of opportunity. Dogs that perform to a suitable standard are then tested under the second judge. As in the UK, both dogs are worked in front of their handler and judge in their own patch without encroaching on the other dog's ground. When a flush is made, both dogs are required to drop, either to flush or shot, and remain steady until whichever of the dogs the judge decides should make the retrieve is sent for the bird. The usual things are assessed: game-finding ability, facing cover, steadiness, quartering and covering all their given beat, marked and blind retrieves, soft mouth and response to commands.

Stakes usually scheduled are: Puppy, Novice, Amateur All Aged, and Open All Aged. There is sometimes a Shooting Dog Stake where the handler is also the gun and shoots over his dog. Both All Aged stakes carry qualification for the Nationals. Two wins in the relevant All Aged Stakes will give the titles Amateur Field Champion (AFC) or Field Champion (FC). The Nationals differ from the above in that they are run on wild game augmented by birds released several days before the Trials. This gives a much sterner and more natural test of a dog's capabilities.

AUSTRALIA
SHOWS
The system used in Australia is an amalgam of those used in the UK and US. The classes are basically the same as those used in the USA, with the important exception that Champions can be shown in the ordinary classes. The CC equivalent is simply known as the "Challenge" but is worth points, as under the American system, depending on the entry, except that the CC is worth five points, plus one point for each dog beaten in its sex (puppies under six months excepted). The maximum score obtainable in the breed is twenty-five, a group winner gets twenty-five points, BIS is worth twenty-five points. A total of one hundred points is required for title of Australian Champion. Each of the States has its own Kennel Control organisation, with the Australian National Kennel Council as a "father-figure". Canine affairs come under the Department of Agriculture. Australia is one of the countries where disqualification ensues if the BOB winner does not present for all subsequent Challenges, e.g. group, and then all breed wins are void.

FIELD TRIALS
Field Trials in Australia are run under the rules of the Australian National Kennel Club and are grouped into three categories: Pointers and Setters, Utility Gundogs (HPR breeds), and Spaniels and Retrievers. This means that All Varieties Spaniels and All Varieties Retrievers compete against each other in a live game, rough shooting format. The dogs work in pairs (as in the "run off), working the same ground, the handlers walking together. There is only one judge, and the handlers shoot their own game. The Trials are run on a "knock out" basis – one dog from each pair going on to the next round. I understand that there are proposals in hand to change this to a two-run, total score system. Whether this will entail two judges I have no information; time will tell. The requisite number of wins at these Trials gives the title of FT Ch. There are also Retrieving Trials, open to all breeds of gundog; these are, basically, cold game tests. The dogs are required to retrieve from land and water, perform marked and blind retrieves, and also single and multiple retrieves. The title earned by success in this type of trial is Retrieving Trials Champion (RT Ch.). Of course, there are different stakes in both these types of trial, and the title is only gained by virtue of wins in the open stake.

NEW ZEALAND
SHOWS
To qualify as a New Zealand Champion a total of eight Challenge Certificates are needed under eight different judges. CCs are all of equal value as in the UK. No working qualifier is required.

FIELD TRIALS
These are run under the rules and regulations of the Dominion Gundog Trial Association (affiliated to NZKC). There are four events at which dogs can obtain Challenge points towards the title of FT Ch. A total of six Challenge points are required for the title. The major event is the All Breeds where all gundogs compete over the same two courses. There are three specialist events: 1. Retrievers; 2. Spaniels; 3 Pointers and Setters. The winner of the All Breeds receives two Challenge points and the specialist winners get one point. Trials are run under simulated conditions, and game used is normally pigeon, although provision is made for the use of any fur or feather game. Trials consist of two separate tests. Tests are worked on a points system, each dog

starting with 100 points for each test, with points being deducted for each misdemeanour. Commands are also penalised. The winner of the event is obviously the contestant with most points from the two tests except that no Challenge point is awarded if the winning score is less than 150.

Test 1. A double bird Heel and Retrieve across water. In this test the dog is required to heel from peg to peg (approximately 5 metres) then wait at the front peg while a blank is fired at each dead bird thrown across the water. The dog must remain steady at the peg until directed to retrieve the first bird across the water to the handler. The dog is then required to return across the water and retrieve the second bird. Points are lost for any deviation from a straight line to and from the birds.

Test 2. A Range, Find and Flush exercise. The handler walks in a straight line between two markers set at about 100m apart, with the dog ranging the ground on either side, seeking hidden dead game. Towards the end of the ground a live homing pigeon is planted which the dog is required to find and flush. On the flush a shot is fired to test for steadiness to shot and flush. Points are lost for failing to quarter the ground properly and for unsteadiness.

FEDERATION CYNOLOGIQUE INTERNATIONALE

The FCI is a co-ordinating organisation comprising various National Kennel Clubs who accept it as their ruling body. It was first started in 1911 with five member states, Germany, Austria, France, Belgium and Holland. It lasted the three years until the First World War. The second beginning in 1921 was more successful, and there are now 40 full member countries with full voting rights, and about 30 associate countries. The FCI issues Breed Standards to be used in Member Countries, and usually it adopts the Standard of the country of origin. In the case of English Springers this is the UK Standard. The FCI issue their own International Certificates which are on offer at certain shows (Internationales) in the member countries. These Certificats d'Aptitude au Championnat International de Beauté, known as CACIBs, are allocated to the International shows (hence the title), which also carry the National CACs of the country concerned, and the two are awarded from the same entry by the same judge. However, the two certificates need not necessarily be awarded to the same dog, different countries have varying regulations concerning the award of their domestic CACs, and the winner of CAC might be ineligible for CACIB or vice versa. CACIB winners must be over fifteen months old. Four CACIBs are normally needed for the title of International Champion, gained in three different countries under three different judges. I say 'normally' because, due to the spread of rabies in Europe, Denmark and Finland are no longer linked with Scandinavia canine-wise, and the rules have been relaxed slightly for Norway and Sweden. As a year must elapse between winning the first and the fourth CACIB before the dog qualifies for the International title, the youngest age that the title can be attained is 27 months. This FCI definition of International Champion is now generally used rather than the old system of calling a dog with a title in more than one country 'Int. Ch.'.

There is also an International award for working dogs called the CACIT (CACI de Travail). This is graded in a similar way to the bench assessments. In many FCI countries, as well as gaining the relevant number of CACITs required for the FT Ch. title or its equivalent, the dogs have to gain a show grading of Very Good or higher and, similarly, the bench dogs have to get a certain grade at a Trial. Exhibits under FCI rules are individually graded, being assessed against the breed standard. In Scandinavia the system is a numerical progression, Grade 1 (top) down to 5 (disqualified): in other countries the gradings go through Excellent, Very Good, Good, Fair, and the disqualified grade. The critiques and gradings are dictated to the ring secretary, and are recorded on special forms in triplicate. For this reason it is important that the exhibits are paraded in numerical order and the absentees recorded, because the individual forms have been prepared prior to the show with the relevant information. Each exhibitor receives an instant assessment of his dog at the end of the class. The other two copies are for the Show Executive and the relevant Kennel Club. The grading is sometimes known as the quality class and the basic classes for this are usually Junior (9-15 months), Youth (15-24 months) and Open (over 24 months). After the grading or quality class, the class is then judged normally, and placings made in order of merit in relation to each other. These are made from the top graded dogs if there are sufficient for the placings. The CAC or CACIB cannot be awarded to an exhibit graded below First or Exc. In some countries a Field Trial qualification is needed before the bench title can be used, and conversely, to be able to use the title FT Ch. a conformation grading of at least VG is required. Other classes are Champions class and Veteran. Additional awards such as Prize of Honour in the Junior or Youth classes, or Certificate Quality in the other classes, may be awarded if the judge feels the exhibit is of sufficient merit.

Although the dictation and issue of ring critiques is fairly widespread among the European countries, there is some degree of individuality, and in some countries the critiques are not mandatory, and the exhibitors have personal record books in which the judge enters the gradings and awards and signs it. Countries at present not affiliated to the FCI include the UK, Eire, Australia, New Zealand and South Africa. Eire and Australia are in the process of joining the FCI and may well be part of the Federation by the time this is published.

SCANDINAVIA

NORWAY: To become a show Champion, three CCs are required. One has to be awarded after the age of two years; it is also necessary for one to be gained at a Kennel Club show. The KC hold about ten shows per year spread nationwide. No working qualifier is needed. However, for an International title, two CACIBs are required in different countries; in most cases, due to quarantine, this effectively means one in Norway and one in Sweden. The dog must be a Champion in its own country, and pass a Field qualifying test. These FT qualifiers were instituted in the 1960s and are run in three parts – some normal field work, a water retrieve and a tracking test. These tests are not necessarily run at the same time.

SWEDEN: The requirements for the Int. Ch. are the same as in Norway, but for the domestic title it is necessary to gain a field qualification. These are similar to the Norwegian tests.

FINLAND: The rules are much the same as in Norway and Sweden, but since the spread of rabies to Finland the country is now more closely linked with the rest of Europe.

EIRE

The Irish Kennel Club is the organising body. At present, the CC equivalents are known as Green Stars which have a points value dependent on the number of exhibits actually competing. In some numerically small breeds, where mixed classes are scheduled, there is sometimes only one GS offered for BOB. As well as the normal title there is also an award of Annual Champion, which is awarded to the top winner in each breed subject to certain conditions. The IKC has recently rescinded its insistence on a FT qualifier before a dog becomes a Champion. The current show system is run on the same general lines as in the UK, with slightly less formality. Readers might be interested in the fact that in the early 1950s there were no Spaniel Field Trials held in the 26 counties comprising the Republic, and to qualify their dogs exhibitors either had to find a Trial in Northern Ireland or England, or else get permission for the qualifier to be run at Setter or Retriever Trials, which would not necessarily have the same conditions for Spaniel work or judges with the relevant qualifications to give the award. This probably accounts for the dearth of Irish Champions of the period.

REST OF EUROPE
These countries have their own local deviations from the model FCI recommendations, although the International Certificate regulations are standard. France, for instance, is one of the countries where the Bench or Field Championship is conditional on a suitable grading in the other discipline. In Holland, though, a dog can get its necessary quota of CACs and become a Dutch Ch., whereas the poor old working dog gets his two working certificates, and then has to get the relevant grading at a show.

In Germany, and one or two other European countries, some of the regulations are rather stricter than elsewhere. Breeding is conditional on the stock approximating to a fairly high degree with the Breed Standard, otherwise the necessary breeding licence is withheld from that particular animal. In many cases, this militates against the Field Trial dogs. This is particularly distressing if one has a top performing Field Trialler that is assessed as not conforming to the Breed Standard in some respects. It is disappointing enough not to be able to use any titles that may be achieved, but not to be allowed to breed is, to my mind, a short-sighted policy. How can you improve your stock if you are not permitted to try? Surely perpetuation of the brains and working abilities is, at least, as important as trying to breed perfect physical specimens – an impossibility in itself, even if all the various individual interpretations of the Standard, and the periodic fluctuations due to changing fashions, are ruled out. Two things that are anathema to most shooting people in the UK, and are disqualifying faults in Trials, are giving tongue while on a line (and also squeaking when waiting to perform) and killing wounded game. These items are, however, overlooked and, in some cases, actively encouraged elsewhere.

SOUTH AFRICA
To obtain a South African Championship a dog must be over nine months of age. Five CCs are needed and at least one of them must be awarded after the age of eighteen months. A further proviso is that one of the CCs must be gained outside the home province. The five provinces are Transvaal, Natal, Western Cape, Eastern Cape and Orange Free State. The show season runs from late February to early November, with a recess during the high summer period. There are 36 general Championship shows spread nationwide. There are also many local open shows held over a similar period. Springers at present have no breed Specialty shows at either level. The breed standard at present in use is the UK version.

Chapter Ten

THE TRANSATLANTIC ENGLISH SPRINGER

The watershed caused by the upheavals of the Second World War is reflected in the UK registration figures. Nearly 1,200 Springers were registered in 1938 but this dropped to just over 600 the following year. This was not, I suspect, due to the imminence of hostilities, but because the KC stopped the then current practice of giving free registration to unregistered parents of any dog for which a registration application had been made. However, the next two years did reflect what was going on outside the canine world and the figures hovered around the 200 mark. In 1942 there was a significant jump to 386, just three short of the total of the previous two years. 1943 saw another jump of 100 per cent, whilst the total of 1,326 in 1944 was the highest since 1927. The figure of 2,000 was passed for the first time in the history of the breed in 1945 and the following year the undreamed of total of 3,250 was reached.

THE IRISH INFLUENCE
With the resumption of Shows and Trials after the War there was a need to get the breed on an even keel again. The advent of Boxer of Bramhope was one factor in helping to achieve this, another was the appearance of W. Rankin Hepplewhite on the scene. His Happeedaze kennels were mostly based on a foundation of Irish blood descended from the pre-war lines of Tom Meageen and MacNab Chassels. His first stud dog, Start of Happeedaze, was by Tomtit from a daughter of Whaddon Chase Anthony and Mountain Breeze. Ch. Solitaire of Happeedaze was by Peter of Shotton out of Irish Ch. Drumcree Joan, whose grandsires were Winning Number of Solway and Dalshangan Tiptop. Ch. Sprightly of H. was by Ir. Ch. Templecorran Spotback.

Ir. Ch. Templecorran Spotback.

More of the Irish bloodlines were brought in through a litter by Ir. Ch. Templecorran Spotback out of Glenmount Lass. This litter was bred by Mr Ritchie and reached England by way of Bob Cleland of County Antrim, although he later settled in Liverpool. Of the two bitches he had from the litter, only Jordanstown Lass seems to have produced anything noteworthy, in Sh. Ch. Grand Lodge, a son of Boxer. The others in the litter to make a mark in the breed were a liver-and-white dog that joined Joe Braddon's kennel and was renamed Invader of Ide (he went on to take the breed record from Ch. Roundwood Lass) and his black-and-white brother who was bought by Mary Scott. She kept his name as Ideal Stamp and he sired several winners including Ch. Bramhope Recorder out of Boxer's dam. Spotback was by (Sh. Ch.) Mockerkin Domino, a Marmion son owned by Tom Meageen. Domino's dam was a grand-daughter of Champions Nutbrooke Boy and Nuthill Dignity. Spotback's mother T. Saddleback had, as sire, Dalshangan Tip Top (Sh. Ch.), bred by MacNab Chassels from Inveresk Cameronian and I. Congress, and eventually owned by W. J. McCoubrey, of Ballynahinch, Northern Ireland (a district that has had its fair share of dog people over the years). The dam of this litter, Glenmount Lass, was sired by Orpheus of Canfordbourne out of a Domino bitch.

Later on, in the early fifties, Miss Francis brought in from Ireland Higham Blarney Blazer, bred by Con O'Connor. He was sired by Ir. Ch. Advent of Leeside, a son of Grand Lodge out of Tan of Leeside. Tan carried the blood of Douglas of Doralan, as well as one of the few lines left by Am. Ch. Stingo of Shotton before his export. Blazer's dam, B. Bramble, was by Towermount Thrasher, owned by John Dring of County Cork, but bred by W. R. Gardiner (more noted for his Pointers) from Higham Tristram out of his Ir. Ch. Margaret's Fancy (alias Meg's Fancy in the English KC Stud Book). Fancy was a M. Domino daughter from Ir. Ch. Eithne's Pet sired by Allegro of Canfordbourne. Bramble's dam was by T. Spotback and there was a further line to M. Domino further back.

FIELD TRIAL CHAMPIONS IN THE POST-WAR PERIOD
As in the post-war period of twenty-five years earlier, the breed attracted many newcomers to both Bench and Field ranks. Some of these would make their mark and grace the breed for several years while others would simply be ships passing in the night. During the war the Ranscombes had been kennelled with Dr Esther Rickards and her Tarbay Cockers at Windsor. Dr Rickards also owned a Springer bitch by Winning Number of Solway out of Mockerkin Myrtle (Ch. Pierpoint Perfection ex Ch. Admiration of Solway). This bitch, Uspup of Tarbay, had a litter to Replica of Ranscombe, one of which, Chris of Tarbay, found its way to Kent and became the foundation for the Woodbay strain of Mrs Frances Sherwood. Mrs Sherwood also had a sister of Chris but I cannot trace any stock descending from her. Chris had a litter by Hood of Horsford, owned by Major Horsbrugh. Their daughter, Amber of Woodbay, mated to Northdown Maquis produced the Field Trial winner Mack of W. along with Biddy of W., a good brood bitch. The Woodbay line really took off when Mrs Sherwood joined forces with Bill Manin in partnership with the descendants of Ch. Northdown Donna. The alliance of Northdown and Woodbay is still an influence in the Scandinavian lines.

Among the newcomers to the training world were the Chudley brothers with their Harpersbrook kennels, but in the years since they started in 1946, they have owned, bred and trained many FT Champions and Winners. I think I am correct in saying they handled all the FT Champions and Winners belonging to Mr and Mrs F. George, including FT Ch. Harpersbrook Reed, who surely must have been one of the most typical Springers to win the Spaniel Championship. In 1946 John Kent bred a dog that would come to figure quite a lot in Springer bloodlines, especially the Trial ones. This was FT Ch. Silverstar of Chrishall. Not only is he behind most of the modern working

*FT Ch.
Rivington
Glensaugh
Glean.*

*FT Ch.
Markdown
Muffin.*

stock, but he caught the attention of many of the dual-purpose breeders. His sire, Whittlesford Bee Sting, was by FT Ch. Beeson of Blair, as his name implies, and carried FT Ch. Bee of Blair on his dam's side as well.

Silverstar's dam, Teggie of Chrishall, was bred by Andrew Wylie out of the pre-war FT Winner Pine Hawk, by Edgar Winter's Staindrop Spitfire. This litter also produced FT Ch. Pinehawk Roger and a dog called Spy Hawk. Spitfire was out of Eng. and Am. FT Ch. Noranby Pelican, his sire being Staindrop Stopbright, a FT Ch. Jed of the Cairnies son ex Renrut Tansy (FT Ch. Banchory Boy–Renrut Patsy). Teggie also produced Harpersbrook Apethorpe Teazle. This time the sire was Roger of Yelme. Roger was out of Grock of Blair, one of the FT Ch. Don O'Vara–FT Ch. Hillhampton Susie litter. Mating Teggie to Mrs B. Beales' FT Ch. Racedale Rover (FT Ch. Beeson of Blair–Pine Hawk), John Kent bred Racedale Revor.

Andrew Wylie's Pine Hawk was by FT Ch. Spy O'Vara out of Rip of the Cairnies. Her son P. Roger made his mark on the breed through various channels, the first of his progeny to get his title being FT Ch. Spurt O'Vara, born in 1947. But the most telling effect Roger had on the breed was undoubtedly via his "get" out of a litter bred by W. G. Sheldon in 1949 from Victory Vee, bred from the pre-war Eromtew line of the Calvert family. These were FT Ch. Dauntless Monty and FT Ch. Ludlow Gyp. From the time Sheldon bred that first litter, until his early death in 1955 he had a remarkable, if brief, career at Trials. In those six years he bred seven FT Champions and his stock had influence on many other lines. Gyp was the dam of FT Champions L. Darkie (by FT Ch. Spark O'Vara), L. Bruce (FT Ch. Rivington Glensaugh Glean), Rivington Michele (R. G. Glean) and L. Socks (FT Ch. Micklewood Scud). From Gyp's daughter Beauty came FT Ch. L. Ruby (M. Scud). Diana, litter sister to Darkie, although not getting her crown, was instrumental in giving the breed FT Ch. Markdown Muffin and FT Ch. Micklewood Slip, both by Glean. Darkie sired Stripe O'Vara, and L. Shelly produced FT Ch. Richard of Elan, whilst Socks is probably best known as the sire of FT Ch. Pinehawk Sark. Bruce went to the US in the ownership of Joseph Quirk and took the US Nationals back-to-back in 1954 and 1955. Socks also went to America and gained his US FT title, as did Scamp. Both were placed in the National Stake. Glean was by Silverstar.

The brother of Victory Vee was Eromtew Flash, who was used by the Rouse Boughton family to sire one of their Downton litters. From one of the bitches in this litter, D. Mischief mated to FT Ch. Sarkie O'Vara, two pups have been of importance to the Trial lines. The dog Longnor Splash was incorporated by Lord Biddulph into his Conygree strain and was the grandsire of Conygree

Simon; the other was Micklewood Sue, dam of Eng. and Am. FT Ch. Micklewood Scud, another double winner of the National. Spy Hawk was the sire of the litter bred by Captain McNeill Farquhar in 1947 that contained the FT Champions Acheron Spot, Pat and Trick. Their dam Dochfour Trixie was bred by Baroness Burton. Trixie's sire Gruline Trash had been bred by the Baroness in the early twenties by FT Ch. Banchory Boy from her Castlehill Reece, who must have been one of the last of the Cornwallis Cavalier progeny. Certainly the Acheron litter having him in the fourth generation would have been the closest descendants to him. The dam of Trixie, Dochfour Fire, was by FT Ch. Bryngarw Firearm out of Noranby Rubbish. Pat went to Dick Burton and is behind most of his Brackenbanks. Trick was owned by Dr E. B. Sunderland. Spot, a black-and-white dog, was sold to John Lukies, whose Cammas dogs were well-known in Trial circles. Harpersbrook Apethorpe Teazle, although not gaining his title, sired several FT Champions and Winners with probably the most influence coming down via his son FT Ch. Harpersbrook Sammy.

NEW BREED CLUBS
Early in 1946, Mrs Nellie Howard of the Chastletons, together with several other interested parties, thought the time was ripe for a second Breed Club, so an inaugural meeting was held in Birmingham. Among the management team were Nellie Howard as Secretary, Colonel Carrell, Mrs Travers, Dick Morgan and Mary Scott. The new Club held its first Open Show in April, less than four months from starting up – some feat of organisation! With today's Kennel Club requirements it now takes a new Club nearer two years to be recognised. The first Championship Show was held that year in October with William Humphrey as judge. Again, this would not be possible quite so soon today as, under modern KC requirements, applications for CCs have to be made two years in advance. The Club also ran its first Trial. I am pleased to say that the Midland English Springer Spaniel Society not only survived but is now a much respected Club approaching its fiftieth anniversary.

The next year another Breed Club was formed. The London Sporting Spaniel Society was an umbrella for the Spaniel sub-group and, as such, had been running Open Shows. However, with the large numbers of Cockers being registered there were spare CCs and the Society applied to run a Show with CCs solely for Cockers, with the other breeds having Open Show status. For some reason the KC refused permission and the Cockers ended up withdrawing from the Society to form The Home Counties Cocker Club. This resulted in the rest of the Society breaking up. From the wreckage emerged the London and Counties English Springer Spaniel Society, which became the Southern English Springer Spaniel Society in 1973, when it was decided to cover the needs of the growing numbers of members in the Southern half of the country.

ESTABLISHED LINES OF THE EARLY 50S
As yet the Boxer influence had not begun, and the Champions and Winners were still all coming from established lines such as Whaddon Chase, Sandylands and Carnfield. Among the others were kennels like the Belchamps of Brian Chambers, although this was basically a Cocker kennel. Hepplewhite had Belchamp Cedilla from whom he bred a litter by Peter's Benefactor. A puppy from this litter, Soubrette of Happeedaze, went as foundation bitch to another Cocker breeder, Mrs F. Thompson of the Beechfields, and won a CC. A dog, Skipper of Happeedaze, gained his Sh. Ch. title. Cedilla was out of Belchamp Clover, one of the litter that contained Sandylands Showgirl and Starshine of Ide. The sire of Cedilla was by Sh. Ch. Knighted, so Cedilla was very strong in the Shotton blood.

D. C. Hannah's first litter from Clintonhouse Elizabeth was by Mountain Crest and proved successful, producing Ch. Carnfield Florrie and Swedish Ch. Miss Greta of Ware. The next litter, in 1947, was to Ch. Whaddon Chase Bonny Tom and contained Ch. Stokeley Bonny Boy and a bitch called Cecil's Choice. This mating was repeated the following year and produced Ch. Stokeley Gay Boy. The most important of Elizabeth's progeny, however, was in her litter to Ambergris Sportsman, one of the Mountain Crest–Sue of Amberside litter. This produced Ch. Stokeley Lucky, possibly the nearest thing to a Dual-Champion since World War Two. Lucky won almost thirty awards at Field Trials but never quite made the two placings in the prize lists which mattered.

The first post-war crop of Champions or Show Champions were: Whaddon Chase Snipe and Bonny Tom, Invader of Ide, Sandylands Showgirl, Starshine of Ide, Sandylands Sherry, Carnfield Christabelle, Sandylands Shot, Grand Lodge, Cavehill Maid, Ambergris Alert, Roundwood Haynford Lady, Roundwood Roger the Rake, Sandylands Shrubby, Sandylands Soubranie, Solitaire of Happeedaze, Stokeley Bonny Boy, Painted Lady, Sprightly of Happeedaze, Staitley May Queen, Carnfield Chick, Carnfield Florrie and Higham Topsy. Of these the Sandylands contingent were all Shotton-based, as was Starshine of Ide. Cavehill Maid, Painted Lady, Invader of Ide, Solitaire and Sprightly of Happeedaze, and Staitley May Queen were all Irish-bred. Two of the Carnfields were mother and daughter, Chick being by Carnfield Commodore out of Florrie. Christabelle was a daughter of Clintonhouse Janet by a brother of Belchamp Cedilla. R. H. Lady and A. Alert were both by Replica. The interesting name in the above "hall of fame" is that of Grand Lodge, a pointer to the shape of things to come. He was the first of the Boxer progeny to get his title.

KENNELS OF THE EARLY 50S

Among the kennels of this era which had an influence on the breed was that of Mrs Sowter, of Ilkley, Yorkshire. Her Stonebrig kennels owned three quite well-known and well-used stud dogs – Stonebrig Sentinel, Ace of Coates Park and Chief of Staff. Sentinel was bred by W. Stordy by Mountain Crest out of Dawn of Dhunean and was the sire of many Winners of the late 1940s and early fifties. Ace of C. P. was by Higham Tomtit out of Jillcote of C. P. (one of the Knighted/Ambergris litter). Among his grandchildren was the dual CC Winner Colmaris Toreador. The most influential of the progeny of Chief of Staff has to be a bitch that Mrs Sowter bred in partnership with a Mr Edwards. Sold unregistered, she was registered by her new owner as Susan of Stubham. Her various litters to Boxer of Bramhope not only enhanced his reputation as a stud dog, but placed Mrs Kay Till in the forefront of Springer breeders for some fifteen years, until her retirement due to ill health in the early sixties. Chief of Staff was by Thornel Browne's Hercules of Rafehill, a double grandson of Showman of Shotton. Following her purchase of Susan, Kay Till acquired a black and white stud dog, Shaughan of Stubham, by the Irish-bred Ideal Stamp out of Bramhope Bonnyface (Totonian Finder ex Bramhope Suzette). Shaughan mated to Susan and, more especially, to Susan's daughters by Boxer produced a whole string of Winners, and when one of the Boxer litters produced the immortal Alexander, the strain was assured of a place in Springer history. Another bitch bred by Mrs Sowter was Stonebrig Seraph. She was by Sentinel out of Seonaid of Dhunean (another owned by W. Stordy out of Mountain Breeze, this time by Ch. Pleasant Peter) and amongst her progeny were the two brothers by Boxer, Sh. Ch. Bonaventure of Bramhope and the CC Winner Beagle of B.

The Clintonhouse kennel of Mrs G. Thomson, apart from providing stock for the Carnfield revival and the foundation of the Stokeleys, was also important to the Colmaris lines of Mr and Mrs "Sandy" Davies. Their interest in the breed extended back to the days when they mated their foundation bitch (another of the many wedding presents that have had an influence on the breed)

Ch. Alexander of Stubham.

to Carnfield King. In the first years after the war they were showing stock by the brothers Carnfield Fieldmarshall and Monarch. The litter by Monarch was out of Coates Park Enterprise and contained the aforementioned dual CC Winner Colmaris Toreador. Mrs Thomson at this time owned a bitch, bred by Mrs Bamford, called Clintonhouse Hazeltong Judith. She was by Replica of Ranscombe and her dam, Judy of Hazeltong, was one of the George and Greta litter. Owing to Mrs Thomson's ill-health, Judith was campaigned by the Davies and, on the death of Mrs Thomson, joined the Colmaris kennel, as did her son by Boxer, Clintonhouse George. Judith and George both got their titles followed by Judith's daughter, Ch. Comaris Contessa, by Toreador. Mary Scott later purchased Judith and she produced several winning pups with the Bramhope suffix. The best of these was probably the Boxer daughter, the great Ch. Bathsheba of Bramhope, who numbered among her descendants the foundation stock for many of the later kennels such as Majeba, Kennersleigh (and via this line the Cleavehills), and the Hortonbank line of L. Charlesworth who, although he did not show very much, provided the link to the Whitemoor strain of Beryl Carstairs.

In 1947, Mr and Mrs Crawford (Winch) decided to mate their shooting bitch, third generation from their original working bitch. Fate led them in the direction of Replica of Ranscombe and thus began a strain that lasted for two decades, producing Champions in the UK, Australia, India and Holland, as well as many good workers. This first litter produced the CC Winner Winch Agate, and careful line breeding to this litter and the subsequent use of Replica's grandson Rollicker fixed the type. Boxer was used as an outcross on one of the Rollicker bitches and, later, by using a son of Clintonhouse George and Contessa, the same Boxer/Replica combination was strengthened.

In the late forties Ernest Froggatt started his renowned Moorcliff kennel. He acquired the black and white Bramhope Recorder (by the Irish-bred Ideal Stamp out of Boxer's dam B. Suzette) from Mary Scott. Sandylands Secret followed from Gwen Broadley and both got their titles. Vicky of Stubham also joined the kennel later.

Another person who founded her strain at the tail-end of the forties and is still active in the breed is Mrs Dorothy George, popularly known as "Mick". She started her current Mortondawn line with Serenade of Happeedaze. Alexander of Stubham was used on Serenade with success, and a sound, typical strain has gradually been built up over the years. At this time the Studley kennels were founded with the purchase of Bountiful of Beechfield from Mrs F. Thomson. Bountiful won one CC and her litters to her grandsire Boxer produced several Champions. She was also the dam of Champions to Banker of Bramhope. She was sired by the part Irish-bred Sh. Ch. Grand Lodge out of Soubrette of Happeedaze. The litter also contained Ch. Banner of Beechfield owned by Miss Joan Wilkins, who later became Mrs Dinwoodie. In the meantime, Lady Belhaven bred from

Staghorn Pinkfoot and her Tillan prefix had started to make its mark both at Trials and on the Bench. A litter by Ch. Solitaire of Happeedaze gave the breed Ch. Tillan Toddy, progenitrix of the Pencloe line of Jack Bolton and his daughter Morag. Tillan Tango (by Boxer), after some winning, eventually joined the Lochar kennels of Mr and Mrs Dinwoodie. After a brief spell in the Show world, Lady Belhaven concentrated purely on Trials, developing a line from Pinkfoot via such top Trial dogs as FT Ch. Kinmount Pat, Criffel Patrick and Saighton's Saint, and resulting in, among others, Am. National FT Winner, Tillan Ticket.

EARLY 50s USA

One of the stars of the US scene in the early fifties was the great Am. Can. Ch. Frejax Royal Salute. He was one of the many Am. Chs. of the forties, but quite a few of them faded into oblivion and, like their counterparts in the UK, only a minority became links in the chain between the birth of the breed and the present day. The main lines of the forties that are ancestors of the modern dogs are of course Melilotus, Salilyns, Green Valley, Greenfairs, Sandblown Acre, Runors, Cauliers, Rumak, Frejax and Donniedhu. Others that appear occasionally are Eldgyth, Macmars, Hunters Hill and Maquams. One of Salute's most important progeny was Am. Ch. Melilotus Royal Oak, owned and bred by Mrs Gilman Smith, who followed his sire as a great stud and Show dog. Born in 1949, he was BIS at the first National Specialty Show run by the parent club, the English Springer Spaniel Field Trial Association, in 1956.

A Salute grandson was also born in 1949. This dog, Ch. King Peter of Salilyn, was a son of Salutation of Salilyn (she obviously being by Salute, mated back to his grandmother, Nancy of Salilyn). Salutation had two litters to Firebrand of Sandblown Acre. An obedience-qualified dog, he also had well over his quota of "beauty" points but not the "major" required to give him his title. However, his progeny from Salutation contained eight champions. Peter had a younger brother, King William of S., who was also quite useful at stud. Firebrand was heavily inbred to Rodrique of S. A., carrying five lines to him, including a father/daughter mating both sides, which accounts for the success of the two brothers at stud. Royal Oak's dam Tranquillity of Melilotus also carried five lines back to Recorder through various of the Green Valley dogs but without Rodrique's sire Donald Dhu.

Norman Morrow's Runors were based on Am. Ch. Audley Farm Judy. The Audley Farm lines of Robert Morrow were based on Ch. Field Marshall, one of the Recorder/Woodelf litter, mated back to Green Valley stock, and were thus strong in the Recorder influence. Judy was the dam of Ch.

Ch. Northdown Donna.

Sh. Ch. Stokeley Sea Sprite.

Runor's Agent by Showman. In a litter by Rufton Breeze of Rob Roy she produced Ch. Runor's Deacon who sired, among others, Ch. Syringa Sue, dam of many winning offspring with the Syringa prefix. Another daughter was the foundation of the Wakefields kennel. Breeze was another example of the borrowed prefix syndrome and was American-bred by Can. Am. Ch. Fleetfoot Dan out of Frejax Dream Girl, the nearest English Rufton being at least three generations back. Dan was by Can. Ch. Royal Flush of Avalon who was a son of Int. Ch. Jamson of Ware. Salilyn's Nancy was another sired by Breeze. Others of Judy's progeny to get their titles were R. Rock and R. Radiance by Rodrique; to Ch. Field Knight of Hampton she produced Rising Star, Rhapsody and Rip. In 1955 the complete stock of the Runor kennel with the exception of Agent was acquired by Leonard Grunwald as foundation for his Ascots line.

CHANGES IN THE ATLANTIC TRAFFIC

After World War Two traffic across the Atlantic had continued, but with a shift of emphasis. With the growing divergence in type between Bench and Trial Springers and the demise of most of the dual-purpose strains, the hiatus in the British breeding programmes caused by the hostilities meant that there was a shortage of quality Show stock to attract American fanciers. The probability was that the standard in the US was higher at that time, due to the importation of a lot of the best UK dogs prior to the War, and there was nothing being bred to take their place. This state of affairs continued until the British breeders managed to restore the breed. However, the split between Bench and Field was increasing in America and, as the standard of work improved, more and more of the top British Trial dogs found their way to American enthusiasts. One of the more prolific contributors to the US Field Trial scene was Talbot Radcliffe. Like Bob Cornthwaite in the twenties and thirties he had his own individual strain which suited the American market and, I suppose, the influence of the Saightons on the post-war workers could be equated to the effect the Ruftons had on the Bench lines some years earlier.

THE US NATIONAL

In 1947 the US National Championship Field Trial was inaugurated and the first Trial was held in Illinois. This is similar to the KC Spaniel Championship in the UK in that dogs need to qualify for entry via awards at other Trials. They are also alike in the fact that a win gives the FT Ch. title – another reason for the increase in British Field Trial dogs being imported. The "National" was an idea that had been formulated just prior to the War but, for obvious reasons, did not come to fruition until normality prevailed. The first Winner was the American-bred Russet of Middle Field handled by Roy Gonia but owned by Dr Charles Sabin, of Oregon, who had been highly successful on the Bench in the thirties with his Am. Ch. Newt Dignity and his progeny. Dignity was a son of Am. and Can. Ch. Norman of Hamsey. Dr Sabin also had Am. FT Ch. Newt Sir Malcolm, grandson of the imported Inveresk Clip. Tragically, Dr Sabin was killed in a car accident during the following year's Trials. The "National" was held over several days and the awards were made on the basis of the standing at the end of the second day, resulting in a win for Stoneybroke Sheer Bliss owned by Mr and Mrs Philip D. Armour. This was a title that they would win several times in following years with imported dogs, usually handled by Steve Studnicki. But in 1960 the Eng. FT Ch. Carswell Contessa took the title. This performance was historic for two reasons: Contessa was the first owner/amateur handled to win and she was the first Trial Winner handled by a lady, Mrs Julia Armour.

BOXER'S INFLUENTIAL SONS

The early part of the fifties was the era of the Boxer sons – Peter of Lortonfell, Clintonhouse

Sh. Ch.
Studley Brave
Buccaneer.

George and Alexander of Stubham, although Peter was an overlap from the forties, being born in 1948. Alex and George were born in 1950, in February and July respectively. George's main lines of descent are via the Stokeley/Colmaris strains to the Teesviews and the predominant influence of Alex is through the Hawkhills. These three "greats" won many certificates between them; Alex took 23 including Crufts 1953 and 1960, George won 18 (sadly he died five months short of his fifth birthday, the day before Crufts) and Peter's tally was a dozen, one of them taking him through to BIS at a General Ch. Show, a feat shared with his litter sister Ch. Light of Ashleigh. Not bad going for a pair bred and reared in an upstairs flat in Newcastle!

Others of the Boxer progeny who achieved either the Ch. or Sh. Ch. title were: Studley Major, Bonaventure of Bramhope, Camdin Chief, Duchess of Stubham, Bathsheba of Bramhope, Northdown Fancy, Banker of Bramhope, Studley Brave Buccaneer, Grand Lodge, Dinah of Stubham, Belarosa of Bramhope, Wollburn Wallflower, Camdin Blazer. There were many other CC Winners as well as several abroad. One of the latter was the litter brother of Studley Major, Studley Hercules, who joined the Timpanagos kennels of Robert Allen and finished his Am. Ch. Bonaventure almost added the American "crown" to his English one after arriving in the US in the late 1950s when his owner, Ted Stevenson, emigrated. Bonaventure was nearly ten when he left England and his age, plus a hot summer when he was being shown, meant he finished one or two points short of his target. One important dog of this era was the previously mentioned Ch. Stokeley Lucky: he was born two days after Ch. Alexander but was one of the few not to carry Boxer blood.

SHOW STOCK EXPORTS
Of the Show stock that went to owners in the US, apart from Studley Hercules previously mentioned, Simon of Stubham, one of the Boxer/Susan progeny and Honeysuckle of Stubham (by Alexander out of Empress of S.) went to the Swan Point kennels of Christine Phillips, followed by Don Juan of Stubham, Studley Grenadier of Stubham, Sheilah, Marietta, Meteor, Lysander and Escort, all of Stubham. Fransisca and University Don went to Canada, while Mr Monte was sent to Panama. The "M" litter were out of Empress by a dog called Robin of Tarnock who was full of Renrut breeding. The mating was advocated by Warner Hill and the experiment could have been useful to the breed had any of the stock stayed in the UK. Grenadier went to the MacMars kennels of W. E. MacKinney, as did Sheilah (the bitch was bred by the veteran Irish breeder Anna Redlich of the Strathfoyle Springers, by Alexander out of a daughter of Irish Ch. Pat of Ardrick, and should not be confused with Sheila of Stubham, one of the Boxer/Susan pups). The MacKinneys had been breeding dual-purpose Springers since the mid-thirties and, post-war, still had stock descended from Dual Ch. Green Valley Punch. A son of Grenadier and Sheilah finished his Bench

title and also gained WDX qualification. In 1950 Miss Francis mated her Ch. Higham Topsy to FT Ch. Silverstar of Chrishall. In the first litter only one puppy survived, a very good-looking bitch called H Titbit, who won on the Bench and at Trials. Unfortunately, an internal infection meant she had to be spayed, so her breeding potential was lost. But the mating was repeated, this time with with better luck, and the next litter contained Whaddon Chase Boy, Higham Test and Stokeley Higham Tonga. These matings of Topsy to Silverstar were the start of a very successful combination for the two strains. Test mated to FT Ch. Harpersbrook Sammy gave us Am. FT Ch. Towser of Chrishall. Topsy mated to Acheron Spot produced Higham Tell, dam of FT Ch. Speckle of Chrishall. Also in the litter was H Turvey who won his Italian FT Ch. title after joining the then young kennel of Marco Valcarenghi.

THE EFFECT OF MYXOMATOSIS

During the early part of this decade an event occurred in the UK which, although not directly connected to the canine world, had a marked effect on gundogs in general and Spaniels in particular. This was the disease myxomatosis which practically decimated the rabbit population. The virus had been introduced in an attempt to control the rabbit population, an objective which was certainly achieved but in rather horrifying fashion. The effect on Spaniels is reflected in the figures for English Springer registrations which showed a gradual decline from 2,300 in 1950 to 1,300 in 1957. It really was a disaster as far as rough shooting and training Spaniels was concerned, and many small-time breeders of working stock dropped out of the breed. Another result was the shift of emphasis at Trials from ground game to birds. This reduction in training facilities also affected the Show dogs with regard to the qualifier. Finally, in November 1958, the KC responded to pressure from the gundog breeds by creating the new title of Show Champion for gundogs which have been awarded three CCs. The old title of Champion was retained for those gundogs which had passed the Field Trial qualifier. Some of the Setter breeds had actually been using the unofficial (and illegal as far as KC rules were concerned) title of Bench Ch. for several years.

NEW STRAINS OF THE 50s

The early fifties saw the beginnings of one or two strains that are still in existence today. Judith Robinson (now Hancock) returned home from a spell learning Springers with Kay Till, bearing Starlet of Stubham as foundation for a line which has now spread worldwide. Judith bred strongly to the Stubham stock and also used Ch. Studley Major. Starlet had already produced Ch. Floravon Silverstar when in the ownership of Hugh Sweeney and, later on, she also became Judith's property. A repeat mating produced Ch. Hawkhill Brave. Judith had many Champions and CC Winners early on from various Stubhams and allied stock, but the litter that did most for posterity was Silverstar mated to Alexander. This gave Hawkhill Harmony of Stubham and Ch. Hyperion of Stubham. Hyperion won thirteen CCs for Kay Till but, unfortunately, died at five years of age. He did, however, sire a fair amount of good stock, the most influential being the bitch Quaker Girl of Stubham who was out of Brandyhole Fleur de Lys of Stubham. A daughter of Quaker Girl, by Sh. Ch. Whaddon Chase Drake, fortunately came into the hands of Judith. This was the legendary Sh. Ch. Slayleigh Paulina, who was to set new standards for the kennel; her litters to Ch. Moorcliff Dougal gave the breed many of the top Winners of the late sixties and early seventies.

The Stubham kennel also provided foundation stock for Jeanne Spence's Brandyhole strain. At one time she owned both Hazel (who won the kennel's first CC under Warner Hill) and Duchess of Stubham, although Hazel returned to the home kennel to get her title and was eventually exported to Ceylon. Mrs Spence made up Duchess, who was by Boxer, and trained her for her working qualifier in a London park. She built up her strain by coupling Duchess with her half-brothers, Clintonhouse George for the "B" litter and Studley Brave Buccaneer for the "C" litter. Berry Brown went as foundation to Isla Campbell Durie of the Kildusklands and gained her title. Bellflower was retained and won one CC. Commodore got two CCs. These two were combined in the "D" and "F" litters. The former contained the dual CC Winner Dynamic (owned by Derek Williams) and the home-based Ch. Diadem. Diadem had two litters. The first, by her litter brother Dynamic, did not contain anything that seems to have bred on, but the second was by Hyperion of Stubham and contained the Dutch Ch. Happy Returns, Aust. Ch. Forest Fancy of Stubham, Hadji (French CAC), Harmony (CACIB, Belgium), and the UK CC winner High Spirits. There was also Fine Feathers of Stubham, who went to the Hawkhill kennels when the Stubhams were disbanded, and stock from him comes down through the descendants of Sh. Ch. H Hello Dolly. The Brandyhole line does not seem to have gone to Scandinavia, although there were quite a number of exports to the European mainland. Isla Durie mated Berry Brown to Alexander, breeding the Dual CC Winner Eriska of Kilduskland, she then used Melilotus Shooting Star on Eriska as an outcross before mating a daughter, Ailsa of K, to Northdown Diplomat for the third generation. Diplomat being by Stokeley Sea Sprite out of Northdown Donna brought in two lines of C George. The Duries at this time retired to Italy and the line faded out, although I had one of the Diplomat bitches, Kildalton, which was incorporated into my lines.

Of similar vintage to the Brandyholes is the Teesview strain. Gamekeeper George Dobson showed his working dog Bass Rock (by Boxer) quite successfully on occasions, as well as Whintonhill Raider and Wollburn White Chief, but the kennel really took off with the purchase of Tyneview Margaret from George Scott. Mr Dobson's wife Ellen piloted the bitch to her title and founded a top dual-purpose line from her. The kennel also owned Stokeley Toreador who, before his export to the US where he finished his title, sired the more-than-useful stud dog Titus, from whom many Champions descend. Mr and Mrs Pratt started their Bricksclose kennels with stock from the Stokeley and Yarningale lines, winning quite well on the Bench, but success in an Amateur Handlers Stake with Stokeley Sultan led to a change of direction. The couple obtained a bitch from Miss Francis – Higham Tally, a grand-daughter of Ch. Higham Topsy and FT Ch. Silverstar of Chrishall, her sire being FT Ch. Harpersbrook Sammy. Tally had a successful Trials career and was joined by Posterngate Jo from Dr White. These two were a nucleus of a well-known Trials line that produced among others Am. FT Ch. Dewfield Bricksclose Flint.

Although my family had owned Springers since 1937, I started again from scratch after completing my National Service. The bitch I obtained was virtually all Trial-bred on her sire's side and her dam was by the Bench and Trial Winner Dagnall Duncan. I mated her to a young dog of almost pure Ranscombe breeding that eventually became Dutch Ch. Winch Crocidolite. At the same time I bought Winch Ryolite who was also inbred to Replica of Ranscombe, but with a Boxer outcross. My strain is descended from this pair with suitable outcrosses to both Bench and Trial lines over the years.

In 1956 the Eastern English Springer Spaniel Club held its tenth annual Specialty Show at the US home of Mr and Mrs Gilman Smith in Bethel, Connecticut. The Club honoured Mary Scott with the invitation to officiate as Judge. One spin-off from this was the importation to the UK two years later of Am. Ch. Melilotus Shooting Star as an outcross to the many Boxer descendants. Benny, as he was known, was born in 1954 and was the winner of the 1955 Futurity Stakes. Although he was not widely used by British breeders he did have some effect on the British lines.

SPRINGER EXPORTS

In other parts of the world the breed was continuing much as in pre-war days with the stock that had been imported. Fresh blood was introduced to South Africa when Polish exile Princess Radziwill emigrated there in the latter part of the 1940s taking Whaddon Chase Harmony and Roundwood Laddie with her. Mrs Penney imported Hope Mountain Stronghold in 1948. Candyfloss of Crosslane by Ch. Clintonhouse George went out to Mr Jordan, becoming a Rhodesian Champion. Totonian Charmer also went out to Southern Rhodesia, to Mrs Raesides, as a mate for her Bob of Ira, bred by Princess Radziwill. As was usual with countries colonised and developed by Britain, the sporting dogs followed, and I believe the working dogs were descended from some O'Vara dogs. In Kenya, there had been imports from the Sandylands and Chastleton kennels. The result of the colonies gaining independence was unsettling to both political and economic affairs with an obvious effect on the dog scene. One factor that caused problems was the currency restrictions which blocked further imports. The Indian sub-Continent was the destination of one or two Springers during the 1950s with Winch Kainite, Jeremy of Stubham, Integrity of Stubham and Royal Flush of Stubham going to India, and Sh. Ch. Hazel of Stubham and Hawkhill Dambuster going to Ceylon. Freckles, one of the Hawkhill "F" litter sired by Dambuster before his export, went to George and Margaret Johnson and founded their Ambridge kennel.

BREEDING IN THE 60s

The sixties had started off with the deaths, in 1961, of Lady Howe and George Taylor and this period was to see the loss from the Breed of many of the other early stalwarts. H. S. Lloyd, one of the founder members of the parent Club, passed away in 1962, and in 1965 Mason Prime (Wakefares) and A. E. Curtis (Whittlemoor) died, as did Reg Kelland who had held most of the offices in the English Springer Spaniel Club and whose Nobel prefix had graced one or two Champions and Field Trial Winners. In 1967 the dual-purpose adherents of the Breed were diminished by the loss of three of the greats, MacNab Chassels, Lady Lambe and D. C. Hannah. Lady Lambe's last judging engagement was at Crufts in 1965 and her BoB Winner was a young bitch at virtually her first show. This bitch, Slayleigh Paulina, was a recent acquisition of Judith Hancock's, and the CC was the first of many.

Mrs Gilman Smith took a son of Studley Major, called Rostherne Hunter, back with her to the US after a visit to England in the latter part of the 1950s. He had not done much winning in the UK and was in fact out of a bitch, Rostherne Beauty, who only had a Class II registration, as her mother was unregistered. However, Beauty was, like Major, a grand-daughter of Grand Lodge. Hunter took his Am. Ch. and also his WD qualifier. He sired one or two Champions for the Melilotus kennels, but the most important of the Melilotus stock by him was an uncrowned bitch, M. Hufty Tufty. She was a winner producer, being the dam of Am. Ch Canarch Sunnyside CD whose Champion children and grandchildren are widespread, one of the most well-known being Am. Ch. Chinoes Adamant James, winner of BIS at Westminster two years running. Possibly Hunter's most effective stock was owned by Mrs Henriette Schmidt who successfully incorporated him into her Hillcrest lines. Gingerbread Boy of Hillcrest finished his title, qualified CD and was reasonably good as a stud dog, his Champion progeny reaching double figures.

When Mary Scott acquired Melilotus Shooting Star, the intention had been to mate him to the Bramhope bitches Ch. Bathsheba and her daughter Barnadine, but a misalliance between Barnadine and her son, Black Buster, postponed her litter. However, the daughter from this mating, Blakantan, when mated to Shooting Star, produced Belize of Bramhope, foundation of the Kennersleigh kennels of Margaret Keighley. Belize, in her first litter to Ch. Studley Major, gave the Breed the black-and-white Sh. Ch. Bella Bee of Kennersleigh, the primary foundation of Jean Taylor's Cleavehills. Her next litter, by Major's son Sh. Ch. S Oscar, contained the two Sh. Chs. Drummer Boy, who stayed in the home kennel, and his black and white sister Dulcie, who went to

Cleavehill. Besides Belize, the litter also contained Bunny Hug and Bali-Hi. They, like Belize, were both mated to Studley Oscar, Bunny Hug producing Aust. Ch. Scottann Samson. Bali-Hi founded a minor line for Pam Podd, a Lowestoft vet who had spent her teenage years helping Mary Scott. A grand-daughter of Bali-Hi, Onward Avidity, was the dam of the two litter brothers Sh. Ch. Sotherton Sky Warrior and Ch. and Irish Ch. Sotherton Phantom of Shipden.

When the Barnadine–Shooting Star mating was eventually achieved, one of the bitches it produced, Brandy Sour, went to Alastair Wylie in Scotland and was the dam of several top winners including the BIS Ch. Show winners Sh. Ch. Majeba Mac and Sh. Ch. Lochardils Ghillie of Bramhope. These were by the Alexander of Stubham son, Sh. Ch. Douglas of Freetwood. Another bitch, Bye Bye of B., went to Ernest Froggatt, gaining her title before leaving these shores for Australia. Barnadine's dam, Ch. Bathsheba (a repeat of Ch. Clintonhouse George), in her progeny to Shooting Star, numbered Ch. Blossomtime of B. who went with Margaret and Jeffrey Backhouse to the US and back. She was the dam of Aus. Ch. Majeba Mystery. Brown-ee, although not winning much in the UK, was the dam of Baba of Bramhope (by L. Ghillie), a winner in Finland. At the same time as she bought Baba, Kirsti Örö imported Majeba Maybee. Maybee was from Blossomtime and Majeba Mac. A daughter of Blossomtime by Am. Ch. Dr Primrose of Wakefield, Woodbay Majeba Memory, went to Norman Jenkins, who already owned Ch. Woodbay Gay Charmer, a tricolour Bench and FT Winner. Memory was never bred from.

OBEDIENCE DOGS
Gay Charmer was the dam of Brian Choat's Wyedowns Wild Bryony, winner of over fifty first prizes in Obedience, including an Obedience CC. An unkind remark by a fellow exhibitor about Bryony at one of her early shows led Brian to the Obedience circuit. Sharn was the first of the breed to win the Obedience "Ticket" and is the only bitch to do so, and I was thrilled when Brian mated her to our Ch. Swallowtail. Two of the resulting litter founded two separate families. Otterspool Allouette was the beginning of the late Angela Choat's Wellonhead line that was starting to achieve success as a dual-purpose kennel until Angela's early death. Brian's own O Andromeda followed in her dam's footsteps as an Obedience performer and then produced a winning family of descendants culminating in Sh. Ch. Otterspool Just Jade.

KENNELS OF THE 60s
The first few years of the 1960s saw the foundation of two kennels which are still going strong today and have had a considerable influence on the Breed. The Cleavehills of Jean Taylor have already been mentioned and of similar vintage is the Loweview strain of Colin Jackson. He founded his line on a bitch acquired from Ernie Woodall. Registered as Judy of Loweview she was mated to Douglas of Freetwood, producing Sh. Ch. Cavalier of Loweview, who combined with the Hawkhill lines successfully. Another to come into the breed at this time was Madge Alder who had Lessudden Linnet from Mrs Robin Clarke and made her up. Like Judy of Loweview, her association with Douglas was successful in giving the breed a Champion – Dougal of Truelindale. Dougal first went to Jack Bolton but was later owned by Ernest Froggatt who added his Moorcliff prefix. Madge retained a bitch from this litter, Morag, who, although not reaching the same heights as her brother, did do her share towards the future of the Breed. When mated to Ch. Teesview Titus she gave us the "P" litter which contained Sh. Ch. Teesview Pandora of T., winner of 40 CCs, Ch. Pericles, an important sire and foundation male of Keith Hubbard's Malacou kennel, the CC Winning Poseidon, sire of winners, and German Ch. Pan of T. Petronella who went to the McKnight family. Although Petronella's highest award was a Res. CC, she was the dam of Sh. Ch. Rebecca of Knightward (by Titus). The Ps were a repeat of an earlier litter which had not been

Sh. Ch. Lesudden Linnet.

Sh. Ch. Feorlig Beautiful Memory.

quite so successful in the ring. The middle to late sixties saw the beginnings of several kennels that would be assets to the Breed over the next quarter of a century. Morag Bolton, who later took up her father's Pencloe affix, supplied the foundation stock for the Feorlig kennels of Don and Jenny Miller with Miss Jennifer of Feorlig and then Pencloe Clearway of Feorlig. Miss Jennifer left no stock, but Clearway was usefully combined with Dougal and Lochardil's Ghillie to great effect and, later on, to Hawkhill Connaught. Clearway was by Ch. Pencloe Driftwood from a daughter of Ch. Pencloe Dynamo. These two brothers were by Douglas of Freetwood out of Dalhanna Dew, daughter of Ch. Whaddon Chase Bonny Tom and the top winning Ch. Tillan Toddy. As with most of us, the Feorlig bloodlines incorporated the American imports to some degree or other. Mating Clearway to Sh. Ch. Lochardils Ghillie of Bramhope, brought in Melilotis Shooting Star and produced their first Show Champion, the lovely F. Beautiful Memory. Some Cleavehill-derived outcrosses brought in Shooting Star again, and also Dr. Primrose. Later on, the kennel was fortunate enough to be involved with the litter born to the Hilray pair en route to New Zealand, a black/white bitch F. Rosholl Ebony Emblem, producing the very smart I've Got Pzazz from Feorlig, thus another American line being assimilated into the strain. These influences would appear to have been beneficial, although integration of English and American bloodlines in some other parts of the world do not seem to work.

Beryl Carstairs started her Whitemoor strain with two sisters by Ghillie, Sh. Ch. Lady Caroline of Hortonbank and Whitemoor Contessa of H. Their dam, Lady Jane of H., was a daughter of Sh. Ch. Kennersleigh Drummer Boy out of Black Duchess of Hortonbank. Duchess was by Am. Ch. Dr Primrose out of Beccy of Bramhope, a Melilotus Shooting Star–Bathsheba daughter. Although Ghillie and Drummer Boy were grandsons of Shooting Star, making three lines to him and one to Dr Primrose, all this American blood did not seem to make any difference and the Whitemoors always seemed typically English. Hot on the heels of these two kennels emerged what looks like becoming the most successful UK Springer kennel ever. When a very youthful Frances Bagshawe became the proud owner of one of the Dougal/Paulina litter it was the start of a line that has made its mark worldwide. Commencing with Hawkhill Derby Daydream, the number of CCs won by the Mompessons is incalculable.

US WINNERS

It would be impossible to mention all the many Champions in the US during and after the fifties in view of the different system of judging in force, where the finished Champions do not qualify for Championship points, and of the vast number of dogs that were crowned. One of those whose influence spread beyond his home shores was Am. Can. Ch. Salilyns Macduff, his son Ruleon's

Pal Joey being the sire of the Hilray pair that went to Australia. At home his importance to the breed was mainly via his son, Am. Ch. Salilyn's Inchidony Banquo. Macduff was by King William of S. out of a daughter of Sir Lancelot and was strongly inbred to Rodrique. Banquo was out of S. Cinderella dam of I. Prince Charming. Cinderella, being out of a King Peter bitch, intensified the Rodrique/Nancy lines, especially as her mother, Am. Can. Ch.. Walpride Gay Beauty, brought in four more lines of Rodrique, plus three more of Rufton Breeze.

Three kennels that were linked and are behind many winners, were the Kaintucks of Stuart Johnson, Mrs W. Borie's Wakefields, and the Syringas owned by Mr and Mrs A. Whitaker. The Kaintucks were descended from Beau Geste of Sandblown Acres, the kennel's main stud dog, the bitch lines being various combinations of the Melilotus Champions. The other two strains were very similar in breeding to each other, the Wakefields being based on a Runors Deacon daughter mated to Royal Oak, giving us Am. Ch. Wakefields Fanny. The Syringa line was a reverse cross of this, Oak's sister being put to Deacon. The salient pup from this litter was Am. Ch. Syringa Sue. These two lines were both bred to Kaintuck Chs., Fanny to Christmas Carol, a litter which produced the great W. Black Knight, immortal as the first of the breed to take BIS at Westminster. Sue had two fairly important progeny in her litter by Am. Ch. K. Mark Anthony. Am. Ch. Claudette was the dam of Am. Ch. Doctor Primrose of W. (by Black Knight) eventually to go Australia. Claudette's brother, Am. Ch. S. Disc Jockey, was one of the major sires and was responsible for, among others, the CD award-winning Am. Ch. Canarch Sunnyside, dam of so many winning progeny, not least being the famous Am. Ch. Canarch Inchidony Brook, producer of five Champion sons, including the record-setting Am. Ch. Chinoes Adamant James.

Another Champion to carry the Inchidony prefix and to make a distinct impression on the Breed was Prince Charming. Although he was the only pup in his litter, he turned out to be a prolific sire. His Champion progeny included Salilyn's Aristocrat, Charlyle's Fair Warning, Canarch Inchidony Brook, mentioned above, along with C. I. Sparkler and C. Yankee Patriot from the same litter. His son and daughter, Aristocrat and C. I. Brook, mated together produced Adamant James. Aristocrat also sired S. Colonel's Overlord out of S. Radiance, who carried two lines to Macduff and a line to Kaintuck Mark Anthony. Fair Warning was bred by Charles and Lyle Clement but, after getting his title, he joined the kennel of Ann Pope. While in her ownership he was handled by Laddie Carswell who handled the Kaintucks. On his dam's side Fair Warning was a grandson of the outcross Ch. Banneret's Regal Brigadier, but his bitch line stretched back to 1933 bringing in Ch. Co-pilot of S. A. and Ch. Frejax Royal Minstrel. It was only natural that with the Laddie Carswell connection, Fair Warning should be incorporated into the Kaintuck lines. A bitch in the kennels at the time was Ch. K. Fortune's Huntress, a daughter of Ch. K. Vicar of Wakefield (full brother of Black Knight) and Ch. Fortune's Dorsue Diana of Day. Diana was by S. Disc Jockey out of his half-sister, Ch. Fortune's Lucky Penny, a Christmas Carol daughter out of Syringa Sue. This breeding produced the two Champions, K. Tolstoy and Serendipity. Tolstoy went into the ownership of Ann Pope and was the sire of Ch. K. Heir Apparent.

SHOW SPANIELS IN FIELD TRIALS

During the second half of this decade a rather important and historical event occurred. The gundog breeds had prevailed upon the UK KC to permit the organisation of special Trials at which the "FT qualifier" (now the Show Gundogs Working Certificate) could be competed for. To make these Trials financially viable, the KC further agreed to open up the Trials to First Prize Championship Show Winners. Prior to this the Qualifier had been restricted to CC Winners and was only competed for at recognised Trials with "A" list judges. There were several drawbacks to this system, including the fact that by the time a dog was mature enough to pick up CCs he was probably harder to train and many Show people were hesitant to demonstrate their inexperience in front of the Field Trial set. Another problem was the time and space taken up by the qualifying test, which meant the FT organisers would probably only accept two per Trial. And yet another difficulty was the difference in the Judges' attitudes towards Show dogs, some expecting a much higher standard than others. Accordingly, the Midland Society decided to organise the first of these special qualifying Trials. In this they were joined as equal partners by the Parent Club and also had the support of the London Cocker Club. The trial was open to all the Spaniel sub-group. The objectives of the Trial were to ensure an even standard of judging for each competitor with adequate time to allow for this. The qualifying certificate is a test of the basic working qualities of a gundog (the full details are found in Chapter Three). The organisers were determined that the standard would be as high as possible and no

Moorcliff Dougal pictured after winning SGDW certificate at the first Field day.

"cheap" qualifiers would be obtained. To this end top-class judges were appointed and this first "Show Spaniels Field Day", as it is now popularly known, was judged by John Forbes and John MacQueen Junior, both highly experienced at handling various types of Spaniel and thus eminently suitable to assess the Breeds competing. An advanced test, much on the lines of an Amateur Handlers stake, was also held, but with cold game, judged by the same judges. A novice test with dummies was judged by Miss C. M. Francis. The award for Best Qualifier went to Chipmunk of Stubham owned by Joe Robinson. Among the other dogs to qualify was Ernest Froggatt's Moorcliff Dougal of Truelindale. F. Oughtred Till (Stubham) was Chief Organiser on behalf of the Midland on the day.

THE SPLIT BETWEEN BENCH AND FIELD
In 1966 a decision by the KC to make entry to the following year's Crufts contingent on wins at Championship Shows during the previous year was, albeit unintentionally, to further increase the split between Bench and Field factions throughout the Gundog Group. When Crufts was a two-day affair, Gundog day was traditionally held on the second day of the Show and was the meeting point for gamekeepers and shooting men. Since 1950 Crufts had been held in early February, straight after the shooting season and the opportunity was taken for a bit of relaxation. The Gamekeepers' classes were usually well filled: there would be entries in the FT classes and, in the Breed classes, some of the dogs would be making perhaps their only Show appearance of the year. Many of the dogs were Show-derived and gave a good account of themselves. A lot of the trade stands were geared to game and shooting requirements. Several of the Breed Clubs would hold their AGMs at Crufts and the two sides would meet socially. But, gradually, this tradition faded and in its place came the Game Fair, started in 1958 by the Country Landowners' Association and now renowned world-wide. The Fair is held at a different venue each year in late July. All aspects of country sports and pastimes are catered for and gundogs are especially well looked after with demonstrations and competitions, the premier being the International Team Competition in which combined teams of Spaniels and Retrievers from each of the four UK countries compete against each other. No doubt, if the Rabies problem is ever sorted out and quarantine dispensed with, we could have the exciting prospect of Continental and Scandinavian teams challenging too.

Chapter Eleven

THE INTERNATIONAL ENGLISH SPRINGER

AUSTRALIA AND NEW ZEALAND

By the late 1920s other countries, besides the US, Canada and India, had become interested in importing stock from the United Kingdom. Among these were Australia and New Zealand. In an article written in *Dog World Annual* in 1935, W. Calvert, a canine journalist and authority on Spaniels (he updated the late 1940s edition of Phillips and Cane, *The Sporting Spaniel*) mentions being shown some Australian photographs of quite presentable Springer-type Spaniels, said to be very efficient gundogs and descended from a bitch of an old Norfolk strain taken out in the 1850s. The first recorded exports to have any bearing on the modern Springers were a pair shipped out in the early 1930s. Frank Warner Hill sent Beauchief Bocara (by Buchanan), and Beauchief Belle (by Nocbuccaneer) to C. Little of Tasmania. Bocara was a CC and FT winner prior to leaving home. Melbourne was the destination of Research of Ranscombe, a daughter of Noll of Harting and Regalia of Ranscombe. Research went to Dr Corkhill. A bitch, Joy of the Cairnies, went to another Melbourne doctor, J. Silberberg. She was by FT Ch. Jed of the Cairnies ex Mollies Beanie of Landermere, a daughter of Ch. Nutbrook Boy. Later, Mr F. Fildes brought in a grandson of Ch. Marmion of Marmion, called Cavalier of Gilderbrook. Grandmaster and Gretchen of Gilderbrook were also imported. I think Grandmaster was a Nuthill Dignity son out of Melody's Delight, a bitch carrying two lines to the Little Brand–Withington Kate litter. Delight carried four lines to Rivington Sam and three to Susan of the Cairnies. One of the Gilderbrooks brought in more Ranscombe blood through the litter bred by the "Dagnall" Hollingworths by Marmion out of Render of Ranscombe.

FOUNDATION STOCK

Stock from various combinations of these dogs were the foundations of the main strains in Tasmania, Victoria, New South Wales and New Zealand in the period leading up to World War II. A daughter of the Beauchief pair, Bocara Radiant, sold by Mr Little of Tasmania to Mrs Coyle on the mainland of Australia as foundation bitch for her Wialla kennels, had two litters, the first to Research and the second to Cavalier. A brace from each litter were sent to New Zealand as foundation stock: Regal and Goldilocks of Wialla, by Research, and from the Cavalier litter, Cavalier and Artists Model of Wialla. Apart from these imports from Australia, four Springers from the UK are reported to have gone out around 1930 but, according to Miss Morland Hooper, only two left any stock. These were Dickens of Bourne and Horsford Hummingbird (a daughter of Hetman and H. Handsome). However, the first dog owned by Mrs Colleen Cooper was Troublesome Gun, out of Hummingbird, by a dog called Gun who is shown as "imported in dam". I cannot trace Gun's parentage unless Dickens was female. If Dickens was male I cannot find any mention of anything by him. At this time a dog went out from Joe Greatorex named Corndean Merrilegs and Mrs Cooper used him on Hummingbird. A daughter from this litter, called Bridget Adair, gave Mrs Cooper a breeding pair, putting the Sandhurst line on the drawing board. Mating her to Troublesome Gun, a black and white, gave her Lonesome of Sandhurst in the first litter and in the second, Solitaire, who took his Bench Championship easily and had come within one point of his FT Ch. when World War II broke out.

Prior to this, Major Hunter Blair had returned from England accompanied by Rajah of Broomhouse, a son of the Eng. FT Ch. & Am. Dual Ch. Tedwyns Trex, and bred by Miss K. M. Ogilvie of the Holefield Springers. Probably the most important result of this importation was his daughter, Ranee of Sandhurst, bred by Mrs Cooper out of Lonesome. Mrs Cooper was a dominant force in Springers in New Zealand for many years, both at Trials and Shows. I think she was the first lady to train and handle her own dogs at Field Trials, although Mrs Patience Badenach Nicholson in Scotland and Mrs P. D. Armour in the US later emulated her. One of Mrs Cooper's Australian dogs, Regal of Wialla, was later sold, together with Penelope of Sandhurst, to Mrs Helen Sapio, marking the beginning of the Cruchfield kennels. Another bitch that Mrs Cooper had from Mrs Coyle was Wilma of Wialla, by Cavalier of Gilderbrook out of Golda of Wialla, a daughter of Stylish Buster (an import that seems to have by-passed the record books) out of B. Radiant.

Two others to have an influence after arriving in New Zealand in the late thirties were the English FT Winner Whelford Trump (by FT Ch. Don O'Vara out of Whelford Nancy, a daughter of FT Ch. Banchory Boy) and Anthony of Somersby, bred by Dick Sharpe the writer of *Dog Training for Amateurs*. Ranee mated to Trump gave Penelope. At the end of the War the Australian and New Zealand lines were still based on the pre-war imports. These were – apart from the original Ranscombe, Cairnies, Beauchief and Gilderbrook dogs to Australia – a pair of O'Varas, Slice and Strike, and FT Ch. Whelford Trump, imported from Captain Holford immediately pre-war, together with Anthony of Somersby into New Zealand. Trump was born in 1935 and was by Don O'Vara, so it can be seen the lines were predominantly Field Trial-based. Slice O'Vara went to the Brackenfield kennels and Strike was the foundation sire of the Dalkeys combined with stock from Mrs Cooper and Mrs Sapio. Brackenfield Dandyboy (by Strike) is behind some of the winning Australian dogs.

POST-WAR STOCK

Some of the early Springers to win at shows in the immediate post-war period were descendants of Wialla stock. Others were New Zealand dogs that had been brought over, and yet more came from the Sandra kennels of L. Pavey. The Sandra lines were based on Research of Ranscombe and the original Beauchief pair sent to Tasmania and so they probably carried less of the FT blood than some of their contemporaries, although the well-known stud dog Sandra Flash was by B. Dandyboy. The Mowbray kennels of Mrs Hale were started with a bitch called Sandra Jane bought from Mr Pavey; later, a dog called Cruchfield Kiwa was acquired from Helen Sapio. A daughter of these two, M Viva, was put to the black-and-white import of Helen Sapio's Higham Tobit, who had won Res. CC and FT awards in England. The result was mated back to her grandsire C Kiwa, and a bitch from this litter, M Chiquita, went to found the Casa Perez strain.

In 1947 the first post-war import was to be another Trial-bred Springer, Whittlemoor Flicker. She was dam of Dual Champions Curtsey George and C. Chiquita. George was by Rasil of Romford and Chiquita by Ranger of Rathlea (Garry of Gilderbrook–Roma of Romford). Flicker was owned by Dr M. Wilson, who took her to Australia with him. Then, on a visit home to the UK in the fifties, he brought George with him, but subsequently decided not to subject the dog to the

Aust. Dual Ch. Curtsey George.

NZ Dual Ch. Camden Ros-N-Van.

long journey back to Australia, so George remained in the care of Dorothy Hooper, siring one or two litters in the UK. The brother of Ranger of Rathlea, Aus. Ch. Rathlea Larry, was the foundation sire of the Kurramana lines of Mr and Mrs Norman Vanner. Larry and Ranger were born in 1948.

Mrs Sapio had bred from the original pair she had bought from Mrs Cooper, producing NZ Ch. Puni Maiden of Cruchfield. She imported into New Zealand several dogs from England during the late 1940s, including Strathblane Renown and Warspite (both by Hood of Horsford), Sir Echo of Chastleton, and Higham Tobit (by Ch. Whaddon Chase Prince out of a Replica of Ranscombe daughter).

Just after this, Aus. Ch. Winch Pyrites – also by Replica – was imported by Miss Lorne Hood of Victoria. Miss Hood had grown up with her father's gundogs, many of them Springers. She had visited the UK in pre-war days and regretted not buying a Springer on her first trip. After the war she purchased a dog from the Sandra kennels of L. Pavey – a good worker, but not top flight show-wise. A second visit to England, in 1948, was accompanied by a determination to take back a Springer. A visit to Crufts led her in the direction of the Ranscombes, mainly because of their beautiful heads. Miss Hooper had nothing to sell but suggested the Winch kennels. The result was the purchase of Pyrites (Peggy to her friends), who arrived Down Under in 1950.

After making Peggy up, Miss Hood decided she needed a suitable mate for her. Winch Garnet (Sam) was selected and sent out by Dan and Grace Crawford. Unfortunately tragedy struck and, on the day Sam embarked for his new home, Peggy died of cancer. Sam duly arrived after his long sea journey but, unluckily, it had taken its toll and his temperament suffered. He arrived in a very nervous condition, although it improved enough for him to get his title. Apart from these two Champions, Miss Hood bred seven others. Mrs Cooper had built up her Sandhurst strain in New Zealand to a high standard, both in Bench and Trial spheres. She had also successfully developed an interest in obedience circles, writing a book on the subject. This is just a roundabout way of saying that, in the fifties, she imported NZ Ch. Charlemagne of Stubham from Kay Till, and Charlie features as model in the photographs for that book! Mrs Cooper also brought over Jonathon of Stubham.

Major Horsbrough took one or two dogs with him when he emigrated to New Zealand, one of which – Strathblane Garganey, by FT Ch. Nobel Nadir out of S Pintail – appears in the Australian lines of the time. Miss Hood used him on Pyrites to breed one of her Lorne litters. Other imports were FT Ch. Pinehawk Prince and Winch Garnet (mentioned above) by Boxer. The Romford line, bred from Research of Ranscombe and Judy of the Cairnies, through the above-mentioned brother and sister, Rasil and Roma, had an influence on the breed, in conjunction with B. Dandyboy and others. Lorne Jennifer from the Garganey–Pyrites litter went to the Vanners and, as well as Rathlea Larry, she also had a litter by Winch Garnet.

Up to now the Boxer influence was not felt in Australia, as Winch Garnet was out of a bitch line-bred to the Ranscombes and consequently, when used with the stock already in Australia, he strengthened the Ranscombe blood. There was also a Bramhope bitch, Bessie, who had arrived in whelp to Boxer and, I believe, stock from this litter were incorporated with some Cruchfield blood to found the Edenfield lines. But this second generation Boxer progeny had nothing like the impact that Boxer had made in England. The result was that the breed as a whole had a dual-purpose/working base – mostly good, sound, typical, honest Springers, but lacking the glamour to progress very far in the group competitions. I do not think any stock from either Charlemagne or Jonathon found its way from New Zealand. The importer of Bessie also imported a son of Ch. Invader of Ide, but, again, he does not seem to have made much of an impression.

LATE 50s AND EARLY 60s
These were the bloodlines new breeders had to found their kennels on in the late fifties and early sixties and both the Karroola kennels of Graham and Val Coulter and the Cranlochs of John and Lily Tulloch, both domiciled in Victoria, carried them. Mrs Sapio had moved to Queensland from New Zealand and, probably, the next new blood to arrive in Australia was her import from the US, Am. Ch. Dr Primrose of Wakefield. A black-and-white, he had served his quarantine in England and spent some time there before continuing his journey. He sired one or two litters while in the UK, but did not really seem to suit the English bloodlines.

Other imports from the UK at about this time included Helen Sapio's bitch Majeba Mystery by Eng. Sh. Ch. Colmaris Bonny Lad out of Eng. Ch. Blossomtime of Bramhope. Another to go out was Aus. Ch. Scottann Samson. His breeder, Ann Penny (née Beattie), sometimes handled the Bramhopes and, naturally, had a Bramhope bitch. This bitch, Bunnyhug of B. was, like Blossomtime, a daughter of M. Shooting Star. Samson was by Eng. Sh. Ch. Studley Oscar, a Studley Major son. Samson sired several titled offspring mainly for the Tallawalla (Jarvisto) kennels out of their foundation, Aus. Ch. Casa Perez Chestnut Teal, bred by Mrs Linsen-Perez.

Mrs Linsen-Perez had mated her Mowbray Chiquita to M Emperor, a half-brother, and their daughter, C P Juanita, produced Chestnut Teal by Aus. Ch. Lorne Lucky Star. A younger sister of Teal, Aus. Ch. C P Lady Syringa, was put to Dr Primrose and a daughter from this, Aus. Ch. C P Perla Negra, was later mated to another American import, Aus. and NZ Ch. Hilray's Avant Garde who was imported in the mid-seventies by Rosalind Holland of the Adroch kennels in New South Wales. With him came his three-quarter sister Aus. Ch. Hilray's Aurora. They were by Ruleon's Pal Joey out of different daughters of Salilyn's King Hi. This pair had an accidental litter while they were in quarantine and left a legacy through their daughter, Rosholl Ebony Emblem, to the Feorlig kennels.

Dr Primrose was heavily marked and bred through the Kaintuck and Syringa lines to the Green Valley and Melilotus strains. The Hilray pair were very strong in the Salilyn's stock but, surprisingly, were comparatively lightly marked and probably would have been out of place back home at a time when the stylised saddle-backed marking and the sharply defined trimming of the saddle was becoming the norm.

Samson was used to good effect on Majeba Mystery, producing the Drembrook litter, among them being Aus. Ch. Drembrook True Jade, who produced stock by Avant Garde and Ch.

*Am. Ch.
Primrose of
Wakefield.*

Tallawalla Brigadier. Her sister Amethyst was the foundation of the Darrajem strain. Among her litters were those by Australian Special Edition of Cleavehill and Ch. Maidenvak Sabuesco CD, who was by Eng. Sh. Ch. and Aus. Ch. Moorcliff Freetwood Gamecock ex Ch. Casa Perez Doña Minerva. A Samson–Mystery daughter mated to Dr Primrose produced Aus. Ch. Cruchfield the Squire.

IMPORTANT NEW IMPORTS

There were two importations in the late 1960s that really brought the breed in Australia into line with the UK. These were the pair from Ernest Froggatt, Eng. Sh. Ch. Moorcliff Freetwood Gamecock and Moorcliff Pintail, who went out in whelp to Ch. Moorcliff Dougal of Trulindale. The litter was born on the boat and are sometimes shown as imports, but nowadays, when everything is sent by air, these puppies would have been born in quarantine and shown as "imported in dam" (i i d).

Pintail was by Sh. Ch. Moorcliff Keeper, whose sire was by Ch. Studley Major and whose dam, Moorcliff Suzette, was a daughter of Ch. Bramhope Recorder and Sh. Ch. Sandylands Secret. The maternal grandsire of Pintail (Moorcliff Gamelad) was by Am. Ch. Melilotus Shooting Star out of M Suzette. Gamecock and Dougal were both by the Alexander of Stubham son, Douglas of Freetwood (Gamecock was actually a father/daughter mating on Douglas), who carried Boxer and Sandylands blood through his dam. Dougal's dam, Lessudden Linnet, carried no less than seven lines to Boxer through such sires as Ch. Irish. Ch. Print of Ardrick, Sh. Ch. Studley Brave Buccaneer, Ch. Peter of Lorton Fell and others. Linnet was a double grand-daughter of Conneil owned by Connie and Neil Crawford, she being by Neil's Boxer son Birselees Beacon out of Moorcliff Morack, a Sandylands Secret daughter by Peter of L. F. These were an entirely new set of bloodlines bringing in the Bramhope influence and, through the Sandylands, the Shotton blood which had not previously reached the Antipodes. Pintail and Gamecock went to Adelaide in the ownership of Mr Nelson, and one of the daughters of the Dougal litter was purchased by Mr and Mrs Tulloch. This bitch, Aus. Ch. Oak Sprig of Heather, set their kennel on the road to success and, mated to Gamecock, produced four Champions in her first litter. The sister of Pintail, Sh. Ch. Moorcliff Wigeon, went out to Helen Sapio in 1967.

Another kennel to start with progeny from Pintail was the Hampshires of Mrs Rita Ogilvie. She had imported Teesview Tyrone, a double grandson of Ch. Teesview Titus. His dam, T. Majeba Meliza, was out of Blossomtime of Bramhope and was a half-sister of Mrs Sapio's M. Mystery.

The late Mrs Esme Westbrook, one of the founder members of the NSW English Springer Spaniel Association, was another to achieve success with a bitch from the Oak stock, Ch. O. Game Law, by Gamecock out of Pintail. By mating Law back to Gamecock several Champions with the Crawney label were produced. Mrs Westwood was honoured by the Association by being invited to be a judge for their first Club function to promote the Breed, held in conjunction with an All Breeds Show, during their two-year "gestation period" prior to their acceptance for affiliation to the Royal Australian State Kennel Control in October 1971.

It was fortunate for the breed that many of the people taking an interest at this time were young, and so they are still actively breeding and either showing or working their dogs today. They include Mr and Mrs D. Cheetham, Tees (originally Bardenvale), of Queensland, John and May Peters, Drumhill, NSW, Mrs Linsen-Perez, sole surviving founder members of the NSW Ass., Peter Cousins, Equity, of QLD, Mr and Mrs Hank Dobrowolski, Briarknoll, formerly of QLD but now NSW, Mr and Mrs J. McNeill, Inniskilling, NSW, Diane Seymour, Stephdie, NSW, Kevin Farmer, Oakspur, QLD, David and Stephanie Rickard, Wongan, of Victoria and Phil and Marie Merchant née Forrester, Clanach, of South Australia. Another who was involved at this time and, although no longer active in the breed, still retains a strong connection through his daughter and two sons, is Brian Keely of NSW. Most of these breeders had stock from the Oak litters and some of them later imported stock that was germane to these bloodlines or brought in some outcross blood.

UPGRADING THE BENCH LINES
By the middle of the 1970s the Australian bench lines were needing a further influx of fresh stock. In 1975 Stephanie Rickard imported the two Connaught youngsters, Mompesson Midsummer Lad and Monclare Sugar'N'Spice. She also imported Hawkhill Crepello, by Sh. Ch. Cavalier of Loweview out of a Connaught daughter, Hawkhill Milly Moss. Spice was out of the Cavalier bitch M. Chantilly Lace so these two were similarly bred. Another import to join the Wongan Kennels was Eng. Sh. Ch. Mompesson Sleeping Partner, a daughter of my Ch. Swallowtail and the lovely Derby Daydream. Sleepy did not make any impression herself, but a great grand-daughter of hers would produce a litter that had a great influence on the breed a decade later.

Chantilly Lace was the dam of a litter that produced three Springers that feature prominently in the modern Australian lines. Eng. Sh. Ch. Monclare Jennifer Eccles, when mated to the brother of Milly Moss, H. Mon Fils, produced Chasmar Charlie, who was for a time in South Africa, and Chasmar Penny Farthing of Moorcliff (Aus. Ch. and Eng. Sh. Ch.). The latter was imported by John and May Peters, and went out in whelp to Eng. Sh. Ch. Thornlea Cascade, a son of Con, but with some useful bloodlines through his dam Inverruel Lyric. The brother to Spice and Jennifer, Mr Chips, would show his influence later on through his son.

Further imports of the late 70s and early 80s were Cleavehill Morning Post by Peter Cousins; the Cheethams brought in Cleavehill Heilan Eriskay; both dogs gained their titles. Diane Seymour imported Marshring Invincible, a great grandson of Con on his topline, the rest of his pedigree containing much outcross breeding, bringing in Stokeley, Teesview, Cleavehill, Woodbay and Brandyhole lines. There were also Special Edition of Cleavehill, Cleavehill Pink Panther, and Cleavehill Heather Cream. Special Edition also carried Con blood. Heather Cream went to Diane Seymour and went out in pup to Frenchgate Marcus, a Teesview Titus son, who was the grandsire of Invincible. A further Hilray dog, Meritorious, had been imported to New Zealand from the US and stock descended from him found its way to Australia. Phil McNally's employment took him to the US and Cranloch Camora went with him and, as is standard practice, had to return via the UK and do the requisite quarantine, after which she was mated to the Crufts BOB winner, Freeway

Indian Summer, a son of Cleavehill Acorn, and grandson of Cleavehill Titus Oates through his dam F. Anastasia. Camora produced two Champions in this litter, Windmere Summer Knight and Summer Breeze.

John Peters also imported Eng. Ch. Moorcliff Kalico and made him up. He was by the brother of Crepello, Hawkhill Blakeney. The Keely family purchased a young black-and-white from us, Shipden Vienna Song. He carried three lines to the Swallowtail–Derby Daydream litter, his sire Cherrybeck Winter Swallow being by Swallowtail out of a daughter of Mon Fils and Sleeping Partner. Mr and Mrs Bill Hinds imported a young dog from Eire by the Eng. and Ir. Ch. Remington Rocking Redwing out of Ir. Ch. Cleavehill Vanity Fair. These imports all helped to raise the standard of the breed, especially when combined with the Gamecock/Pintail lines. Spice did produce two Champions to Midsummer Lad, but she was infinitely more successful when combined with Marie Merchant's Clanarch Argyle Tartan.

FIELD TRIALS IN AUSTRALIA

The Australian Field Trial scene is somewhat different to other countries in that, instead of having separate Trials for Spaniels, they compete against the Retrievers, in the Spaniel and Retriever Trials. They are run on a rough shooting basis, using live game, and the handlers shoot their own game. Another difference to other systems is that there is only one judge. This is in comparison to the two judges, and separate guns, of the UK trials where the dogs are worked in pairs similar to a driven shoot, or the planted birds which are used in some US trials. Some of the Game laws in some of the Australian states are strict and for nearly two decades trials in NSW were severely restricted. The season is also very short (July and August). The few trials that were organised during the 70s were held using released game and resulted in two Springers getting their FT Ch. titles, the bitch Glenmazeran Heather, and Demoka Daniel. Both these were from show lines and were NSW dogs.

There are also Retrieving Trials which are open to all gundog breeds, although in the early days they did not attract too much in the way of Springer competition. One who did take the plunge successfully was Don Livingstone, of the Tulgiva kennels, with Ch. Casa Perez Favor. These Retrieving Trials are basically cold game tests. Victoria was the only state to have been regularly running trials for over thirty years. The two Curtsey Dual Champions won their FT titles at the Victorian KCC trials in the fifties, as did FT Ch. Pinehawk Prince. The NSW trials only started in earnest in 1973, with the Queensland trials being of a similar vintage. Supporters of the breed in Queensland were Kevin Farmer, Oakspur, and Peter Cousins, Equity, and, of the two NSW FT Champions of the 70s, Heather was by an Equity dog and Daniel owned an Oakspur dam.

During the early 80s interest in trials picked up and the breed began to challenge the ubiquitous Labradors. This was due, in no small measure, to the efforts of two ladies and their UK imports. Rachel Greaves, of the Wrangham kennels in Victoria, brought in the bitch Cuchullin Beag in 1976, and, of very much more importance, the dog Bellever Raffleson in 1979. A winner at Trials in the UK, Raffleson was bred by Rupert Hill and, as his name implies, was by FT Ch. Crowhill Raffles, his dam being FT Ch. Nell of Bellever. These two, in their first litter (1979), produced three trials Champions – Wrangham Sradag Beag getting her FT title and her brother, W Urusig, becoming Retrieving T Ch. as well as qualifying CD in obedience. Number three did rather better – W Faolan Ban added FT Ch., Ret. Ch. and CD to his name; he also proved a good sire, having seven FT Ch. progeny. Urusig went up-country to Amand Golle of Queensland, and trials are not so regularly held there. Their 1980 litter contained FT Ch. W Tannasg Ban (male), and in 1982 they produced the bitch FT Ch. W Cuilean Beag. Two more imports arrived in Australia that year, Crowhill Floss to Rachel Greaves, and Kirtdon Minstrel to Linley Fox-Cumming of NSW. Prior to this, in 1978 T. Carter of Tasmania had brought over Pinehawk Jim. These five Springers, used in conjunction with each other, did much the same job of up-grading the working lines as the Moorcliff Dougal/Pintail progeny and Gamecock had done for the show lines.

In 1986 a further influx arrived when three from the same litter, bred by Tim Healey, were imported, a dog and a bitch by Rachel Greaves, Glencaol Farway Rory and G F Sine. Their sister G F Sari went to J. Cole of NSW. Another addition to the breeding stock was made in 1990 when Linley Fox-Cumming brought in Gelli Goch Tessa in pup to the prolific sire, Eng. FT Ch. Cortman Lane. Lane carried the same blood-lines as Raffleson and Floss. I mentioned earlier, when detailing the influence of the Monclare Chantilly Lace litter by Con on the Australian stock of the late seventies, that a dog from the litter would also have an effect on the breed later on. I also indicated that Sleeping Partner would provide an important influence through her great grand-daughter. Ch. Swallowtail's last litter was out of his grand-daughter Hawkhill Sleepytime (Mon Fils/Sleeping Partner) and a bitch from this, Cherrybeck Crackling Rose, was the dam of the last litter by Connaught. Their daughter, retained by Judith Hancock, Hawkhill One in a Million, was later purchased by Phil and Marie Merchant in 1984, and was mated to Genghis Khan (which is where the Monclare Mr Chips connection comes in) prior to embarkation. The result must have been gratifying to the Merchants, for the litter contained the four Champions, Clanarch Union Jack, British Raj, Rule Britannia, and the outstanding C Wrath O'Khan, who was co-owned with the Rickards, who campaigned him to many outstanding wins. This litter combined well with previous imports and Wrath O'Khan proved as good a sire as show dog, especially when combined with the Crepello, Midsummer Lad and Spice progeny. Strangely enough the wheel has now completed a full circuit and stock from the Clanarch lines are now finding their way back to the UK and Norway. At the time of writing, the Mompesson kennel have in quarantine a Clanarch import, by Aus. Ch. C. Union Jack, a litter brother to C. Wrath O'Khan, and Ann Buvik in Norway has imported Alhambra Larry Olivier, also by U. Jack, out of a daughter of Ch. Aus. Ch. Bomaris Envoy to Shipden and Aus. Ch. Wongan Dynasty, a W. O'Khan daughter. These lines have already had an effect in New Zealand and South Africa.

SOUTH AFRICA

Whilst the Australian breeders in the 1950s and early to mid 60s were still relying on the older bloodlines that had gone out before the Suez Canal was closed, making the journey twice the length, the breeders in Southern Africa were able to import stock from the top winning English kennels and improve their show lines. Mrs Penny, breeder of the Renfrew Springers, who had moved from South Africa to Salisbury, Southern Rhodesia, imported Studley Hussar of R. from May Smithson, and Diamond of Stubham of R. from Kay Till. Hussar was by the Boxer son, Sh. Ch. Banker of Bramhope, out of Studley Flamingo (Alexander of S. ex Studley Bernadette – litter sister to Brave Buccaneer). Diamond was a daughter of Alexander and Anita of Ruro (Ch. Clintonhouse George ex Ch. Dinah of Stubham who was one of the many repeats of the Boxer/Susan matings). Hussar and Diamond both gained their South African and Rhodesian titles.

One of the pups from this brace, Kim of Renfrew, was purchased by Mr and Mrs Harry Foden, also of Salisbury, and he too attained the double Ch. The Fodens also imported Janey of Stubham: needless to say she became Ch (S. Af.) and Ch (Rho). Her breeding was obviously selected to suit Kim, her sire being younger brother of Flamingo, and her dam Candida of Cloudbrook was by Alexander out of Nanette of Stubham. At the time Kim was the only English Springer to go BIS all breeds under South Africa Kennel Union rules, and Janey was the only ESS bitch to take BOS awards at all breeds under the same rules. Their son, Ch. (S. Af.) Rannerdale Breck rather upstaged them by taking his title at his first four consecutive shows beating his parents for BOB each time, and also taking BPIS at three of the shows. Unfortunately, the uncertain political situation and the eventual emergence of Rhodesia as an independent nation put an end to canine affairs for a period and the Fodens returned to live in the North of England, at one time showing a Hawkhill Springer.

After a lull, following the imports of the late fifties and early sixties, a more settled period ensued and some fresh stock was imported. In 1973 the Veritys imported Cleavehill Highland Magic, followed the next year by Cleavehill Trace of Gold. These two produced a brace of Champions: Wharfedale Simon and Wharfedale Mist, and later came Carry on Talking of Cleavehill. A son of Mist, Wharfedale Its Magic, also became a Champion. The Sirlands kennel of Geoff and Karen Finney had been around for some years, starting with a working line which they combined with Belinda Rourke's Bonfire of Tullamore a couple of times. Two of the second litter were made up, S Brut and S Youthdew. Brut went as the first

S. Afr. Ch. Alresford First Tri.

show dog of Bob Barnett and his wife, while Youthdew remained in the home kennel. After making up Brut the Barnetts bought in another dog, Keresley Avenger, to which they added their affix of Alresford. Avenger was bred by Mr and Mrs Symonds from their imported foundation bitch Knightward Strawberry Fair (Cleavehill Huckleberry Finn ex Petronella of Truelindale). The sire was also an import, Chasmar Charlie, another of the Hawkhill Mon Fils – Monclare Jennifer Eccles litter. The Barnetts later imported Cleavehill Dorothy Brown as a mate for Avenger. Two Champions were produced from the resultant litter, Alresford First Tri and A Sweet Potato.

Chasmar Charlie had gone out with his owner Bill White, who had emigrated, and he later imported Robil Laura Ashley. These two bred a pair of Champions: a dog, Whyteleaf Wide Boy, and a bitch. When Bill White returned to the UK he brought back both parents and their daughter. The Veritys mated Youthdew to Avenger twice and produced top winning Champions in both litters. In the mid-eighties Ardencote Adventurer went out to the Tullamore kennels and gained his his title. In 1991 Joan Whittingham imported Wongan Moody Blues from Australia. He was from the first litter by Eng./Aus. Ch. Bomaris Envoy to Shipden out of Aus. Ch. Wongan Dynasty. The South African lines now look to be firmly based on most of the best UK lines, and should make progress.

SWEDEN

Those litters from Invincible George and Graceful Greta in the 1940s were helpful in establishing the breed in Scandinavia. A quarter of a century after Eudore Chevrier had been instrumental in taking fresh bloodlines to North America, Stig Onnerfelt, who could be considered to be his Swedish counterpart, did the same for the Nordic countries. Onnerfelt was generally recognised as the founding father of the modern English Springer in Sweden and thus an influence on Scandinavian Springers in general. In the earlier years the working Spaniels were mostly of

Am. Ch. Timpanagos Adonis (exported to Sweden).

UK. Sh. Sh. Fin. Sh. Ch. Mompesson Special Dream

German origin and, like the Continental dogs, they were prone to give tongue while tracking the game, basically working more like hounds. Stig Onnerfelt wanted something that would work on birds in proper Spaniel fashion and, through contact with Bert Lloyd (of Ware), brought in some Springers from England. These were: Miss Greta of Ware (exported by H. S. Lloyd but bred by D. C. Hannah, Stokeley) and with Carnfield Craftsman, her cousin, bred by George Taylor.

In 1947 Onnerfelt imported two Springers from the US, Am. Ch. Timpanagos Adonis (by Showman of Shotton ex a Rufton Recorder daughter) and Timpanagos Anita (a double granddaughter of Recorder). The English dogs brought in, through Dry Toast and Higham Tomtit, the Marmion of Marmion blood not generally found in the American lines. Craftsman died at the age of twelve months but, fortunately, he did sire one litter to Anita which contained the first post-war Swedish bred Champion – Sport av Bjerkefall. In 1953, Am Can. Ch. Frejax Royal Minstrel, a black and white son of the great F Royal Salute, was imported together with his half-sister, Frejax Royal Suzette. Later, Onnerfelt also owned Norw. Ch. Petersborgs Peggy, a daughter of Eng. Norw. Ch. Sandylands Showgirl (imported in whelp to Eng. Ch. Sandylands Shrubby). Peggy thus carried three lines of Showman.

All the Swedish-bred Champions of the 1950s descend from various combinations of these half-dozen dogs. Showgirl was imported by the Petersborg Cocker kennel of Oslo. The first Swedish FT Ch. was out of Peggy, by Royal Minstrel. This bitch, FT Ch. Penelope av Bjerkefall, was later mated to Swe. Ch. Garr av Bjerkefall, an Adonis son out of Greta. The result was the first Dual Champion in Sweden, Pelsös Don. It is interesting to note that, at a time when the breed as a whole was developing a schism between the Bench and Trial sides, a Dual Ch. should be bred from a combination of pure Show lines from America and England. Prior to this, the breed was very scarce in Scandinavia and any Springers were likely to be from European sources. There were some earlier English imports but I have been unable to trace any records for these in Sweden.

FINLAND

In Finland, however, the first breeder as such was Väinö Donner, who founded his Woollen Mill kennels in 1923 with a pair of Ruftons – Kid and Curley. He continued breeding through the twenties, but any further details concerning his activities are unavailable. The family of my friend,

Kalle Örö, had imported a dog from England in 1931 but the details of Jack's pedigree and breeder were lost when the family home was destroyed during the War.

IMPORTANT SCANDINAVIAN IMPORTS

In 1974 a further influx of American blood was imported into Scandinavia. This was through Can. Ch. Salilyn's Passkey, a son of the back to back Westminster BIS winner, Am. Ch. Chinoe's Adamant James, bred by Karen Pricket from Loujon Amy, a combination of Salilyns and Wakefields bloodlines. With Passkey came Salilyns Electra, a daughter of Am. Ch. Salilyns Colonel's Overlord bred by Julia Gasow. This pair were bought by Berit Kauppinen of Finland. She bred Americano of Finnline from this pair and he had some influence on the stock at the time.

In the 60s and 70s several imports from the UK had gone across to the Scandinavian countries. Marianne Ahrenbech had taken the previously mentioned Ambridge Bystander of Stubham, to Sweden. Fru Ahrenbech was the owner of Bårrings Fifi, by Dual Ch. Pelsös Don out of Ch. Gavotte av Bjerkefall, her affix was av Börsesjö. As well as Fifi she also owned Petersborgs Lady, one of the import litter from Sandylands Showgirl. Other imports by Fru Ahrenbech were, Wollburn Windjammer, Int. Nord. Ch. Carwinley Copper Coin (later to go to Finland) and Int. Nord. Ch. Whaddon Chase Storm. The Mustela lines of Baroness Hermelin were strongly linked with those of Fru Ahrenbech, her early stock coming from Fifi and Bystander, and a daughter of Copper Coin and My Fair Lady av Börsesjö (Bystander ex Petersborgs Lady). Sigrund Wallquist took over many and incorporated them into her Brigadoon kennel, which she had founded on Northdown Donnetta, a daughter of Ch. Northdown Donna and Stokeley Sea Sprite. Her first litter was by P. Don and produced five Champions. Next came Larkstoke Capercaillie who went out in whelp to Higham Ted. She was followed by numerous Woodbays, and the Woodbay affix passed to the Wallquist family on the death of Mrs Sherwood.

The many imports later from the Cleavehill kennel by Frank Bjerklund and Terje Johnsen of the Inu-Goya kennels in Norway, and Kristina Korhonen (Pygmalia's) and Margareta Nyström-Paulin (av Simmatorp) in Sweden, blended in with Teesview and Cliffhill stock that had also gone out. The Inu-Goya kennel had imported Teesview Tycoon of Lynsett, but acquired Travis Aelia from Kari Haave when she moved to Sweden. Aelia was from a litter born to Silveroak Ysenne, imported in whelp to UK Ch. Cliffhill Julius. Ysenne later went to the Hey-La Cocker kennels as foundation. Another influential import that Fru Haave made was Cliffhill Huggy Bear. Some Hawkhill and Mompesson dogs also found their way across: Mompesson Fisherman (Lochardils Ghillie–Derby Daydream) had quite an influence, as did Crepello of Classicway (Sh. Ch. Teesview Twister–Sh. Ch. Hawkhill Riding Low). There were also one or two Inverruel-derived imports.

THE EUROPEAN SCENE

With regard to the European mainland, it has been difficult to pick up a definite pattern of imports and breeding trends since the Second World War. In the late forties or early fifties M Jean Trubert of Paris imported a dog and bitch of Totonian breeding. These were Fr. Ch. Xam and Xamia. He also imported the trial winner Higham Thimble. From these he founded the Du Haguedick line which were still a dual-purpose line prominent two decades later. A daughter of Xam and Thimble, Brunette Du Haguedick, was owned by Mme Alexis Blot (maiden name Guinand), who had imported Fr. and Lux. Ch. Babillard of Bramhope, and had the de Ternay dual-purpose line. Amongst the early Dutch imports from the UK was Winch Crocidolite who was, I believe, the first of the imports to get his Dutch title. He went out in the late 1950s, having sired several winners in the UK, one of which was Ch. Winch Starturn. At about this period the top winner, Winch Topaz (a son of Boxer) went to France.

In the early sixties three of the progeny from a litter by Ch. Hyperion of Stubham ex Ch. Brandyhole Diadem were exported to France to the brother and sister partnership of M Milleret and Mme Bigot, of the Springtower affix. B. Happy Returns gained his Dutch title as well as winning CACs and CACIBs in France and Belgium. He went as replacement for his brother Hadji, who died at an early age after winning one CACIB and four CACs and before he was due to run for his working certificate. Their sister, Harmony, won several CACs and CACIBs. Another from the litter, Highlight, went to Italy. The Springtower kennel housed both bench and trial winners, their Eddie de Vetoise siring top winners in both disciplines in the forepart of the 1960s.

SWITZERLAND
Brandyhole Good News, from a previous litter, went to Switzerland. In the fifties Frau Luise Richei had imported stock from Sandy Davies' Colmaris kennel, while Leonie Bernhauser founded her Windrush kennels with an Irish-bred bitch from Anna Redlich which eventually became Swiss Ch. Stream Nymph of Strathfoyle. Later, in 1969, Sw. Ch. Larkstoke Waxwing went to Frau Bernhauser.

HOLLAND
Imports to Holland during the sixties make interesting reading. They include the two Mortondawns, Hawk and French Fern, Larkstoke Sarcelle who gained her title as well as winning CACs and CACIBs in other continental countries, Winch Kernite, Corrlough Carry from Ireland and two from rather further afield – the US-bred Waiterock California Pancho and the Australian bitch Casa Perez Alteña. Following these came Gaudins Jester, a combination of Larkstoke and Field Trial blood and one or two of my breeding. One of the latter was owned by Dik Galjaard, who is still exhibiting at the present time, as is Anton Viergever, owner of Sarcelle.

Norfolk's Moby Dick: Imported from the UK to Holland.

FRANCE

The late M Gilbert Thorp was the President of the French Spaniel Club and their Club Championship Shows used to be held at his country estate, Le Rouge-Pommier, at Bouafles, south of Rouen. He imported Int. Ch. Larkstoke Nuthatch around 1970, and later on Thornlea Golden Dawn from George Leckie. Prior to this M. Thorp had imported Bracken of Bramhope. Mme Sainson founded her de la Tour du Bon L'il line with the Stud dog Bedouin of Bramhope. Her famous Int. Ch. Lamy was by him. She also imported Kennersleigh Beefeater.

Others to go France in the seventies were: French Ch. Cliffhill Gareth (M Moles); Novacroft Freestar Forest Ranger (M Bayles); Fenway Speculator (Mme Sainson); French Ch. Silveroak Sir Brandelles (Mlle Yvette Chavernac); French Ch. Silveroak Octavia (M Jean Valery); Rocket of Larkstoke (Mme Guinand, later owned by M. Sorin); Valtos Amorello Lisa (M. Valery); Sh. Ch. Cleavehill Harvest Gold (M Dath); Cleavehill Morag (M. LeBrun) and the English FT winner Peat Inn of Pinewarren (M. DeVilder), a black-and-white who had won the FT class at the English Breed Parent Club's Championship Show and went on to win a CAC and CACIT in his adopted country. There were also Rodway Superb (M. Trubert); Baltwood Surveyor, Silveroak Sir Sagramore, Woodbay Fleurs Countrymaid and Countrygirl, Hawkhill Majestic Prince (M. Milleret); Carwinley Cosy Corner, Cleavehill Goldfinger, Eydon Roma (Yvette Chavernac); Cleavehill Hunting Pink, and again surprisingly, a bitch from Australia, Casa Perez Doña Estima; Larkstoke Peregrine; Larkstoke Marjayn Matthew (premier stud dog for the des Mirkalines kennel of M. Chevallereau); Ch. Tr. Rivington Chester; Kylemore Ambassador; Whitebrook Cybele; Moleside Gold Digger and Trewsville Benevolent Boy. Much earlier Ch. Tr. Breckonhill Burglar had gone out. Apart from Harvest Gold none of these had really made any impression in England, although some of them perhaps would have done if they had stayed in the UK.

GERMANY

English exports to Germany during this period included Teesview Tensing and Woodbay Dilly's Dancer.

DENMARK

In the seventies and eighties, many of the Danish dogs were derived from Swedish lines, the Saxdalens kennel of J. K. Bjorn being founded on the Int. Ch. Reviret's Adam, a son of Norw. UCh. Americano of Finnline out of Reviret's Fancy, bred by Carl Elofsen in Sweden, although, as his name implies, Americano was bred in Finland and descended from the Adamant James son, Salilyn's Passkey. The Saxdalen kennel also housed Creation of Finnline and Flamebird of Finnline. A very nice bitch from Adam and Creation, named Saxdalens Dette de Vette, went to Holland as an outcross for the v. d. Lage Noord kennels of G. M. C. de Vette. Flamebird was out of Int. Nord. UCh. SF J. Ch. Alibi of Irac, a daughter of Passkey and SF Ch. Classicway Highland Wedding (Grand Black Rod–Shipden Gay Trip). Flamebird's sire was another of Berit Kaupinnen's American imports, SF Ch. Salilyn's Viewpoint.

Earlier in the sixties Kay Till had sent out Renrut Brunette of Stubham, but I have not been able to trace any stock descending from her. Most of the Danish stock was basically for work. Prior to this Axel Petersen bred under the Solveigs prefix and made up two Champions in the mid 1950s, Bob and Leila. At this time Denmark was closely linked to the rest of Scandinavia as the spread of rabies had not yet reached Northern Europe, and the few hundred yards of water between Copenhagen and Malmö was no great obstacle to canine traffic in either direction. One or two Danish dogs were exported to the other Scandinavian countries. Solveigs Lussi and Dk. UCh. Saxdalens Chang are behind the Hazelwood lines of Thorkild Mogensen in Sweden. During the early part of the 1980s, Alfred Dideriksen purchased Swallowhill of Shipden from us, and on his trip to collect him was delighted to handle him to first place in WELKS Championship Show, in spite of not speaking a word of English. Other imports to Denmark during the eighties were from Sweden – Brigadoon Claudi's Remainder Man (by Inu-Goya Autumn Dew), and a Mompesson bitch who went out in pup to the black and white Sh. Ch. Romaline Country Squire. More recently, further Swedish stock has been introduced via Nobhill Upper Class Delight and his son Hammersmiths Real Magnum Smash. Delight was sired by Berit Kauppinen's American import SF. UCh. Willowbank's Bolero. On the working side, during the mid-1970s several dogs were exported from the UK. Unfortunately, some of these were not properly registered, due to the English KC bringing in a new system in an attempt to relieve congestion on the KC registration files.

A current dog that I think is in Denmark is Strathnaver Barley Wine. I say 'I think' because that is where he was last based. Originally he was exported to the Canary Isles, and was then resold to Svend Lovenjar, and since then he has become quite a traveller, winning "tickets" in most European countries at the International and World Shows from Scandinavia to Spain. He followed on, in this respect, from the American import, Expert of Kirwin, who was in Europe for three or four years in the late eighties and early nineties. Based in Denmark, Expert accrued several European titles before returning to the US, where he then added Am. and Can. Chs. to his tally.

NORWAY

At the beginning of the 1980s, the Inu-Goya kennels imported the first of their Cleavehill stock. This was C. Hunting Habit, and she went out carrying a litter by Freeway Indian Summer, three of which got their titles. Others to join the kennel were Coorigil Limelight from Peter and Shirley Wood, after being mated to Sh. Ch. Cleavehill Johnny Walker. Again the resultant litter produced a triumvirate of titleholders. A later import was also from Coorigil, C. Limelight, and she, naturally, was in pup. This time it was Ch. Bowswood Barleycorn whose seed was to be spread abroad, and again it was a case of "good things coming in threes", as a trio from this crop got made up. Recent imports are the dogs Cleavehill James Herriot, and Sh. Ch. C. Indian Tree, plus the bitch Sh. Ch. C. Brown Sauce.

The Inu-Goya endowment to the breed in Norway cannot be underestimated. Whereas the Petersborg kennels were virtually in isolation when they tried to establish the breed in the fifties, and there was an almost complete disappearance of English Springer Spaniels for well-nigh twenty years when they ceased breeding in the late 1950s when Fru Haave moved to Sweden, it was fortunate that Silveroak Ysenne and Travis Aelia went to enthusiastic breeders. Following on from that, Inu-Goya stock went as foundations to other keen exhibitors. Tove Solberg founded her Salix line on N. Ch. Inu-Goya Autumn Lily, one of the Indian Summer–Hunting Habit litter. Lily's sister, N. Ch. I-G Autumn Rhapsody became the matriarch of the Lajban kennels of Laila Dysjeland. Rhapsody emulated her dam in producing three Champions in her first litter. Interestingly this was not, as one would expect, by an established stud dog, or by the latest champion, as would be the case with most novice breeders and their first litter. Instead, perhaps unknowingly, Miss Dysjeland followed Warner Hill's dictum that type and linebreeding were more important than actual show awards, and opted for an unknown, unshown dog. This dog, Nordstrandhoydens Guts, was the result of a nephew/aunt mating based on the Julius–Ysenne litter, being by Travis Choerilus out of a daughter of Tycoon and Aelia. The brother of Lily and Rhapsody, N. Ch. I-G Autumn Dew was the top stud dog of his era, siring well over a dozen Champions, and his sons N. Ch. I-G Summer Blues and N. UCh Country Squire were also quite useful sires.

I suppose it was logical that, with similar base lines, the Swedish Brigadoons and the Inu-Goyas should be used in conjunction with each other. Sigrun Wallquist mated her imported Sh. Ch. and N. UCh. Cliffhill Juliet, to Autumn Dew, while the Inu-Goya import N. UCh. Cleavehill National Velvet had a litter to Int. SF. N. UCh. Brigadoon New Generation of York. New Generation, as his name implies, carried a different set of bloodlines to the Woodbay-based dogs of the original Brigadoons, although they descended from Titus and Dougal. New Generation was out of the Tricolour Sh. Ch. Skilleigh Tangy, who was all Teesview and Cleavehill breeding. Before leaving

Nor. Ch. Stormbird's Final Whistle.

she was put to Ch. Ardencote Alexander, a son of Julius and Sh. Ch. Ardencote Tapestry (Connaught ex Hawkhill Tranquillity).

The Norwegian blood stock was further increased with UK imports by Harald and Annika Ultveit-Moe, who took over Coorigil Brown Sugar, Int. N. Ch. Melverly Uptown Girl and N. Ch. Salloway Shady Lady of Tasa. The latter was, not surprisingly, in pup. She was almost pure Majeba breeding, and was mated to Sh. Ch. Hawkhill Starsky. One of the pups from this litter, N. Ch. Whisborne Pot Luck, went to the Bjerklund/Johnsen partnership and, like Autumn Dew, became the top stud dog of his period.

The other two bitches were mated to the brothers mentioned above – Brown Sugar to Country Squire, and the lovely Uptown Girl to Summer Blues. Uptown Girl was by Genghis Khan, and produced the beautiful N. UCh. Whisborne Which Witch (Ellen Wold). Another from the litter was Whisborne Devil in Disguise.

Chief among the Mompesson imports was Fisherman, who went to Finland. Breeder's Dream also went to Finland. Breeder's Dream was out of UK Sh. Ch. and Aus. Ch. Midsummer Dream. Hawkhill Madhatter, a son of Sh. Ch. Hawkhill Royal Palace, was another to find a new home in Scandinavia. These imports were combined, together with Crepello of Classicway (grandson of Hawkhill Finlandia, a Fisherman son), to great effect by Britt and Thorkild Mogensen, in their Hazelwood strain. Hazelwoods Red Buccaneer especially, did a lot of winning. Prior to this their Fisherlad had won his Norwegian and Swedish titles. The imported Int. S. N. UCh. Cliffhill Gossip's Fieldday was also integrated successfully into the Hazelwood lines, as was Inu-Goya stock.

On the west coast of Norway Anne Buvik imported two dogs from us, first the black-and-white male N. UCh. Shipden Fiorello, followed by N. UCh. S. Oonah. These two bred one or two Champions under the Stormbirds affix and, later, Miss Buvik joined forces with Miss Dysjeland in importing Wadeson Thomas Magnum who also got made up.

THE LATEST IMPORTS

Recent imports to Europe from the US are Am. Ch. Salilyn's Midnight Sun (Finland) and Am. Ch. Salilyn's Best Seller by Laurent Pichard of Switzerland. Judging recently in Holland I had another young American import, McScotts Foreign Affair, entered under me. However, to my great disappointment, he was absent on the day. Two English exports to Holland during the early part of the nineties were Feorlig Welcome Edition and Wadeson Private Collection, both of whom made their titles. Prior to this, Dik Galjaard had imported Norfolk's Moby Dick, and Mompesson Going

Dutch had joined the Soothers kennel. Crichview Cognac had also gone out with his English owners. All of these became Dutch Champions. The Soothers kennel had introduced Mompesson and Romaline blood previously, via the Danish dog Fondantes Quincy, bred by Kjeld and Connie Buus, who imported Mompesson Foolow Folly in whelp to Sh. Ch. Romaline Country Squire. Among the various Dutch imports of the seventies were a pair of Teesviews, Traveller and Trinket, that went to J. C. Arendse-Rozenbrand. This pair produced a number of good winners, under the v. d. Dongemond suffix. One of these, Dutch Ch. Billy v. d. Dongemond, owned by R. W. Stuyvenberg, was a dog I particularly liked. Stuyvenberg later made a notable import of his own, Dutch FT Ch. Bonny of Cilcraig, a daughter of FT Ch. Hamers Hale, and quite a good-looking bitch. She had progeny by another import, Kentoo Donald (by Farway Mac), brought over by J. Brouwers. These puppies were quite presentable, as were those of an earlier litter from Bonny, by Hauks Be Lucky, owned by B. Boers, and the Dashill kennel is building up into a strain of quite good-looking triallers. Dutch FT Ch. Brown Speedy of D., one of the Donald litter, was mated to Int. Belg. Dutch FT Ch. Cy of Gwibernant, another import. This mating contained a very nice-looking bitch, Discover Cilla of Dashill. J. v. d. Vlasakker was another who used Cy, on his imported Drilladee Pep. He also imported Flaxfield Sam, one of the legion sired by FT Ch. Cortman Lane.

Browsing through sundry catalogues and breed books, it is interesting to note the various imports from different countries and the intermingling of the bloodlines. Modern transport and general interest in the breed has led to a broadly-based mix that could be useful when all the effects of the imports have filtered through. As well as the Dutch imports mentioned, Lochar Border Patrol and L. B. Silk went to Western Germany, as did the two Chetrudas, Daisy Chain and Leather Man. Another German import was Debanza Society Belle, her litter to the much-travelled Barley Wine ought to be beneficial to the European bloodlines. Another English dog that is doing a useful job for the European stock is the Swiss-based Bomaris Orient Express, a son of Aus. Ch. Benefactor to Bomaris. There has also been a fair bit of traffic from Scandinavia, with Hazelwood and Nobhill blood being introduced. There have been one or two Brigadoon dogs taken into Germany, and some French dogs have brought in some top English lines through descendants of Fenway Speculator and Thornlea Golden Dawn.

RABIES

Sometime in the mid to late eighties, in a similar fashion to Myxomatosis in the UK thirty-five years earlier, the spread of a disease was responsible for a change in canine affairs. This time it was rabies. The disease had gradually been spreading across Europe and it finally reached Finland by way of Russia. The result this time was the divorcing of Finland from Sweden and Norway. This meant that access to each other's shows and, more importantly, bloodlines, was denied them. From the show point of view, the Finns, although losing the opportunity to campaign for the CACIBs at the comparatively easily-reached Swedish and Norwegian International Shows, had the rest of Europe opened up to them, although the distances were greater. Thus it was still possible to get the four CACIBs in three different countries, necessary for the International Title, although rather more expensive. Due to the quarantine required in Norway and Sweden, it is impossible for them to fulfil those requirements and for the present it is only necessary for the relevant Certificates to be awarded in two countries.

At the time of writing, I believe, moves are afoot to rescind the Nordic quarantine regulations and bring Scandinavia back into Europe, which will eventually mean the situation reverting to the state which obtained some years ago, before rabies spread across Europe.

Chapter Twelve

THE ENGLISH SPRINGER SPANIEL TODAY

An innovation for the UK in September 1970 was the formation of the United Spaniel Association and the hosting of the European Spaniel Congress. This, as its name suggests, is a meeting-point and debating chamber for all the Spaniel Clubs in Europe. The Congress is held triennially at different locations in member countries in conjunction with a Show weekend. Of course, with the UK quarantine laws there is not the excitement of International competition. The inaugural Congress in the UK was held in association with Birmingham Championship Show. The breed judge was the late Mary Scott, and her CC winners were both black and whites – Jean Taylor's Sh. Ch. Cleavehill Corn Dolly and our own Ch. Swallowtail of Shipden, who took BOB. These two still hold the breed records for CCs won by black-and-whites of their respective sexes. They were also both Ch. Show Group winners.

The 1991 English Springer Spaniel Club Championship Show: Frances Jackson with Ch. Mompesson Remember Me (left) and Mrs C. Muirhead with Sh. Ch. Shipden Chuckberry.

Photo: A.V. Walker

Sh. Ch. Graftonbury Genghis Khan.
Photo: P.A. Timmings.

Sh. Ch. Monclare Mr Chips.

MAJOR INFLUENCES

The rest of the early seventies in the UK was dominated by Sh. Ch. Hawkhill Connaught on the show scene; Con went on to win 50 CCs, with multiple Championship Show Groups and BIS wins. Naturally, with all these wins he had a useful stud career and produced many winners. His breeding was a repeat of the Dougal–Paulina mating that produced the three Show Champions, H. Royal Palace, Derby Daydream and St Pauli Girl. These all followed their dam in winning CCs at Crufts. Like Paulina, Derby Daydream took two, Palace and Pauli Girl had one each and Con won two, one with the Group as well. Con's son Sh. Ch. Thornlea Cascade also won two BOBs in 1979 and 1980, with a Con daughter, Sh. Ch. Monclare Jennifer Eccles, winning the bitch ticket in '79.

A combination that was to produce winning stock for various lines was that of Sh. Ch. Hawkhill Finlandia (Mompesson Fisherman–H. Hello Dolly) and Teesview Telma, a Connaught daughter. From these two came Sh. Ch. Hawkhill High Society of Lawnwood, foundation of the Graftonburys, H. Tranquillity, the start of the Ardencote line, and Sh. Ch. H. Hazy Idea, who began the Robil kennel; Ellen Dobson had Sh. Ch. H. Riding Low, and H. High Line got his title in the ownership of Mick Friel. The mating of High Society to Sh. Ch. Monclare Mr Chips resulted in the successful Sh. Ch. Graftonbury Genghis Khan. During the first half of the eighties Khan made Crufts his own special show. Starting in 1980 under my wife he took Res. CC to Cascade. The next three years saw him win the CC. He was not entered in 1984, but came back with a bang the next year to take BOB and the group. The 1981 bitch winner was "Auntie" Jennifer Eccles again. The connection was carried on in 1986, when a Chips' son, Ch. Risdene Devil's Advocate, was BOB, and Khan's daughter Sh. Ch. Bomaris Coral Dancer took the bitch CC.

Two current kennels that started in the seventies were the Wadesons of Kay and Colin Woodward, and the Lyndoras of Tom and Dorothy Bury. The Wadeson line was founded on the kennel's first dog, Sh. Ch. Barlochan Engineer, a blend of Cleavehill and Hawkhill lines, and Feorlig Just Jolene, by Connaught out of Sh. Ch. F Beautiful Memory. The foundation of the Lyndora kennel was Sh. Ch. Hildarry Roast Chestnut, by Con out of the same bitch line as the Monclare foundation which went back to Roydwood Russian Silk (M. Shooting Star–National Velvet of Stubham). At the end of the shooting season in 1977 the breed lost John Kent at the age of 91. His career had spanned over 70 years in Field Trials; prior to this he had trained Sheepdogs. He first won awards at trials in 1905 with a Cocker and with a Springer in 1909, and he was still handling his Springers at the Spaniel Championship when well into his eighties. He actually passed away while saying goodbye to two old friends who had spent the day visiting him to see a

Sh. Ch. Wadeson Jessica Fletcher.

Sh. Ch. Chuan Chablais at Lyndora.

couple of young Springers in training. One of the friends was Larry Macqueen, the top American trainer, who himself died some two years later.

FIELD TRIAL PEDIGREES

Trying to trace successful strains in the post-war Trial world is difficult. This is due to the practice of breeders only registering one or two in the litter and letting the rest go unregistered to other trainers. Consequently one can find two or three siblings entered in the KCSB as FT winners, or even FT Champions, all with different affixes. With the exception of the older-established names such as the Criffels of Tom Laird, the Rivingtons and the Saightons, very few entries would appear to be from recognised strains as such. This arrangement gives the breeder rather less than their due share of credit. Some that would appear to qualify to be regarded as strains are Jack Davey's Wivenwoods, who seem to have been around for a very long time, the Parkmaples of Rachel Gosling, who are also well established, and the strong line of Staxigoes developed by Danny MacKenzie, and the Berrysteads of W. Williams.

The career of Keith Erlandson and his Gwibernants has spanned over thirty years and has been associated with many well-known dogs. His first FT Ch. in his own name was Gwibernant Aberneithy Skip, bred by W. Llewellyn from his top-producing bitch Dinas Dewi Scottie and FT Ch. Pinehawk Sark. Before this he had already handled Major Spittle's Dinas Dewi Sele to her title – she was also out of Scottie but by Rivington Sailor. Probably the best-known Springer connected with him is Hales Smut, born 1960, which he bred and sold as an unregistered pup. Although he never made his title, he was unplaced at only one trial in a four-year career, and his FT Champion progeny reached double figures. In this respect he was like his sire, Conygree Simon, owned by Lord Biddulph, who sired at least four FT Champions. Among those who used Smut were Dr T. K. Davidson, to breed FT Ch. Jonkit Joel, Captain Corbett (FT Ch. Micklewood Story), Mrs M. Pratt (FT Ch. Bricksclose Scilla), Mike Scales (FT Ch. Layerbrooke Michelle), Jack Davey (his FT Ch. Wivenwood Fofo produced FT Ch. Braiswood Pimm, owned by Mrs Madge Hartt), and Tim Healy who bred the two siblings, FT Champions Farway Skipper and Shann. Another sire of importance by Smut, was FT Ch. Crowhill Raffle.

In the early 1980s Mrs Audrey Erlandson became the owner of a dog bred by P. Onslow and handled by Keith, which was descended from Smut on several lines, through Raffle, Farway Tina, FT Ch. Gwibernant Ashley Robb, FT Ch. Macsiccar Mint, and possibly one or two others. The dog in question was FT Ch. Cortman Lane, who was a very prolific sire, with a total of some 210 litters in the UK, with a further five abroad. There was somewhere in the region of 1250 puppies actually registered by him at the UK KC. He died in January 1993 at ten-and-a-half years of age. At that time his tally of FT Champions was seven in the UK and five abroad, with the possibility of further additions from the later litters. He sired winning stock in France, Canada, USA and Australia. One spin-off of this success was an invitation for Keith Erlandson to judge at Trials in Scandinavia.

W. Llewellyn's brood bitch Dinas Dewi Scottie was the dam of several FT Champions and winners of the sixties, and carried Rivington, Micklewood and FT Ch. Dauntless Monty lines. Hal Jackson founded his later Barnacre line with a bitch from Talbot Radcliffe. She was FT Ch. Gwen of Barnacre (Searle O'Vara–Saightons Slice), and she produced FT Ch. Willy of Barnacre to Conygree Simon. A repeat mating resulted in FT Ch. Kate of Barnacre. FT Ch. Joss was by Markdown Muffin ex Tuft of Barnacre. Muffin was also the sire of FT Ch. Sallie. She, in turn mated to FT Ch. Markdown Mag, was the dam of FT Ch. Robbie of Barnacre. The Jonkits of Dr Davidson provided foundation stock for one or two people. His first FT Ch. was Jonkit Jasper by Pinehawk Sark ex J. Julia, the litter sister of Jasper. FT Ch. J. Jandy became the foundation bitch for Bernard Dutton and the Hamers strain. Others to benefit from the Jonkits were Frank George, who had FT Ch. Wilby Trigger, and W. Charles Williams, whose foundation bitch was FT Ch. Berrystead Freckle, both bred by Dr Davidson. These two were litter brother and sister and were by Jandy out of J. Juno. I have mentioned Joel in connection with Hales Smut: Joel was one of the many of Smut's offspring to make it in the US.

One of the many breeders to emanate from the Essex Field Trial Society was Jim Lock. He started with a bitch obtained from Madge Hartt, bred from her FT Ch. Braiswood Pimm by FT Ch. Berrystead Factor, the same litter that produced FT Ch. Philray Tern. This bitch, Misty Muffet, after getting FT awards in the UK, went out to Oregon to Dr and Mrs Christensen, although it was Janet Christensen who handled her to win awards in Amateur and Open Championship Stakes. Jim Lock later took the affix Dewfield and, after winning numerous awards, his Dewfield Bricksclose Flint also went to the Christensens and was one of the half dozen or so UK imports to take top place at the National FT Championships twice. Flint was by Factor out of a Markdown Muffin daughter and, like many of the Factor progeny, was quite a good-looking dog. Jim has on occasions judged at Trials in the USA. A later acquisition was FT Ch. Concraig Rock

US BENCH LINE MARKINGS

It was in the seventies that certain of the American bench bloodlines began to specialise in producing Springers with a standardised pattern of markings, with a solid blanket or saddle on the back, and a white collar and evenly marked faces. The fashion also crept in for a pristine white background with an absence of freckles. At the same time backs were getting shorter, and a sloping topline developed. Probably the dog who crystallised the gradual trends of the previous two decades was Inchidony Prince Charming. The solid markings were, in fact, endemic in the breed, as most of the early imports such as Chancellor, Springbok and Jambok were very heavily marked. Little Brand was almost solidly marked, while Recorder was responsible for the lack of flecking, and also the white collar. I think it is possible that the now-classic American markings came about by chance. The American breeders followed a much closer breeding pattern than their counterparts across the Atlantic, and for that matter still do – most of the Sandblown Acre Champions were the result of Rodrique covering various of his daughters. Their breeder being a horticulturist, he applied his knowledge of plant genetics with a fair amount of success – but, of course, his failures are not recorded. One of the more successful stallions of this period, Co-Pilot of S.A., was bred this way.

The early Salilyns were full of Rodrique descendants, combined with Nancy of Salilyn who brought in two further Recorder lines. One of these was through her sire, Rufton Breeze, who seemed to click with the Rodrique lines. As well as Sir Lancelot of S. this combination of Co-pilot on to a Breeze daughter produced Ch. Chaltha's the Gainer, sire of Am. Can. Ch. Walpride's Flaming Rocket and W. Gay Beauty. Their dam, W. Sensation, was a grand-daughter of Sir Lancelot and Breeze. Salutation of Salilyn, also a grand-daughter of Lancelot, was mated to Firebrand of S.A. Firebrand carried at least seven lines to Rodrique, including three father–daughter matings. This pairing of Salutation and Firebrand was responsible for the Champions King Peter, King William, King Arthur, as well as their sister, Queen Victoria.

All these divers lines of Rodrique were gathered together in Prince Charming about thirty times, his dam S. Cinderella being by King Peter out of W. Gay Beauty, and his sire, S. Citation had, as grandparents, Queen Victoria and King Peter. As I mentioned earlier, Prince Charming was the only pup in the litter and, contrary to what normally happens in such cases, where the singleton turns out to be so much garbage and a complete waste of time and energy for all concerned, Prince Charming eventually proved to be a top stud dog and sired over fifty champions. Of his progeny, Ch. Salilyn's Aristocrat and Ch. Charlyle's Fair Warning were alike in type and markings, although Fair Warning had virtually an outcross bitch line. Aristocrat's dam brought in Citation again, and King William. This intensive breeding fixed the blanket markings and pure white background with an absence of freckling. Some artistic tonsorial expertise produced a crisply delineated saddle, and the Salilyn's look was born. In-breeding to Prince Charming and Aristocrat over the next few generations by most of the breeders meant that most of the dogs were very similar in shape and markings. This succeeded to such a degree that when a representative of the UK Parent Club visited a Specialty Show in 1993 all 57 exhibits for BOB were almost exactly alike in size, type, presentation and markings.

One of the breeders who did not believe in too much in-breeding and also appreciated ticking (and also tan markings, another victim of fashion) was the veteran Juanita Waite Howard, of California. Her Waiterock line was founded about the same time as the Salilyn strain, with an Avandale bitch used for work. This was mated to one of the Elysian dogs and the line started. Juanita Howard's philosophy was to breed working gundogs to the standard so they looked like Springers. She gained many awards at Trials with her dogs although never the top placings to get a FT Champion. Juanita owned Eng. Sh. Ch. Brown Bess of Bramhope, who was bred by May Smithson out of Studley Bernadette (dam of Am Ch. S. Grenadier owned by the MacKinneys) by Bentinto of Bramhope, one of the many Boxer–Judith progeny. Bess went to the US with May Patey when she emigrated, and was taken out in whelp to Melilotus Shooting Star. Juanita Howard also acquired a pair from the litter, Waiterock Amerigo and her brother Messenger.

RECENT KENNELS

There are several successful kennels founded in the last fifteen to twenty years which have settled down to producing good stock, many of them also taking an interest in the working side through the "Field Day". Joan and John Palmer of Sussex have gradually built up their line, producing two or three Show Champions, although disaster struck when their dual Group winner Sh. Ch. Roandew Gemima Jones died before her career had really begun. The Bomaris kennel of Dick and Carole Sheppard came into prominence when they used Genghis Khan on B. Hideaway, which was basically Shipden with some Teesview and Hawkhill. The resulting Show Champion, Bomaris Coral Dancer, was then mated to the black-and-white Ch. Esholt Beaujolais, a son of Sh. Ch. Malacou Dusty Miller and Barlochan Ebony Lace (litter sister to Sh. Ch. B Engineer), and I was more than happy to purchase one of the ensuing litter.

In all breeds there have been kennels that have burst into prominence like shooting stars slashing

Sh. Ch. Chaigmarsh Sudden Impact:
Winner of 10 CCs and 4 Reserve CCs.

across the dog scene, only to fade as shooting stars do, with equal rapidity. This can be for many reasons – family commitments, career changes, health reasons or, in the case of gundog owners, getting involved with the working side rather than shows. This last is a classic road trodden by many in the past. Apart from the well-known examples such as Stokeley, Higham, Ranscombe, etc., who simply extended their activities to include Field Trials, some made the switch completely. Among these were H. F. Lock, who made up Ch. Glenford Gamester, and, after doing well at the inaugural Show Spaniels Field Day with Gamester's daughter, Teal of Halamy, faded out of the show scene to concentrate on the working side. Joe Robinson, for many years Field Trial Secretary of the Parent Club, followed much the same pattern. After making up Ch. Chipmunk of Stubham (another to do well at that first Field Day), and showing and working his progeny, he ended up with a Field Trial-bred dog purely for work. Keith Hubbard has also forsaken the show circuit for the shooting field – or, in his case, the grouse moor. After campaigning Ch. Pericles of Truelindale to his title, he bred and made up the influential stud dog, Sh. Ch. Malacou Dusty Miller, who was out of Majeba Melody Maker, a Connaught daughter. Fortunately Joe and Keith still make the occasional appearance as judges, so their experience is not completely lost to the breed.

A contemporary and near neighbour of Keith Hubbard is Peter Wood, who seldom shows now due to pressure of business, his Coorigil line being quite successful, having more than a little influence in Scandinavia. Like Keith, Peter was one of three protégés of Ellen Dobson, and his foundation bitch, Sh. Ch. Coorigil Starshine, was in fact bred by the third member of the trio, Les Soley, by Teesview Titus out of his Whintonhill bitch. The breed parted company with Les when he emigrated to Australia after he had piloted Teesview Twister to his Championship and bred one or two litters. Perhaps an indication of some deep-seated yearning for foreign shores was shown when he named one of his bitches Healsville Waratah Blossom. She made her mark in the breed as the dam of Sh. Ch. Windydale Whimsicle Ways of Calvadale. Glen Miller, after campaigning Graftonbury Genghis Khan through to his many top wins, is also now only seen as a judge occasionally. Doug and Jean Sheppard (Cliffhill) are also quiescent at present, although they have been an influence over several years, especially in Scandinavia, where the combination of Teesview Titus on their Woodbay-derived bitch lines, has meant that the Cliffhill exports have nicked in particularly well with the Northdown-descended stock already over there. One could be forgiven for thinking that Colin Jackson (Loweview) was a member of the above club of "retired" Springerites. Not so! As far as the breed is concerned the affix might be in abeyance, but Colin and his wife, Hilda, are now in partnership with Sue and Tommy Aston showing the successful Tasa exhibits.

Graham Rogers founded his Chaigmarsh line on Cliffhill stock, combining it with lines from Dusty Miller, and back to a Cliffhill Julius son. Mrs Eunice Ward (Wardhill), also used Dusty Miller to good effect on her Sh. Ch. Wardhill Whistling Magic, breeding Sh. Ch. W. Whistling Miller, who has sired one or two good winners at the moment. Mrs G. Badcock has been breeding her Frenchgate line for quite a number of years now, in spite of all the periodic upheavals associated with being the wife of an Army Officer. One of her earlier bitches, back in the 1950s, carried vintage Bramhope and Stokeley blood via Merrydais Brigadier. Later generations brought in Larkstoke and Zoybank lines. Then came a reversion to the Stokeley lines when she used Sh. Ch. S. Son of Laddie. Laddie's daughter, mated to Ch. Teesview Titus, produced what is probably the best-known of the Frenchgates – Marcus, who was left with Mrs Pat Hollywood when an overseas posting came up. On returning to England Mrs Badcock purchased a Cliffhill bitch who was mated to M. Dusty Miller. This new line was then combined with progeny from Marcus.

Janet Wood founded her Ardencotes with one of the Hawkhill Finlandia–Teesview Telma litter, first breeding Sh. Ch. A. Tapestry, sired by Connaught. This litter also contained the multi-CC winning A. Autosport. The next generation, Julius out of Tapestry, brought forth Ch. A. Alexander, sire of Sh. Ch. Chaigmarsh Sudden Impact, who turned out to be an influential stud dog. Valerie Lockhart (Chetruda), transferred her affections from Irish Setters some years ago. One of the early dogs, Diggle Jackadandy, a black and white, has left his mark through one or two of his progeny. Her first Show Champion, C. Pearly King, was also black and white (by Shipden Pearl Diver ex Melverly Penny Black of C.). Since then several Champions have derived from the Chetruda stock, mostly Lochar based. Penny Black was mated to Hawkhill Starsky, and their daughter, C. Miss Tilly, produced Sh. Ch. Chetruda Premier Rose by Sh. Ch. L. Nice an Easy. Recently, Ray Smith has made up Sh. Ch. Melverly Lois Lane, and Sh. Ch. Chetruda Lancashire Rose of Melverly, descended from Penny Black. Ken Green has quietly been building up his Kennair strain for several years, mainly based on the "Grand" lines of Bob Cleland originally. Inverruel Nicola was the foundation for Diane Scott and her Lossiedoon strain. Winner of one CC, she was one of those rare bitches to take a BOB from the great Connaught. Bred to Teesview Titus, she produced stock that had an influence in Scandinavia. More recently, combined with Lochar and Wardhill blood, the Lossiedoons have won quite well with CCs and Res. CCs. The Lochar strain is now in the hands of Mrs Dinwoodie and Nina Best, the two ladies joining forces after the death of Mr Dinwoodie, with Nina lapsing her own suffix. After Sh. Ch. Loweview Temptation had been made up, an unfortunate accident curtailed the career of the promising Freestar Fellwalker of Lochar, although he recovered and left behind some descendants, siring Ch. Lochar Delilah to a daughter of Temptation and, also, through the Plaiglen and Beaters kennels. Acquisition of some of the late Bob Cleland's bitches added a broader base to the line, which is another to have benefited by the introduction of Dusty Miller blood.

Ann Corbett, although her present Trimere lines are descended from two Abbeygate bitches (A. Tudor Jewel, by Hawkhill Mon Fils ex Mompesson Paper Doll, and A. Tudor Silk, bred from Sh. Ch. Romaline Country Squire and Chasmar Jennifer Juniper, a grand-daughter of Sh. Ch. Monclare Jennifer Eccles) first showed Bellaw Beau Brummel, a son of Monclare Moon River, litter sister to Chips and Jennifer Eccles. Jewel was mated to Hawkhill Starsky and founded the main line, coming down through their daughter, Sh. Ch. T. Trinity. Silk had a litter to Raenstor Country Boy at Mompesson, producing Sh. Ch. T. True Grit. Later links with Ardencote and Mompesson have produced the kennel's latest Show Champion, T. Terrahawk. Mr and Mrs J. Lillie's Freeway is based on Teesview Tarrana in combination with various Cleavehill dogs, with Cliffhill lines brought in. Mr and Mrs Pidcock, Ketsby, brought in Bowswood Billie Jo to mate to her Ketsby lines founded on Firsby Portia, mated to Cleavehill Titus Oates, owned by John and Lynda Lillie (Freeway). The Ketsbys and Freeway are closely linked. The Westerton kennel of Dora Yates is another that is in abeyance at the present time, although there are some of her bloodlines behind one or two of the later kennels, one being the Wardhill. Jan and John Eteo, Jancliff, basically Hawkhill in origin, lined up with Whitemoor and other suitable lines. The kennel is only a small one and not much breeding is done, but it has housed several Champions over the years. The Morrivale kennel of Mr and Mrs Ron Morris is another that has quietly made progress over the years. Their original bitch was by Healsville Digger Boy out of a bitch by Westerton Dusty Miller, eventually going back to Titus and Swallowtail. Their first litter was by Barlochan Engineer and, since then, their lines have become strongly Mompesson. Mompesson Pride and Joy became a Show Champion and since then CCs have been won by Morrivale Simply Red and M. Milli Vanilli.

The Swales family, starting with a foundation bitch that combines Mortondawn and Cleavehill stock, and with the addition of Feorlig and Wadeson blood, have bred several good winners, Sericum Evening Star gaining his title and siring CC-winning progeny. Dawn has progressed from being a Top Junior Handler to Championship show judge. Fran Glendinning first started showing a litter sister of Lochar Delilah and has stuck close to the Lochar lines in building up her Plaiglen strain. For the past few years Fran has been involved with the organisation of the Southern English Springer Spaniel Society. She did however manage to find time to make up Lochar Great Expectations of Plaiglen. Graham Osborne is also involved with running the Southern and, by coincidence, his Beaters line is also Lochar derived. A son of Fellwalker, Springbay Fellsman, actually carries Mrs Carrie Osborne's suffix of Derohan, which can be confusing. A mating of Lochar String of Pearls at Beaters with Wardhill Whistling Miller gave the kennel Ch. Irish Ch. Beaters Brigadoon.

The Catraz story reads like a fairy tale. Fred Rothwell, looking for another gundog, acquired Sophie Duchess Chanelle who was advertised in a national weekly sales magazine. His wife, Linda, started showing her at the age of two. She bred a Show Champion, C. Annacereece, and a CC winner, C. Apache, in her first litter and gained her own crown a few days after her daughter was made up, so I think Sophie was a bargain! There are other CC winners among her descendants during the last decade and a half, in what is essentially a small, fun kennel. The Calvdale kennel of Nichola Calvert and her husband started in the late 70s with the liver and white Windydale Whimsicle Ways of Calvdale, eventual winner of 19 CCs, by Sh. Ch. Hawkhill Highline (one of the Finlandia–Telma litter). The black and white Black Ebony of Burmon at Calvdale followed. She too gained her title. A later addition was Esholt Carafino, another to be campaigned to her title. From these bitches several Show Champions and CC winners have derived, at home and in Scandinavia. Apart from Whimsicle Ways, most of the other stock is a blend of Teesview–Cleavehill lines. Mr and Mrs Guy (Fenaybrook), had, as a foundation, Oakenwood Hot Chocolate at Fenaybrook – sired by Thornlea Cascade out of Hilaw Enclore, bred from Sh. Ch. Majeba Mac out of Sh. Ch. Meadow Mint. They incorporated Titus lines through Sh. Ch. Mastermind of Mordax. A daughter of this first litter, when mated to Cleavehill Ginger Ale, produced the first Champion for the kennel, F. Lady Madonna. Madonna's younger sister has produced a CC winner in her two litters, both by different dogs. Mr and Mrs Gunn, together with daughter Diane, have been successful over the years with their Strathnavers, making up Sh. Ch. Cleavehill Ginger Fudge. They also owned Dallowgill Woodwych who, apart from producing winning stock in the UK by Cleavehill John Peel, when combined with Sh. Ch. Bowswood Barleycorn gave the breed Strathnaver Barley Wine.

Debanza is the prefix of Alec Geddes and his wife, and it has come to the fore in recent years, starting with Silver Spoon of Hawkhill (from one of the daughters from Connaught's last litter) who bred the kennel a Champion, D. Lucky Charm, in her first litter by Sh. Ch. Whitemoore Hill Billy of Jancliff, although her son, D. Buccaneer, by her grandsire, Hawkhill Starsky, beat her to the title. Jill O'Keefe (Drakespur), after steadily breeding several generations from her Feorlig Anais Anais without any really spectacular success, has suddenly made it, campaigning Sh. Ch.

Jennich Joe Sugden to his title, breeding D. Different Strokes at Wadeson and, finally, making up her first homebred Show Champion, Drakespur Forget Me Not. Eric Chadburn, after winning several CCs with his Connaught daughter, Trand Bren Ragapple, suffered the ultimate in misfortune when she proved barren, and he has not really been seen in the show ring since, although he did breed Silver Spoon of Hawkhill, mentioned previously as the foundation of the Debanza's.

Although Wendy Minshull is better known for her Labradors, she has just made up Sh. Ch. Sidelock Chippendale and is, at present, showing some nice bitches, these being mainly Kennair breeding, and Ken Green is also showing a Sidelock. Wendy, in fact, bred a Springer litter as far back as 1978. The sire was Anacapa Bosun. Anacapa, owned by Mr G. J. Wright, is one of those small kennels that are the backbone of most breeds. It was based on Merseyside and consequently was conveniently situated to use Bob Cleland's dogs. This leads me very nicely to Ron and Yvonne Billows. Prior to having Sh. Ch. Hawkhill Hazy Idea, matriarch of the Robils and foundation of their current lines, one of the early Robils was a daughter of Bob's Sh. Ch. Grand Black Rod and an Anacapa bitch. Among the people to benefit from the Robil stock is Ken Carter who, although not breeding himself, has made up two Show Champions, R. Handyman and Owen Glynn of R., father and son. Handyman was also the sire of Mr and Mrs Dempsey's Sh. Ch. Arngeirr Viking Saga, whose son, Kennair I'm a Driver, sired Chippendale. I mentioned Pat Hollywood earlier, in connection with Frenchgate Marcus. She founded her Marshring kennel with a Woodbay bitch, and during the last few years has supplied foundation stock to quite a number of people in the south-east corner of England. Sheila and Barry Turk have also given steady support to the breed and, although not yet hitting the high spots themselves, their efforts have appeared in other people's lines. Perhaps their most successful litter was by Freeway Last of the Summer Wine out of a Genghis Khan–Cleavehill Easter Bonnet daughter. This contained the CC winning Spankis Squadron Commander, as well as Spankis Lily Marlene, dam of Sh. Ch. Penygader Chrystal Star. Joan Hill no longer shows, but after gaining experience with one or two dogs, put this to good use when she bought Barlochan Ebony Lace, sister of Engineer. Lace won one CC, but was important as the real foundation of the Esholts. She was the dam of Ch. E. Beaujolais and his sister, Sh. Ch. E. Carafino. The black and white Beaujolais was an important stud dog, siring Sh. Ch. E. Muscadet and our own Eng. Australian Ch. Bomaris Envoy to Shipden. Carafino has done her part in providing a tertiary bitch line for the Calvdale kennel, producing Sh. Ch. C. Campanologist. On the cessation of the Esholt activities, the sister of Muscadet, E. Beau Peep, joined the Bomaris kennel, and gave them two Champions, B. Moonlight Gambler, out of Genghis Kahn's last litter, and B. Rose Marie, by a son of Envoy.

The Bowswood line of Mr and Mrs A. Bower – not to be confused with the other Alan Bower (Bowsmiths) who campaigned Ch. Conneil Covergirl to glory over thirty years ago – had a successful run during the eighties, making up three generations: Woodgill Shadowfax of B., her son B. Botany Bay, and grandson B. Barleycorn. Since moving they have not been so much in evidence, but are still breeding the odd litter, including Ch. Bowswood Bijou of Heulyn for Dave and Angela Mitchell. Lyn Gregory started the hard way, campaigning an undocked Springer some years before the regulations were changed. The fact that Cliffhill Cleopatra got one CC and the odd Res. CC in spite of this proved her quality and, no doubt, she would have been made up had she been docked. Her son, A. Augustus by Wardhill Whistling Miller, won his title, and she has winning grandchildren via her daughters. Pat Leslie and her daughter Sally began their Risdene line some twenty years ago, breeding the occasional litter in between campaigning Sussex Spaniels and Border terriers. One litter by Monclare Mr Chips contained the two black and whites, Ch. Risdene Devil's Advocate, owned by Colin Jackson, and the Res. CC winner, R. Debutante.

At present they are showing R. Happenstance, a Res. CC winner. Among other breeders who have developed in the last few years and achieved some success are Mr and Mrs Ray Jaggers, who made up Sh. Ch. Jaraina Jaqui Tin. Janice Bates made up Sh. Ch. Salloway Dom Perignon, but has not shown recently. These two kennels share the same basic roots originally. Someone who has bred an occasional litter, but who probably equates to the old style "fancier" rather than a breeder, mainly due to reasons of space, is Mary Lyons. Over the years she has made up Irbyfield Commodore of Cleavehill, Zoybank Iced Ginger, and Cleavehill John Steed – all dogs – and the bitch Carwinley Coral of Kylemore. Lesley Bloomfield also breeds very little but has won fairly well with dogs bought from other kennels, including several with Res. CCs, among them Linsun Yussuf, Moorcliff Liam, Hawkhill James Stuart, Fenaybrook Chocolate Fudge and Pencloe Daybrake. Homebreds being shown at the moment are Fernlin Weave a Dream, Fernlin Chance to Dream and Fernlin Moonlight Escapade. Marian Stowe has been showing and breeding now for many years, originally under the Bellaw prefix, lately using Stowequest. Always having had a fondness for a black and white, she has won a CC with one of that colour, Bellaw Gadhelic. She currently has on circuit one or two nice black and whites.

There are some exhibitors who have joined the breed in the last year or two and are winning well at the moment, but as yet have not become established. Time will tell whether they join the ranks of serious breeders or become part of the "five-year turnover" that besets all breeds.

CURRENT ISSUES

Coming right up to date, the first triennium of the nineties contained one or two controversial issues as far as the breed was concerned. Chief among these was the edict from the British government forbidding tail-docking by lay persons. This, of course, affected more breeds than just the English Springer. It is still legal for breeders to amputate dewclaws before the puppy's eyes are open, just as in the past, but tails must be done by a veterinary surgeon.

Another point of discussion that is in the debating chamber at the present time, is the suggestion, put forward by the UK Parent Club, and supported by some of the European countries, that in view of a proposed change in the US standard and the fact that some show points were being enhanced overmuch, so that the top US winners were deviating too much from the desired UK ideal type, that the US type become a separate breed in its own right. This, if it comes about, will, of course, have repercussions world-wide, especially in Scandinavia and Australia, where the UK and US bloodlines have been intermingled, sometimes successfully and other times not. With the increased interest in dog shows and canine affairs generally throughout the world, combined with the ease of travel occasioned by the improvement of air transport, the availability of stock has become easier. The virtual one-way traffic of pre-war days from the UK to the USA has been replaced by exports from the US to other parts of the world, and most of the Springers to be found in Japan are American-bred. This does mean that the practical application of a split has its difficulties.

In view of the fact that there are many variations in type from country to country, and from kennel to kennel, a split seems to me somewhat irrelevant. The roots are all shared from common bases, and therefore Springers, like "Judy O'Grady and the Colonel's Lady are sisters under the skin". The US FT and hunting strains are like their UK counterparts, of a different type to the show dogs. Some of the West coast show lines are different to the stylised type favoured by the Mid-west and Eastern breeders. As a result of the approach by the UK Parent Club to their counterpart in the US, a representative was invited from the UK Club to the Specialty weekend of shows and field trials. This invitation was accepted and the public relations exercise was reasonably successful. In the event, the more radical changes to the Standard were never implemented, and the new version as adopted is given in Chapter Eight. This proposed split hit the

Am. Ch. Salilyns Condor: Best in Show at Westminster.

headlines at about the same time as Ch. Salilyns Condor was going BIS at Westminster. Following on from the discussions on the differences between the UK and US types, and the judging of an American Specialty by one of the English judges, a reciprocal invitation was made by the English Springer Spaniel Club, and an American judge is due to officiate at the Parent Club Open Show in 1996. Ch. Mompesson Remember Me continued to pile up a heap of CCs, easily surpassing the 40 amassed by Teesview Pandora, to take the bitch record, and eventually achieving the seemingly impossible task of overhauling the breed record of 50, set by Connaught, finishing with 55 CCs at present. During this period Sh. Ch. Wadeson Miss Marple notched up 32 CCs, a creditable total. Late in 1995 Ernest Froggatt died. He had been associated with the breed for almost half a century.

ADVERTISING SECTION

The advertising on these pages has been charged for by the Publisher and its inclusion in no way implies any endorsement or otherwise by the Author.

ENGLISH SPRINGER SPANIEL BREEDERS DIRECTORY

SOUTH EAST
FRENCHGATE
Mrs JMW Badcock,
Antrum Lodge, Stodmarsh Road,
Canterbury, Kent CT3 4AH.
Tel: 01227 470340
Dogs at Stud/Puppies occasionally for sale.

EAST MIDLANDS
MOMPESSON
Mr & Mrs R.W. Jackson, Mompesson
Kennels, Tideswell Lane, Eyam, Derbyshire
S30 1RD.
Tel: 01433 630020
Dogs at Stud/Puppies occasionally for sale
Boarding facilities available.

WEST MIDLANDS
REULEMILL
George Clarke,
Dale Croft, Dale Lane, Haughton,
Stafford ST18 9EJ.
Tel: 01785 282701
Dogs at Stud/Puppies occasionally for sale.